NO ORDINARY SOLDIER

MY FATHER'S TWO WARS

Liz Gilmore Williams

Liz Gilmore Williams

Burkwood Media Publishing

Burkwood Media
P O Box 29448
Charlotte, NC 28229
www.bit.ly/burkwoodmedia

Printed in the United States of America

First Printing, 2016

ISBN 9-7806927799-7-2

Cover design by Heather Kegerreis

To April

Brave, beautiful, beloved

PREFACE

By the time I wrote this book, I had already journeyed far in life. I'd left home to get a liberal arts degree. I'd worked for my county government and flown around mostly the eastern part of the United States as a flight attendant. I'd dated scores of men and married two of them—the second one a keeper. I'd worked as a writer and editor in consulting firms and for two offices of the U.S. Congress as well as in collections management for two museums. I'd lived in four states and traveled to 30 foreign countries, living in one of them, Mexico, for a year.

All of those journeys prepared me in some way to write this book, for which I consulted not only my parents' letters from World War II but also archival records; official Army reports and studies; oral histories; books on World War II; and old news articles, magazines, and photos. I interviewed my sisters and mother; emailed archivists, scholars, and librarians throughout the country; and flew to Hawaii to tour, talk with historians, and conduct research.

When Mother gave me the letters, I asked her why she'd saved them. "Because they were precious to me," she said. I have no doubt they were. But I sensed the real reason she'd saved them, lying just below her consciousness: The letters were saved for me, for my journey to discover not only Daddy but also the truth about our family and a kind of love that hurts and one that heals. This journey made sense of all the others. It took me home, really, for the first time.

ACKNOWLEDGMENTS

How did a confirmed girlie girl like me write a book about World War II? I did so only with the help of many generous souls.

First and foremost is my late mother, Ann Fritz Gilmore, who, while in her eighties and early nineties, kept finding photos and additional materials after giving me her letters. What a woman.

The support of my husband, Charles H. Williams, Jr., was also vital to this project. He sent me to Oahu for research as a Christmas gift. As a former marine, Charlie served in the "Death Dealers," Marine All-Weather Fighter Squadron 114 in Viet Nam. He gave me invaluable insight into military life in general.

My editor Ron W. Starr, a former senior editor for *Reader's Digest* (Canada), used a surgeon's precision to extract the unnecessary words and asides that, though interesting to me, distracted from my story.

Many archivists, librarians, journalists, and historians helped in my research. Jessie Higa, tour guide extraordinaire, former journalist, and amateur historian, showed me around Hickam Air Force Base and answered many questions for me while in Honolulu and by email after I returned. She also steered me to oral histories of men in my father's company. Jodie Mattos, Librarian, Hawaiian Collection, Hamilton Library, University of Hawaii at Manoa, directed me to a scholarly article by Carol A. Stabile and was extremely helpful to me. Her colleague at the Hamilton Library, University Archives and Manuscripts, Sherman Sekai, also helped me greatly when I was researching the book. Scott Pawlowski, Curator of the USS *Arizona* Memorial, took time from his busy schedule to show me the John S. Lopinsky collection at the memorial and other materials. He also steered me to other sources. DeSoto Brown, Curator of the Bishop Museum, provided me with information about and identified Sammy Amalu for me in emails we exchanged. Theodore Kurrus, retired journalist, also gave me information about Sammy Amalu. Barbara E. Dunn, Administrative Director and Librarian of The Hawaiian Historical Society helped me find appropriate sources. Judith Bowman, Director, U.S. Army Museum of Hawaii, took time to help me find pictures of Hickam. Dr. Thomas P. Lauria, of the Air Force Historical Research Agency, provided much information on sources by email. Carol Tuckwiller, former Director of Research and Archives for the National D-Day Memorial, helped me find information on demotions in the army in the 1940s. James W. Morrison, author of *Bedford Goes to War: The Heroic Story of a Small Virginia Community in World War II*, helped me verify the death of Charles Giambrone on D-Day. Carolyn Klepser, author of *Lost Miami Beach* and consultant to the city of Miami, provided photos and other information on Miami Beach in the 1940s.

And, finally, I thank my cousins, Paul T. Gilmore and Dana A. Gilmore, for sharing information with me on their late uncle, Andrew M. Beyer, and their late father, John F. Gilmore.

CHAPTER 1
SEEKING DADDY

They sent me to Hawaii,
Where I became a boot,
They handed me a rifle,
But the damn thing wouldn't shoot.
—Airman's Song, Anonymous

My father fought two wars in his 51 years of life. One he waged with the Japanese as a soldier in World War II. The other he waged with himself.

I tiptoed through girlhood to keep my father's bark at bay. No one knew when Daddy would bare his teeth. He ranted when my sister, April, dated a Catholic boy. He forbade me to wear bangs.

One Saturday afternoon when I was 11, Daddy charged from our living room through the dining room. Glowering and gripping April's gray and pink bottle of hair tint, he pushed open the swinging door to our tiny kitchen. The door smacked the kitchen table. Trying to keep April from bleaching her hair, he splashed the bottle's contents down the drain. I watched, cotton-mouthed, holding my breath as if under water. My stomach churned. I picked and chewed the cuticles on my thumbs and forefingers until they bled.

The week I left for college in September 1970, Daddy died of leukemia. At the funeral, in a favorite brown dress that Mother deemed too chintzy for the occasion, I sighed with secret relief, not heartache: The chaos in our household would end. I could finally exhale. Though Daddy left us, my curiosity about the cause of his rages remained, submerged in my mind like a submarine in the sea, surfacing periodically.

For 57 years, my parents' wartime letters braved the attic of my girlhood home in suburban Philadelphia until I rescued them in 2003. In torn-open, yellowed envelopes, the nearly 300 letters written from October 1940 to May 1945 bore strange addresses and stamps. Some letters Mother had scribbled in pencil; others were carefully scripted with her fountain pen. Some featured her lipstick-print kisses and smelled of floral-scented perfume. Stylish military insignia, airplanes, or tropical scenes adorned Daddy's stationery. The letters urged me to sort them, to read them, to make sense of them.

Handling the letters quickened my pulse. Who was Daddy as a young man? Was he even tempered before the war, as Mother said? What did he do in the war? Did combat plant a smoldering fuse in Daddy's head, sparking his explosions, or was it something else?

My search for answers began with urgency given the uncertain longevity of my then 80-year-old mother. I started quizzing Mother by phone, composed questions for her to answer, and mailed them to her. She lived in a town 170 miles north of my central Pennsylvania home. She responded as best as she could but was mining memories 68 years old. Besides that, she and Daddy were just friends before the war; she knew only basic, but telling, facts about his early life. The sixth child of his parents, he had the status as well as the onus of a firstborn son. His two older sisters, Dorothy and Viola, preceded him by 10 and 8 years, respectively. Viola disgraced the family by bearing three illegitimate children. After Viola came Harvey, who died from pneumonia as a toddler. Then twin boys, Bradford and Harold (nicknamed "Bud"), arrived. Diphtheria took Bradford's life at age 4, and fever from the disease broiled Bud's brain, disabling him physically and mentally. So perhaps his parents gave their next son, my father, Herbert Russell Gilmore, special treatment

2

after he thrived beyond age 4. His brother, John, joined the family three years later.

Months after my first inquiries to Mother, I drove east to my father's hometown. A map, notebook, and directions lay on the passenger seat, within easy reach. A water bottle sat in the cup holder. Only bathroom breaks would interrupt this trip. As I traversed a bridge over the Schuylkill River, I knew where I was: Norristown. "How did I know this?" I wondered. I hadn't been there for more than 40 years. I headed for the Montgomery County Historical Society.

There, in old city directories, I found three addresses for the Gilmore family, all in the city's West End. The last of these, on Kohn Street, was where we visited my father's mother, already a widow, in my childhood. I drove to the house, a narrow, three-story brick row house, which my grandparents had rented. I parked the car. My eyes moistened as I looked at the house and recalled the narrow living room and the pet parrot perched in a cage there. I imagined the pudding NaNa made just for me and my delight in piercing its skin with a spoon before scooping up and tasting its chocolate sponginess. I took in the streetscape: the houses had no front lawn and sat only a few steps from the sidewalk, the street just feet farther away. Seeing the houses intact—now part of a historic district—thrilled me.

I drove around to the alley behind the row of houses. Chain-link fences separated the narrow backyards from each other. In the yard of my grandparents' old house, where NaNa once grew vegetables, two Hispanic-looking men sat in lawn chairs. I waved to them and got out of the car. The sound of a Latin tune floated from the house. I asked them, in Spanish, if I could please enter the house and told them my grandparents had lived here. One of the men answered, also in Spanish: The owner is not home, so we can't let you in.

"Está bien," I said, smiling as I left. No matter, the inside of the house, so changed from the late 1950s, would disappoint me, like finding a parking lot where your old high school hangout once stood.

Still a working-class area, the West End of Herb's day housed the mill and factory workers of Norristown, 15 miles northwest of Philadelphia. According to Mother, he worked in a woolen mill after graduating from Norristown High School, but she didn't recall which one. Hoping the names of the old woolen mills would jog Mother's memory, I'd copied them from the city directories.

Back at home, I called her, reciting the names of the mills, "Wall . . . Scatchard . . . Norristown . . . Smith . . . Bry. . ." Bingo.

"Herb worked at the Bry Woolen Mill," Mother said. Herb, who rarely used "Herbert," had earned $17 a week as a mill hand. A dapper dresser, he'd hated the filthy, steamy, and unsafe mill. From the letters, however, I learned he'd also hated the army. Aside from escaping the mill, why would he join?

Herb, like many Depression-era young men, had never ventured much beyond his hometown or state. Naïve and facing the prospect of low-paying jobs, his generation of men fell prey to recruiting posters promising adventure in exotic locales, such as Hawaii and Panama. Young men trotted off to enlist in the U.S. military's Hawaiian Department, in many cases not even sure where Hawaii was. Though 2,400 miles of ocean separated the U.S. mainland from Hawaii, Herb and thousands of other men bound for Hawaii felt lucky to be so assigned—as if taking a vacation on the government's dime.

Herb had read the news about the pending passage of the Selective Service Act. If he enlisted, he could choose the branch he wanted and get the best possible posting. So, four days after Independence Day 1940, at age 21, he enlisted for a three-year term as a private in the Signal Corps of the U.S. Army Air Corps'

Hawaiian Department. One of 53,500 men who enlisted that year in the Air Corps, he chose Hawaii, Mother said, because he thought it would be lovely.

Herb left for basic training at Fort Jackson, South Carolina, later in July. After that, he headed for California. From San Francisco, he sailed on an army transport ship on August 15, 1940, bound for Oahu, Hawaiian for "gathering place." After climbing the gangplank onto the ship, he entered a troop hole in the ship's hold crowded with men on bunks stacked atop one another at two-foot intervals, a multi-decker sandwich of men and bunks. Once underway, the swaying ship sickened most of the men, whose vomit and body odor stunk up the place.

The ship rounded Diamond Head on August 21 and docked near the Aloha Tower in Honolulu Harbor. Herb arrived to a typical Hawaiian welcome. A rousing march blared from the Royal Hawaiian Band, serenading the men, and Hawaiian girls placed fragrant leis around their necks. Native boys in swim trunks splashed into the harbor, diving for coins the soldiers threw into it.

As Herb formed ranks dockside with the other GIs, beads of sweat glowed on his forehead from the sticky tropical air. Small bursts of sea breeze relieved the heat. He had finally set foot on the land that had lured him there: lush mountains looming over sandy beaches, crystal-blue water, and tall swaying palm trees. After 20 days of quarantine at Fort Armstrong, a coastal artillery post on Honolulu Harbor, Herb reported to Hickam Field, next to Pearl Harbor.

CHAPTER 2
PREPARING FOR WAR

As a . . . Pearl Harbor survivor, I am often asked what ship
I was on. When I reply that I wasn't on a ship but was
stationed at Hickam Field, I am usually asked, "Where is
Hickam Field?" The Japanese certainly knew!
—Master Sgt. Thomas J. Pillion

Fortification pierced the abundant calm of Hawaii. As wavelets lapped at their hulls, warships crowded Pearl Harbor. A khaki green caravan of tanks, armored cars, and jeeps rumbled through Honolulu's streets, where barefoot children walked. Airplanes on military missions roared above. Poised sentries guarded important plants, buildings, and other sites as carefree tourists lounged on beaches. Newspapers reported a possible air attack. In a state of "limited emergency," Hawaii gave way to its military role in the Pacific. There, one of the largest gatherings of U.S. troops anywhere in late 1940 defended Oahu against the Japanese, whose incursion of China raised alarm about Japan's intentions elsewhere.

Like a blade smith tempering steel for a sword, the army conditioned Herb. He pushed his strength and learned to shoot, pitch a tent, and wash himself the army's way—from top to bottom. He marched in close order drills and learned to use a gas mask and patrol inside a building. After additional training, he moved on to the 307th Signal Aviation Company, a soldier.

October 10, 1940

307 Signal Company

Hickam Field

Honolulu, Hawaii

Dear Ann,

    Received your long expected letter. Why do you hesitate to write? Why do you think I've forgotten you? The pictures you sent are lovely. Please send some more. I can never have too many of you. I think you can tell how I feel now. I miss you very much. Your picture is here in front of me. I look at it to get inspiration.

    I worked today in the Signal Corps warehouse; it's not hard but tiresome. I will have a chance to go to school soon to study telephone maintenance. I think I will like it.

    How is the weather back in Pennsylvania? I will miss winter, which is the season I like most. Which is your favorite? The weather here is hot right now. We are in the tropic of Cancer, which is about 20° above the equator. The only relief we have is the cool breeze from the ocean. If it wasn't for that, it would be hot as <u>h</u>. Above all, it is a lovely place, and I wish you were here.

    How are your parents? Give them my best regards.

Love,

Herb

For several months Herb worked on telephone equipment at the Signal Corps warehouse, set in a cable yard outside of Fort Shafter, the home and administrative center of the Hawaiian Department. In the drab warehouse, Building 307, the fledgling Air Warning Service (AWS) took shape. Controllers monitored incoming aircraft using data from mobile radar sites, long-range reconnaissance, or surface ship contact. Aircraft plotters marked planes' flight paths on a huge table map, where the center's director, along with liaison officers from the Hawaiian Air Force, the navy, and civilian aviation would identify any planes as friendly or "unknown." If a plane was unknown, the director would order fighter planes to take off to intercept it. Though the Hawaiian Department acknowledged the importance of the AWS, it would be neglected, much to everyone's dismay later on.

The oldest military base on Oahu, Fort Shafter was far from the only one. The Hawaiian Department oversaw units from all branches of the service. On Oahu, this included those of the Hawaiian Air Force, in which Herb served, and the Pacific Fleet, based at Pearl Harbor. Hickam Field housed the bombardment wings of the air force; Wheeler Field housed the pursuit wings. Oahu also claimed the largest U.S. military base at the time: Schofield Barracks. On a picture post card campus, Schofield hosted knife fights, broken-bottle brawls, sadistic company punishments, and guard house brutality. It provided the setting for the novel and subsequent movie, *From Here to Eternity*.

The information center atop the Signal Corps warehouse at Fort Shafter (Building 307). (Photo courtesy of the U.S. Army Museum of Hawaii)

October 20, 1940

Dear Herb,

Thanks for the swell letters and pictures. You look more yourself in these last ones, and you seem more like yourself in this last letter. It was the nicest one you have written.

It has gotten colder here, and the leaves are turning colors; some of the trees are already bare. In fact, we had our first snowfall last night. We woke up to a two-inch blanket of snow on the ground. You said winter is your favorite season. I think mine is fall. I love the beautiful colors and the crisp, cool air.

It's swell that you are going to study the telephone. It will form a good basis for a life occupation after you leave the Army.
I am still studying away at [Norristown Business] school. I hope I will finish in 5 or 6 months, and then I hope to get a job as somebody's secretary. I think I will like office work.

My next door neighbor, Sara, and I still pal around together. We go skating fairly often. Friday evening, we won first prize for "best dressed" at a masquerade skating party at Ringing Rocks roller rink. I wore one of my tap dance outfits, and Sara wore a matching one that belongs to my sister. We won $4.

Everyone here is fine. Mother and Dad are still working hard, and Sis is busy with her schoolwork. She's a junior this year. She thought it was awfully nice of you to mention her in your letters.

Love,
Ann

As Ann looked at Herb's photos, she admired his classic features: perfect teeth, clear and ruddy skin, straight nose, and dimpled chin. He stood 5 feet 8 inches tall, and his "fighting trim" in the army never topped 140 pounds. His warm green eyes, quick to see the humorous side of a situation, and defined muscles made up for his lack of height. With his city-boy suavity, he could charm

10

the flies away from a picnic lunch. Women loved him. He liked to entertain and make people laugh. His thick, dark brown hair with a slight reddish tint earned him the nickname of "Red" in Norristown, where everyone had a nickname.

Herb Gilmore before the war. (Family photo)

Just 15 miles from gritty Norristown, the two-bedroom bungalow where Ann read Herb's letters sat in an apple orchard in Schwenksville, a town of 483 souls. When graduated from Schwenksville High School in 1940, third in her class of 27 students, Ann knew everyone in town.

A letter addressed to Ann from Herb in 1942.

Sun Krest Orchard stood just up the road from Pennypacker Mills, the country estate of former Pennsylvania Governor Samuel Pennypacker. Across a bridge and up an ascending lane, the "Sun Krest" sign came into view. Beyond the sign stood my grandparents' home, the apple storage building, apple barn, and the home of the Muttarts, who owned the orchard. Across from the residences, the apple trees grew, their blossoms delicately scenting the air in the springtime. In a creek near home, Ann and her sister, Mary, fished for "sunnies"—a type of sunfish—which their mother ("Granny" to me) fried for breakfast, making the kitchen smell like the inside of a greasy spoon.

Ann Fritz in her high school graduation picture, 1940.

At a dance recital in June 1938 given by Miss Annie Louise Herbert, Ann swung her slim hands and wrists above her head and tapped her feet while Herb's sinewy fingers pounded out "American Patrol" on the piano. As Ann danced, she stood out from the other dancers. Herb noticed her slender ankles as well as her exuberance. Her pointy nose made him wonder if she were a rich Jewish girl; her mother did have a foreign accent.

After the recital, Ann stood statuesque next to her mother and sister. Her red frock flattered her hour-glass shape. Her curly dark brown hair framed an oval face, and her tan enhanced her green eyes. Fresh country air and farm produce gave her complexion a healthy glow. Her bearing erect, with her handbag dangled from her forearm, Ann's mother laced her fingers across her waist, looking like a squat Elizabeth, future queen of England. Impressed by Herb's looks and neat attire, she commended his musicianship and introduced herself and her daughters. In the weeks afterward, she prodded Ann in her thick Ukrainian accent, "Vy dun't chu call Hairbrt and aask heem to deennair?" Sent to Germany from her home at age 9, along with her sister, to toil as a farm worker, Ann's mother sailed to America in 1913, never to see her parents again. No one opposed her, least of all Ann, who, from age 3 to 6, had often heard her mother lament the loss of three stillborn babies that preceded Ann. Ever obedient, Ann called Herb, and he came to Sunday dinner.

November 14, 1940

Dear Ann,

Received your letter, which was very brief. What was the trouble? Were you saving paper and work?

Please wear the bracelet, though it is not a good one. I shall try to send you something better.

I miss you very much, Ann, and think of you often. I wonder sometimes what made me drift away from you as I did. But I hope you will forgive me and that you miss me. I never felt this way about anyone else before. I think you understand.

13

Let me know how you feel.

You talk of Election Day. Sometimes the best man doesn't win, as you mentioned. I don't know how you stand on politics, but I have great faith in F.D. Roosevelt and think he is the best man.

I am still working in the Signal Corps warehouse but hope to go to school in about three weeks.

My buddy and I were at Waikiki Beach on Sunday. I am sending you a few pictures that we took. Why don't you send me another picture of you? Please?

Well, I will close my letter. Until I hear from you, I remain

Your

Herb

P.S. If I could only have spoken to you that day in Norristown when I saw you. I would not feel as bad as I do now. I feel guilty. I meant that message on the box the bracelet came in—I love you.

At Waikiki beach, Herb and his buddy swam, relaxed, and ogled women as beach umbrellas flapped in the balmy breeze. Smiling Hawaiian youths—"beach boys"— massaged coconut oil into the pale bodies of tourists and film stars. One beach boy strummed a Hawaiian tune on his guitar. Others, in the water, helped mainlanders learn to surf. Herb, spotting Dorothy Powell, the movie star, grabbed his camera and took a candid shot of her.

Spanning the beach, Waikiki's cottages, hot dog stands, and curio shops huddled as strolling tourists browsed for souvenirs. Honky-tonks, tattoo parlors, shooting galleries, barber shops, pinball machines, massage parlors, and photo booths lay like mouse traps, awaiting the GIs.

Unlike the soldiers who spent a couple of hours at Waikiki Beach, films stars, such as Mary Pickford, Douglas Fairbanks, and Shirley Temple, as well as the super rich, such as the Rockefellers, stayed at the Moana Hotel. The Victorian-style, gray clapboard hotel, the first on the beach, brought European flair to Honolulu's southeast corner.

Dorothy Lamour, Dorothy Powell, and Sonja Henie, three of the movie stars whom Herb saw in Hawaii. The picture of Dorothy Lamour was most likely a publicity shot he got because he knew a photographer in the Signal Corps Army Special Services. He had similar shots of Bette Davis, Esther Williams, and Virginia Mayo. The second two he shot himself. He also took pictures of Jack Benny, Irene Dunne, and others.

Herb dear,

I was awfully glad to get your letter, but I was sorry to hear things are so bad for you out there. Herb, I never said this before because I thought it would make you feel bad, but I regret that I didn't know you were thinking of joining the Army. I would have never let you go that far. Of course, this won't cheer you up any. We have to make the best of it. Remember, I'll always be waiting for you and praying that you're safe.

Friday, I went to see your parents, and your mother told me you wanted me to have this piece of material that you had brought from the mill when you worked there. Thank you for your thoughtfulness. I will make it up into a beautiful skirt and show it to you when it is finished.

Yesterday, Mother, Sis, and I went to Philadelphia to shop, and I got you a box of candy at Lit Brothers and am sending it to you. We saw a lot of soldiers at the Reading Terminal. If there is anything you want me to send you, please ask for it. You know I'll do anything to make things easier for you.

Everything is the same as it was here. Dad has sold just about all the apples and now we can get out a little more.

Well, I'll stop now as I have some typing to do and my music lesson practice. I'll be waiting for your letter and you.

                                    With love,
                                    Ann

—★—

To convey that their letters made it over 6,000 miles of land and sea, Ann and Herb reported the dates of the letters they received from each other. From this, I calculated that about 100 of the letters vanished somehow. I had to infer the meaning of some phrases, such as Ann's noting that "things are so bad for you" in the preceding letter. Herb had anticipated the pleasures of life on a tropical isle but not the rigor of army life. He'd started to grasp how far he was from home there on the most isolated land mass in the world.

—★—

November 26, 1940

Dear Ann,

Received your letter yesterday, but I am going to wait awhile before mailing this one because the end of the month is near, and I haven't any stamps and won't have any until November 30 (payday).

I wrote to Mother telling her to write you and that I asked you and your family to go to see her. I know she will be glad to see you all.

Last Thursday, my buddy and I went to Pearl Harbor and boarded a sub that is the second largest in the navy. A guard directed us over the ship, taking us into every department, which I enjoyed very much. All the parts of a submarine are compact, and we had little room to move around in. What attracted my attention the most were the torpedoes or bombs, which are 12 feet long and 2 feet in diameter. You can imagine the quantity of TNT they contain and the damage they can do once fired. The submarine has a crew of twenty men at a time and enough supplies on board for one month. To anyone who sees a submarine for the first time, it looks as though it is nothing but tubes, pipes, levers, valves, guns, and the like, but it is sufficient.*

Did you have a good Thanksgiving dinner? Our Thanksgiving dinner was as good as you can expect in the Army.

---

*The crew of 20 here refers to the number of crew members on duty to get the ship underway in an emergency. The sub, most likely the USS *Narwhal*, had a normal crew of 88 men. One of five submarines docked at Pearl when the Japanese bombs fell, the *Narwhal* helped to destroy two torpedo planes. Luckily for the sub, the bombers ignored the Pearl Harbor Submarine Base, targeting battleships instead, and it suffered no damage. After receiving 15 battle stars for its wartime service, the *Narwhal* met an inglorious end at the Philadelphia Navy Yard in 1945, when it was decommissioned and sold for scrap.

It is hard for me to make believe that you are here when 6,000 miles are between us. Do you believe that "absence makes the heart grow fonder?" I have found that it's true. I hope you will too. After all, we are still young, Ann, and have plenty of time to think things over. As I have told you before, I have never felt this way about any other person.

I hope you will go out and see and do things with others. After all, I have a little time in here yet. I hope you will give me a little time when I get out.

Until I hear from you, I remain your

Herb

P.S. I love you. If you don't like the picture, tear it up.

While Herb toured the submarine, sailors scurried to complete Pearl Harbor Naval Base on the southern rim of Oahu. But the main machine, torpedo, and battery shops, as well as repair, training, and berthing facilities stood ready. More submarines arrived in the next three years, and by 1941 Pearl Harbor had 22 submarines.

Herb and 18 other men received orders in November 1940 of their reassignment to the newly activated 324th Signal Company, Aviation (later known as the 324th Signal Company, Air Wing). Herb and his colleagues installed, operated, and maintained signal communications for bombardment squadrons of the Hawaiian Air Force.

Signalmen did all kinds of communications work: They took photos to document military life. They used wire, or telegraphy, to send Morse code; telephones to transmit the human voice; and teletype to send printed messages. Wire dominated communications in the war, but signalmen also used radio, critical in tactical communications. In addition, signalmen operated brand-new and top-secret radar devices to determine the range, altitude, direction, or speed of aircraft, ships, and motor vehicles as well as weather formations and terrain. Signalmen also trained non-signalmen to operate communications equipment. Like the Army's Corps of Engineers, the Signal Corps was a combat branch.

Herb outside of an Eastern Air Lines DC-3. In the early days of the war, the military leased commercial planes. (Photo from Herb's collection)

November 30, 1940

Dear Herb,

I'm sorry you found my letter too brief. I wrote two letters to your last one to make up for the first.

I am listening to the Army-Navy football game; Navy is ahead 7-0. This is the first year I am rooting for Army.

We celebrated Thanksgiving this Thursday. I had dinner at Sara's. We had roast goose, and was it good! In the morning we went to a football game at Schwenksville High School, which beat Collegeville for its first win this season. The field was such a mess of mud; you could hardly tell one player from another.

I wish you were stationed closer so you could come home on furlough at least once or twice. When I think that it'll be 2-1/2 years before I see you, it seems awfully long....

I wondered why we drifted apart as we did, too. But I don't think it was either of our faults. Don't feel bad about not speaking to me in Norristown. I could have stopped to talk but saw you were talking to someone else....

I hope you will like school when you start and won't find it as boring as mine. I am half through now, so I don't mind it much.

Waikiki Beach is where all the movie stars vacation in Hawaii, isn't it? Dad, Mother, and Sis send their regards. I hope this letter pleases you more than the last one.

With love,

Ann

As Ann braced for a northeastern winter, Oahu's mountains, beaches, and central plateau basked in warmth year round. The third largest of Hawaii's eight major islands, Oahu was dubbed "Wahoo" and "The Rock" by the GIs.

Herb cut this map of Oahu out of a local paper and sent it to Ann early in the correspondence. It shows Oahu's two mountain ranges, Honolulu's Aloha tower, Waikiki, and Schofield Barracks. Herb wrote in the locations of Hickam Field, Pearl Harbor, and the Mormon Temple, though he was a Methodist.

December 11, 1940

Dear Ann,

I am writing this letter at the Post and it has to go to Honolulu first to be put on the boat, which goes out tomorrow at 5 p.m. I don't know if this letter will make it.

I expect to go on maneuvers tomorrow. I will be stationed at Fort Shafter to take over teletype for three days. I don't know how I am going to like it, but I'll let you know. I think Hickam Field is the best post here.

When you write about winter as you do—especially slippery roads—it makes me feel a little homesick. I hope you will be careful about driving—promise me you will?

21

To me, Waikiki Beach is just another beach. It is small and overrated. This island has more beautiful beaches. I hope someday we can see Hawaii together.

Well, I'm going to hit my bunk. Give my regards to your parents and sister and until I hear from you again, I remain yours.

Love,
Herb

P.S. I spray myself every night on account of the mosquitoes, which are lousy down here. Use 324 Signal Co. in the address from now on. I have been changed to a different unit.

The post flag at Fort Shafter (c. 1942),
Now a site on the National Register of
Historic Places. (Photo from Herb's collection)

Herb's post, Hickam Field, cut a swath of paving and concrete into the 2,200-acre jungle and sugar cane fields from which it was carved in 1940. Only a chain-link fence divided Hickam, known as "Bomberland," from Pearl Harbor Naval Base, its neighbor to the north.

Hickam in the 1940s bustled as the largest U.S. Army Air Corps station, with approximately 100 officers and 3,000 men. In addition to housing the Hawaiian Air Force (except for one pursuit wing), its air depot handled the major overhaul work for Army Air Corps units in Hawaii. Also headquartered there were the 17th Air Base Group, the 19th Transport Squadron, maintenance companies, and other detachments.

Herb's admiration for Hickam started with the architecture. An Art Deco showplace, its new stucco buildings gleamed along broad, brightly lit, tree-lined boulevards. A stunning white, octagonal water tower of Moorish design rose 171 feet at the far end of the parade ground.

The main gate of Hickam Field, early 1940s. (Courtesy U.S. Air Force)

The water tower at Hickam Field in the 1940s.
(Courtesy U.S. Air Force)

Modern, spacious stucco houses for officers sprawled beneath the water tower on manicured grounds. A canopy of monkey pod trees shaded the red tile roofs and overhanging eaves of the stylish homes. Hickam was a city unto itself. Its business and shopping center, including the hospital, administration building, branch Post Exchange (PX), and post office stood between the water tower and the hangar area. The PX had a tailor shop, retail store, restaurants, beer gardens, and shoe repair shop.

In the operations area of the base, five double hangars lined up along the landing mat, or strip, which spanned nearly a mile and resembled an outstretched letter "A." Hickam Field accommodated landings of the Flying Fortress—the B-17—when no other base could do so. Next to the street by the hangars, a railroad track connected the base with the busy port of Honolulu nine miles away. The railway and street extended past the huge air depot building and shops, continuing beyond rows of warehouses and ending abruptly on a concrete dock in Bishop Point, where large oceangoing freighters discharged supplies.

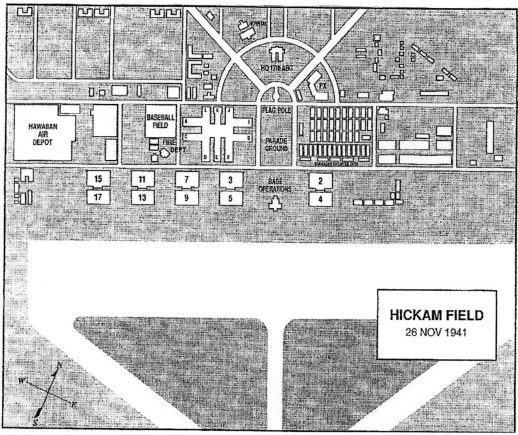

This map of Hickam shows the basic layout of the major buildings. The bottom of the diagram shows part of the outstretched "A" of the landing mat. (Courtesy U.S. Air Force)

Staff began moving into a brand-new barracks, the largest single structure of its kind on any U.S. military post in 1940. The three-story, $1 million consolidated barracks could house 3,200 men. It faced the parade ground and had two barber shops, a 24-hour dispensary and laundry, and a dayroom for each squadron in the barracks. Each sleeping bay had 50 beds, with foot lockers for toiletries and larger wall lockers for uniforms and civilian clothing. After visiting the barracks, Actress Dorothy Lamour noted, "Why I never dreamed that men could keep things so neat." Miss Lamour made several appearances on the base as she romanced a married officer there.

The nine wings of the barracks, called the *Hale Makai* ("inn by the sea" in Hawaiian), surrounded a central mess hall, which fed 2,000 people at a time in a space the size of six regulation-size basketball courts. Enlisted men lined up cafeteria style to get their meals and sat at one of the 104 10-man tables. Along the walls of the mess hall, palm trees and potted ferns cozied up the place, and paintings of squadron insignia adorned the walls. The Hickam Hostess Society, a group of officers' wives, sponsored a monthly dance in the mess hall, inviting more than 200 local girls. Jitterbugging and waltzing beneath colorful streamers, dancers competed for prizes while a civilian or service band played.

Herb's company moved into the consolidated barracks in September 1941 but moved out later into new two-story quarters, known as "Splinter City," on the other side of the parade ground and across from the PX.

— ★ —

To view Hickam, Pearl Harbor, and other places about which my father had written, I flew into Honolulu in late March 2013, filled with excitement. The GPS device I'd brought from home refused to work as I drove my rental car out of the airport into the third worst traffic in North America. Thank goodness I had directions to my rented condo. I found the place, 13 floors up on Kalakaua Avenue in Waikiki. From there, I planned my days of research and touring.

Jessie Higa, the local historian who escorted me around Hickam, gave me an abridged history. Of Japanese heritage, she told me her grandfather had built the buildings on the base. The consolidated barracks had metamorphosed into an administrative building. There, Jessie and the base historian showed me a collection of 1940s *Hickam Highlights*, the post's newsletter, and steered me to three oral histories of men in my father's unit.

From the *Hickam Highlights*, I learned of another move made by my father's company into its quarters. Before the new barracks opened, he and other enlisted men lived in 50-man tents in a temporary "Tent City" built near the hangar line. The large canvas-roofed tents had wooden sides and floors and featured steel lockers and showers. The ambient air smelled like aviation fuel. In Tent City, the men used a separate kitchen, mess hall area, and dayroom tents, where they listened to the radio, nestled in easy chairs, and flicked the ashes from their army-issued cigarettes into smoking stands.

Herb, outside a tent at Tent City with his camera, and a shot of the inside of a tent. (First photo is from Herb's collection. Second photo courtesy of the U.S. Air Force)

After leaving the admin building, Jessie and I walked to the lush garden memorializing those killed in Pacific fighting. A reverence overtook me. On a perfectly Hawaiian day, palm fronds rustled and birds sweetly sang where whistling Japanese bombs once killed innocent boys, whose bodies had piled up where I stood. Native flowers seasoned the once smoke-blackened air. Suppressing tears and the lump in my throat, I shot photos, awestruck by the lives lost and my father's survival. "Who would I be if Mother had married someone else?" I wondered. "Would I even be?"

—★—

As a post, Hickam boasted lots of amenities. A gym, basketball and tennis courts, and baseball diamond hosted a robust sports program full of competitors and spectators. Officers and noncommissioned officers socialized in their respective clubs. In dress whites, officers dined in a large club dining room, danced in the ballroom, drank at the bar, and played games in the fully equipped game room. Enlisted men guzzled Primo or Acme beer in a wooden building across the parade ground from the barracks, dubbed the "Snake Ranch," because "you walked in and crawled out." A glee club and an entertainment troupe occupied GIs with an artistic bent. The troupe, the Hickam High Hatters, sang and performed comedy routines. The post theater featured a nightly movie costing 10 cents. The religious went to chapel.

Jobs at Hickam Field ranged from those of the Commanding General, Hawaiian Air Force, and his senior staff, to pilots, engineers, medical staff, firemen, mechanics, photographers, clerks, drivers, enlisted aides, and others. The base's technical school prepared servicemen for the many specialties required there. The school had high standards and difficult courses; about 25 percent of those who took them failed. In addition to their regular jobs, everyone but officers and noncommissioned officers at Hickam had month-long P&P (police and prison) or fatigue details, including kitchen patrol (KP) and post maintenance, that is, lawn care and general cleaning.

Herb attended telephone maintenance school, training for teletype and message center operation, and army administration training, among other courses. Using the teletypewriter, he learned to send typed messages from one point to another or to several points over communication channels.

Herb's Military Occupational Specialties (MOSs) while in what was then known as "Foreign Service," included Teletype Operator and Clerk Typist. Mainly, he "operated a teletypewriter for transmission and reception of communications and kept a log of all messages transmitted and received," according to his discharge papers. He also operated a switchboard or trained and supervised those who did and drew some maps. In combat, however, the army assigned whatever job needed doing to whoever could do it, and an MOS often ended up including all the jobs in some companies.

December 17, 1940

Dear Herb,

This morning I received your present, which is so lovely and unusual. I appreciate it a lot, especially since it is clearly characteristic of Hawaii. It is beautiful.

One reason I didn't write sooner is that I wasn't home on Saturday, when I usually answer your letters. Mr. Shoop, the principal of the Business School, sent one of the other girls and me over to Summerhill Tubing in Bridgeport to apply for jobs as typists. He thought we would go right to work, but when we got there, all we did was fill out applications and have an interview. He said he'd call us if they needed anyone, but neither of us has heard anything.

Last week, we heard on the radio of some explosion either at a navy or an army base in Hawaii. I hope it wasn't where you are stationed. It seems so long since you've been home and since I've seen you, but I think we are close in each other's thoughts.

I apologize for the lack of Christmas spirit in the

wrapping of the gift I sent you. I hope you like it and it reaches you in good condition. I didn't know what was practical to send and what you could make use of there. I don't suppose you will have much of a Christmas but tell me all about it.

Like every year at this time, everything is decorated in wreaths, lights, tinsel, and so forth. Everyone is rushing around getting their shopping done. Main and Marshall Streets are all decorated with lights, and it all sparkles at night.

I brought home a little Christmas tree. I wish you were home to help me decorate it. I'll be thinking of you while I'm trimming it.

Love,
Your Ann

December 22, 1940

Dear Herb,

Even though it is the Sunday before Christmas, things are a bit dull. Right now it is raining, but I think it will turn into snow and we will have a white Christmas.

In the past few days, I've heard lots of news about Germany's anger that the U.S. is aiding Britain and talk of the U.S. getting involved in the war. This has dampened my Christmas spirit. I certainly dread the thought of war. The newsreels I've seen showing bombings of English towns are terrible. Every time I go to a movie, I come home with pictures of bombings in my imagination.

It was very nice and fair of you to tell me to go out and see and do things, but I don't go out much because of my schoolwork. I usually go to the movies with my parents on Saturday and sometimes skating with Sara and my other girlfriends. When I think of how nice and warm it is where you are and how cold it is here, I envy you, but when I think of the mosquitoes you mentioned, I think I prefer the ice and cold.

I had always liked President Roosevelt and his policies, but I have changed my mind lately, especially since he was so anxious for a third term. I think eight years is long enough for any man no matter how good he is. If the other candidate would have been elected, he would have been more concerned with matters here instead of foreign affairs.

I hope the cookies I sent you arrived in good condition. I sent them as soon as we baked them, so I hope they won't be too stale. I wanted you to have some of our Christmas spirit.

Lots of love,
Your Ann

Though the news of war troubled civilians, such as Ann, it weighed even more on the Air Corps' top brass. In January 1941, the Hawaiian Air Force had 117 airplanes, all obsolete or outdated. The force's officers begged for aircraft, which, along with more personnel, arrived in Hawaii throughout that year. In mid-February, 31 pursuit planes arrived, and by mid-April, the force had 55 pursuit planes. In May, 21 heavy bombers flew into Hickam from Hamilton Field, California, the largest gathering of such planes at any overseas garrison. By the end of 1941, the Hawaiian Air Force had 231 aircraft.

January 23, 1941

Dear Ann,

I am writing this letter at work, that's how busy I am.

I played tennis yesterday and feel stiff today. I haven't played since Christmas. We may play today after work; we finish at one o'clock.

How are school and your music coming along? I expect you to be a second Rachmaninoff. I very much want to hear you play.

I haven't any more pictures right now. I haven't been taking any. The reason I look cross in the last one I sent is because I told my buddy not to take it, but he wouldn't listen. I'm sorry I look mad. I never get mad but I do get hurt by people I like. I try to control my emotions but can't seem to.

Nothing ever happens here—just the same routine every day. Sometimes it's very boring. I hope your life is more

31

exciting than mine right now.

This picture is of the volleyball team. Some team, eh? The two fellows on my left are from West Virginia. Their names, from left to right, are Henry Kohunsky, John Lopinsky, both from Summerlee, West Virginia; Herman Chattin, from Saint Claire, Pennsylvania; and Gerald Stiner, from Renova, Pennsylvania.

So, until I hear from you again, I love you,

Herb

Herb proposed to Ann by letter. With his movie-star looks, Herb could've had any woman he wanted. But besides her virtue, Ann had something special. The wife of the owner of an orchard Ann's father had tended taught Ann's mother to appreciate the drape of a fine linen tablecloth and delicate bone china. Ann's mother passed these inclinations on to Ann. ("Hifalutin," my sister April would call her mother later.) Ann had taste and a knack for design, qualities which, as an artist, Herb shared. They'd make a stylish couple. Ann accepted Herb's proposal sometime between late December 1940 and early 1941.*

—★—

"Why did you accept his proposal?" I asked Mother on one visit amid my years of research. Sitting in her wing chair, she looked right at me through green eyes curtained with sagging eyelids, her hair the color of clouds. Her gnarly, arthritic hands, once as delicate as mine, rested on the arms of the chair. Though Mother's 85-year-old mind was still agile, high blood pressure and diabetes had despoiled her body. For most of the time I'd known her, she'd been overweight: She loved food. I did too, but wearing clothes well and looking good meant more to me than eating, so I'd stayed in shape. Did I have my father to thank for that? He'd

---

*Unfortunately, the proposal letter and Ann's response were lost, perhaps squirreled away so carefully Ann forgot where she put them.

always stayed slim. Mother had given me a petite version of her figure but not her height. Likewise, her eyes and wavy hair, but I had Daddy's straight nose and his sister's full lips and strong jaw line. Both of my parents had contributed to my good looks and those of my three sisters.

"I thought I was an ugly duckling and no one else would propose," Mother answered, sipping her tea. "Besides, I wanted to please my mother, and she liked Herb. . . . She said that one boy I dated, Danny Feaser, looked like a pig. And another one, Pete Fulton, well, we were walking in the orchard one day, and he got fresh. I rebuffed him." Tears tumbled from Mother's eyes. "My mother hounded me horribly for weeks for 'losing' Pete Fulton, our class president . . . . 'What did you do to make him lose interest in you?' she asked me over and over." When I'd heard this story before, Mother had sounded resentful. This time, the corners of her mouth turned down and she sobbed, a browbeaten child once again. I sat quietly and allowed Mother her emotion as she'd allowed mine so many times, hoping my acceptance could purge her pain.

Stroking her hand, I mustered all the gentleness I could. "Why didn't you tell her what Pete had done?"

"I was too embarrassed to tell her . . . I couldn't discuss such things with her," she sniffed through her words. "My mother orchestrated the relationship with Herb," she said, gaining composure, "but I thought he was handsome, decent, and kind. We shared values and interests. It wasn't a giddy romance. I grew to love him." Like a reed bent by the breeze, my mother had bowed to Granny's pressure and made the best of it.

—★—

The Iolani Palace in the 1940s housed the post office from which Herb
mailed some of his letters. It is the only royal palace in the United States.
(Photo from Herb's collection)

February 12, 1941

Dear Ann,

Received your letter, which made me very happy. . . .

I am working back at Hickam Field. So far, it's okay—
nothing to brag about. It seems that I can't be satisfied. I am
tired of the work already. I can't explain it, but it seems I am
not cut out for this or that kind of work. Sometimes, I cuss
myself for being this way, but I can't help it.

Sunday evening, I went to see a buddy of mine in the
Navy, and he took me aboard his ship, a light cruiser.* It takes
50 men to fire one cannon on the navy ships—interesting,
don't you think?

I have been rated PFC, which means Private First Class. I
can't see why I got this rating. I don't deserve it, but, after all, I
won't turn it down because it means more money. Also, I have
to wear a stripe on each arm, which makes me feel self-

---

*The ship was most likely the USS *Philadelphia*, engaged in fleet maneuvers in and
around Pearl Harbor. "Light cruiser," is shorthand for "light armored cruiser." It refers
to a small- or medium-sized warship that carried armor the same way as an armored
cruiser, that is, with a protective belt and deck.

conscious. Hereafter, when you address my letters, be sure to put PFC on the envelope.

You ask me if I get a chance to play piano—no! To read? Well, I take time to read, which I enjoy very much. I have subscribed to *Reader's Digest*. And the books in the library here keep me in reading material. Before I bore you anymore, I shall close. I am sorry for writing just a lot of words and hope you will forgive me. Give your family my regards.

Love,
Herb

P.S. Do you want a grass skirt?

March 1, 1941

Dear Herb,

Today is the first of March, which should be a spring day, but yesterday, we had a big snowstorm. Today the wind drifted the snow and now we are just about snowbound.

I enjoy reading your letters very much. You weren't writing "just words" in your letter. Herb, I'm proud of your promotion. Just for that you get a great big hug and a dozen kisses: XXXXXXXXXXX Keep up the good work.

I would love to have a grass skirt. There is another thing I would like if it wouldn't be a bother or too expensive. I would like to have a photograph of you in full uniform to put on my piano. If it costs too much, let it go. Herb, write more often. If you don't have much news to write, just to hear from you and know you are all right will make me feel much better.

Thanks for the last picture you sent me of you and your friends. You have nice smooth skin so don't go and have it tattooed like some Army and Navy fellows do. I saw a picture in a magazine the other day of an Army fellow who had tattooing, and it looked awful....

I'm still in school, and I have to go about one month more yet. I certainly do wish I could get a job so I could stop wasting time and money at school.

Love,
Ann

Despite Ann's disapproval of tattoos, Herb got tattooed while in the army. A coiled snake on the inside of his right leg, just above the ankle, peaks above his sock in this picture. According to Mother, Herb felt ashamed of the tattoo and, fearing his parents' reaction to it, hid it under his sock. (Photo from Herb's collection)

March 10, 1941

Dear Herb,

You must be feeling blue since you haven't written for so long. I wish I could do something to cheer you up. If there is anything, please ask. In a few months, almost a year will have passed since you joined—only two more years to go.

You can be glad you aren't here right now. Last Friday night, we had a snowstorm and were snowbound all week, and this Friday, the same thing happened and here it is the second week in March. Next time, I'll try to leave the weather out of my letter.

The latest news here is that the Lend-Lease Bill (aid to Britain) is about to be signed by the president. It seems to be a bad step, but let's hope things will come out all right....

Herb, did you get the fudge I sent? I sent it about a month ago, but you didn't mention it in your last letter. If you got it, what condition was it in?

Last night, Saturday, I saw *Road to Zanzibar* at the Norris with Bob Hope and Bing Crosby.* They ran a short reel about enlistment in the Army for Foreign Service, which showed a few scenes of the Panama Canal and one or two of Hawaii. Besides that, they showed other war newsreels. One was about convoying materiel from Canada. It showed Nazi planes attacking and Britain's Royal Air Force driving them off.

This afternoon, we went to a big Air Rally for the benefit of Britain's R.A.F. at Wings Field in Ambler.§ Do you remember the night we bicycled with Gordon and Virginia and we drove past an airport? That's Wings Field. The place was packed with what must have been 25 or 30 thousand people and more cars than I ever saw in one place. Different planes did stunts and men parachuted out of planes. They must have made a lot of money. I certainly hope it gets to Britain.

Thanks for the picture. It is good but you look thinner. Don't they feed you enough?

As ever, with love,

Your Ann

*Norristown's Norris Theater was an icon of Art Deco design with a stunning terra-cotta window grille façade. Six 8- by 4-foot stained glass windows featuring jesters, skyscrapers, musicians, and dancers lit up the interior of the theater. The 1,950-square-foot foyer also had two murals, 50 feet long and 8 feet high, and a fountain filled with fish. Built in 1930, the Norris entertained moviegoers for 52 years. Unfortunately for Norristown, the Norris fell with the rise of suburbia, replaced by a parking lot. And the terra-cotta façade now graces a museum in Miami Beach's historic district.

§At the time one of the oldest continuously operated U.S. airfields, Wings Field designated its "runways" by mowing the grass there lower than the other grass on the field. During its annual wartime rallies, pilots flew their planes over a closed course of about 200 miles, with the winners judged on speed and least fuel consumption.

President Roosevelt signed the Lend-Lease Bill in March 1941, a year and a half after war erupted in Europe. The bill allowed the United States to give 38 nations, including the United Kingdom, Russia, China, and Free France, $50 billion worth of war supplies between 1941 and 1945. And it moved the United States away from a neutral stance and closer to war.

March 29, 1941

Dearest Ann,

If you want to send me the sewing kit that you mentioned, I would appreciate it. We send our clothes and uniforms to the Quarter Master laundry, which does a lousy job of pressing them. And if any buttons are lost, we have to sew them on the best we can, for they don't bother about sewing and pressing soldiers' uniforms. In fact, they almost wash them threadbare. It costs us $1.75 for one month, and we get just $1.75 worth.

It must be wonderful to be home now that spring is almost here. I imagine the orchard is beautiful this time of the year. When I come home, we will take walks the way we used to.

I can see you now, riding to work on your bicycle, which I think is a practical idea. If conditions get any worse, you will not be the only one. It is good exercise for keeping that waistline down. I am trying to stress that exercise is good for people. So far, I have been getting enough for I get to play tennis about two hours per week.

There is a Tech Sergeant who is going to become a Lieutenant, but he is 12 pounds overweight, and he wants me to play tennis with him to lose weight (fatty boy, he could stand to lose some).

I read *How Green Was My Valley* about 7 months ago. I would like to see the picture also. The story is beautiful; in fact, it is one of my favorite books. I don't think the picture can stir your feelings as the book does. I saw a fairly good show the other day, *Sisters in Retirement*, starring Ida Lupino and

Lewis Hayward. The story is morbid, but the acting is excellent.

Until the next time, yours as ever,

Love,
Herb

March 30, 1941

Dear Herb,

I got your letter, picture, and the grass skirt last evening and I just love it. It was awfully sweet of you. Thank you so much. I'll get Sis to take some snapshots of me wearing it.

I've been working. I started at Summerhill Tubing, but then I got a chance at another job in Bridgeport. I have been working at the Daring Paper Company since February 26. The man I am working for has just bought it, and things are awfully mixed up as yet. So far, I like it a lot.

I have stopped taking music lessons since I started working. I haven't finished all my subjects at school, either, so I guess I'll have to go to night school.

I'm sending you a few handkerchiefs. I wasn't sure which color would be the most suitable. Tell me which one you like. I'm sorry the embroidery isn't perfect, but it couldn't be sewn exactly perfect. I hope you will like the other gift I am sending for Easter.

Until next time, Ann

With the number of men in the U.S. military approaching millions, the army continually rearranged units and organizational charts to keep track of its fighting machine. On April 11, Herb's unit, the 324th Signal Company, Aviation, was redesignated the 324th Signal Company, Air Wing, a change in name only. All of the men remained on duty in their respective sections with the same equipment.

April 16, 1941

Herb, dear,

Your letter came last week and the picture, yesterday. The picture is swell. It is so natural looking. It makes me feel as if I am really looking at you instead of a picture.

Herb, I was glad to read that you are now a corporal. It must be a good feeling to know you are getting ahead and that you are "somebody." Keep up your good work.

Both jobs I had were temporary. I am now looking for a steady job, but good jobs are rather scarce.

Mother has quit working at the handbag factory and is at home now, and I am painting the front porch in my spare time and going to school to practice my office skills.

Dad and Mother have gotten me another car. It isn't altogether mine, but it's considered more mine than anyone else's. It is very nice, a 1940 gunmetal gray two-door Chevrolet Coach. I wish you were here to take a ride with me. It rides awfully nice.

This is about all I have for now. Now, write, will you?

Love, Ann

In May, the army promoted Herb from corporal to sergeant. Like the tide in Honolulu Harbor, Herb's rank rose and fell throughout his army career.

[Undated but probably May 1941]

Dear Herb,

The weather has been very hot but suddenly turned cool and rainy. As much as we need rain, it is going to spoil the apple blossoms.

I am back at school again. I have just taken my English final and still have three or four other tests to take. I applied for two jobs in the Penn Trust Bank. One was taken before I got there, and a more experienced girl got the other one.

Your descriptions of war are interesting. We don't have blackouts here, although I believe they have them at the various Army camps. We don't hear much about war preparations, but the mills that produce war materials are busy. Many workers in the bigger mills have struck for more money and fewer hours. Lots of places have had riots and pickets. At Bethlehem Steel, picketers turned over the automobiles of some of the workers. Most of the strikes have been settled now, though.

You shouldn't even think that you will never see me or the mainland again. I have always believed that if one wishes for something hard enough he will get it, so just keep on wishing and hoping as I am doing.

Herb, what does "Aloha" mean? I want to tell you again, your photograph is wonderful. I have put it on the piano so I can look at it every time I play.

"Aloha"
Love, Ann

On Tuesday, May 20, Hawaii had one of many blackouts in preparation for hostilities. Air raid blackout leaflets with the following message in five languages told civilians how to respond:

Urgent!   Warning!   Urgent!

Tuesday night, May 20, 1941, between 9:00 and 9:30 o'clock, "BLACKOUT ENEMY" PLANES will again SIMULATE ATTACK on YOUR ISLAND AND YOUR HOMES! When warning bells are rung or sirens sounded . . . IMMEDIATELY put out all lights . . . inside and outside! TURN OFF ALL SIGNS! Don't use flashlights, matches, etc. BLACKOUT COMPLETELY! While this raid is only make-believe, act as if it were real. Show your patriotism and your loyalty by giving your full-hearted cooperation. We hope the time will never come that Hawaii Nei will actually be bombed but if that time ever does come, we want to know that you know your part in the defense plan. We can only learn by doing. Let's prove to our military forces that we as citizens know how to cooperate in the defense of our Territory . . . . and this means . . . . not going to the hills to see the lights go out. Keep your radio on. Listen for the signal. Then act. Experience is a valuable teacher.

Amid the preparations, the War Department created the Army Air Forces (AAF) in June 1941, and Herb's company became an AAF unit. The Army Air Corps continued as part of the AAF, along with Headquarters AAF and Air Force Combat Command.

With all of the fortifications on Oahu, many in Hawaii felt safe from attack. In fact, some leaders refused to believe that the Japanese would strike Hawaii, despite deteriorating relations with Japan and other signs of impending war. Major General Frederick L. Martin, commander of the Hawaiian Air Force, fired his operations officer, Lt. Col. Albert Hegenberger, when, in July 1941, Hegenberger told the general that the Japanese could make a sneak attack with six aircraft carriers. "I will not have an officer on my staff who thinks like that," the general exclaimed, demoting Hegenberger to commanding a bombardment group.

July 7, 1941

Dear Herb,

I felt like writing tonight, especially since it is the eve of our "anniversary." In a way, it has seemed so long and yet short. I don't suppose that makes much sense, but I think you understand.

We had a miserable Fourth of July. It rained all day Saturday and Sunday. My two girlfriends went to the shore, and they said it was miserable there, too, and yet the papers this morning had pictures of the traffic jams all along the highway leading from the shore last evening.

Since working at the [Penn Trust] bank, I've met a girl named Eleanor Yount, a minister's daughter, and she says she knows you. She has a boyfriend in the Navy stationed at Pearl Harbor. I don't know his last name, but his first name is Bob. I was wondering if you perhaps knew Bob.

Herb, you once wrote to me, "I've never felt about anyone as I do about you," and you asked me how I felt. I don't know if I ever answered your question. I feel the same about you. I, too, am finding out that "absence makes the heart grow fonder." I miss you so much. I sometimes just sit and wish I could see you, even for a little bit. Well, I guess I'll just have to be patient and wait. Please write soon.

Your own, Ann

One day in mid-July, Herb went into Honolulu and mailed some money to Ann to save for their future. Afterwards, he swam at Waikiki Beach, having a "marvelous" time. Herb loved Hawaii's always-warm water. As he strode toward the shore, the soft, sun-scorched sand stung the soles of his feet. He swam gracefully; his strokes barely disturbed the surf. His muscles relaxed and his racing mind eased. He lay on the sand, as the sun swaddled him in its warmth, and listened to the whoosh of the waves rolling in. The almost-constant trade winds blew, cooling his skin. Swept up by the breeze, grains of sand pelted his legs. The smell of the coconut oil he'd covered himself with filled the air. He dragged on his cigarette, one of five he smoked daily, and slowly blew his stress into the breeze. A couple of drinks lulled him, and he felt peaceful, as calm as a lake in summer when no one's around.

Returning to his base and "the same old grind" at 6 p.m., his mellow mood evaporated. When he checked his company's bulletin board, he spied a list of about 25 names of men, including his, to report to the orderly room. Herb went to see why he was listed.

"Take the trash off of the radio by your bed," he was told. The only "trash" on the radio was an empty match box he had forgotten to throw away and a small piece of tin foil. His jaw slackened and he heaved a sigh as he picked them up and tossed them into a waste basket. "How unimportant, how petty—why can't they see the stupidity of it all?" he wrote. The army's discipline still riled Herb, who reacted like a fidgety boy made to sit still, even after a year of service.

Herb on the beach in Hawaii. (Photo from Herb's collection)

July 18, 1941

Dear Ann,

I hope the money I mailed you the other day from town reaches you safely. Next month, I will not be able to mail as much for my transfer has been approved, which means I will be a private again. But this doesn't make any difference; at least I am out of a place where I was unhappy. Happiness means more than money. I like my present job better than any work I've done since in the Army. It's office work; I can't tell you what kind.

I mailed you a model of an outrigger canoe, the type of boat the natives use. I have never ridden in one but have seen them in action and imagine it's a lot of fun. It is not as popular as the surf board, I guess, because it costs more money to own one.

I finished the painting I told you about, so as soon as I get a chance to mail it, you will get it. See if you can get a frame for it; glass is not necessary. When I get enough spirit in me again, I will try to paint something with a Hawaiian effect to it.

Did you read about the V-mail? One of the guys down here wrote a V-mail letter, and the censors sent it back with a note stating that using vulgar language is against the rules and to please use better taste. The guy who wrote it is a little crazy, and he did use harsh words. The censors take pictures of the V-mail, which seems to be much speedier than regular mail, as fast as three days. But it has disadvantages; you can't write much and only on one side of the paper.

Tell your friend Grace not to write to that person I mentioned in my letter. He's a dope. Another chap down here, a nice guy named Wendell Armor, a corporal, saw the picture you sent me and wants to write to Grace. Ask her if she will answer if he writes to her. Tell her that he is from Pittsburgh, Pa., and wants someone to write to. Incidentally, what is Grace's last name? I don't think anything will come of the letters he writes, but he seems lonesome, and if he wasn't any good, I would let you know. He has already asked me twice since yesterday whether I had mentioned his request to you.

If you really want to get me something for my birthday, you can send me some Fanny Farmer candies. That is all. I hope the gifts I sent you arrive safely. The bracelet is the main gift; I put the others in for good measure.

Until I hear from you again, I remain as ever,

Love, Herb

An outrigger canoe and surfers off of Waikiki Beach with Diamond Head in the background, c. 1943. (Photo from Herb's collection)

—★—

The pride of our family, my father's oil paintings graced the living room walls of my parents' Cape Cod, my girlhood home. The still life of a brown jug spouting a rhododendron branch next to a dish towel hung over Mother's secretary. The landscape of the covered bridge in Amish country adorned the mantel. This painting, now in my living room, conjured one of my earliest memories: I played there as a toddler while my father sat in a lawn chair and dabbed paint onto the canvas in the easel before him. The stream beneath the bridge gurgled as I collected sticks and stones. The fresh country air reddened my cheeks and diffused the citified smell of the oil paints and turpentine.

Each Halloween, on a poster-sized piece of art paper, Daddy drew, in pastels, an evil-looking witch, with a hooked nose and warts. He hung it on the top half of our front door. My sisters and I loved the pictures but they frightened some neighborhood kids, who wouldn't knock on our door. Daddy would put a nylon stocking over his head for the occasion, deforming his face, and scare us. We girls squealed in fright, but it was a fun kind of scary, like watching a horror movie.

I'd wondered how my father had learned to paint. Mother called his family "poor," but I began to doubt that. First of all, his father worked continuously at a woolen mill and as a motorman for the Schuylkill Valley Traction Company during the Depression, according to the Norristown city directories I'd consulted. Secondly, how could a poor family with five children afford piano and art lessons?

For several Saturday mornings during my childhood, my father and I drove, wordlessly, from the suburbs to downtown Philadelphia to what I knew only as "Fleisher." There, I took an art class for kids; he took one for adults. Wondering if that was where my father learned his craft, I researched the Samuel S. Fleisher Art Memorial, a product of the altruism of the son of the founder of the Fleisher Yarn Company in southwest Philadelphia. To reward the mill workers for their role in the success of the country's first worsted woolen mill, Samuel Fleisher sponsored free art lessons for their children. The endeavor became known as the Graphic Sketch Club. I called Mother and told her about Fleisher's history.

"Yes, I knew about the free art classes. Herb studied there before the war," she recalled. Though working at another mill, Herb had heard about the Sketch Club and studied commercial art there for a year and a half.

—★—

August 17, 1941

Dear Herb,

I was looking for a letter from you for three weeks, and finally I received two letters and a package within three days. The blouse is simply lovely and a perfect fit. It is such a splashingly gay color....

Herb, would you rather I send you candy or cigarettes? Of course, I don't know much about cigarettes, so you can tell me what brand you like, or is there anything else you would like me to send you?

You say you think the war will start shortly. I want to say one thing. Don't volunteer to "go across" if you should have a choice of waiting until they make you go or volunteering to go across on an expeditionary force. Please don't go unless they make you. You've gone far enough away from home.

I learned to run the bookkeeping machine and enjoy my work now. I will have to take some courses in banking at a school in Philadelphia, so that will take up my spare time these winter evenings.

Herb, I hope you will get a good job when you come home. I am very flattered that you think so much of me that you want to marry me, and I think that someday we will be able to get married. However, it will be some time before we can seriously think of this. Lots of good jobs are available now, but if the U.S. enters the war, many of the soldiers will come home at the same time, and good jobs will be hard to get. I don't sound very encouraging, do I?

Have you read about the new legislation lengthening the term of enlistment of all soldiers? I am sending along a clipping from *The Bulletin*. It sounds as if you have 2-1/2 or 3 years instead of 1-1/2 or 2 as I was thinking. I guess Eleanor and I will have to come over there to see you and her "Bob." I heard a senator say today that the U.S. is no nearer war today than it was a year ago. So maybe things aren't so bad after all.

48

I'm sorry this letter isn't more cheerful, but I am in one of my serious moods. Don't let this letter get you down.

Your loving,

Ann

With all of the war preparations, all but the naysayers in Hawaii must have felt the way Herb did: the war would soon begin. In fact, the military elite and Roosevelt's cabinet thought that Japan would attack the United States in late 1941.

On October 1, Herb's company stopped work for the day to celebrate the company's first anniversary. Leaving behind a skeleton crew to handle communications for the bomber command, the company headed for the Shriner's Beach home on the windward side of Oahu. There, the men enjoyed a distinct change of scenery: the jagged cliffs, lush valleys, and dense foliage of the Koolau Range of mountains. Blue skies and sunshine smiled on the partiers swimming, relaxing, socializing, playing games, and drinking. "Morale and behavior was [sic] excellent," wrote the unit's historian.

November 5, 1941

Dear Ann,

Why haven't you been writing? A boat came in today from the mainland. I was expecting a letter from you, but none came. Did I say anything that made you mad? Let's have a letter to let me know you are still alive.

Things here have not changed; they will always be the same. If they would take the tennis courts away, I would go crazy. That's about the only worthwhile thing I do besides swimming. If you don't exercise in this climate, you become lazy. The natives are an excellent example of climate disease!!!

I don't want to write about war and am getting tired of waiting for it. I wish it would start, so we can have some action around here. Fortunately, we are in a good spot for war. But our country is still not prepared.

I was swimming at Waikiki Beach this afternoon and few people were on the beach. It was the first time I ever saw it so deserted.

My buddy and I went to town yesterday, and I had an excellent steak; in fact, it was the tenderest steak I ever tasted. We went to the Wagon Wheel. It's expensive, but if you want good food, you have to pay for it, and you really don't mind when it's good.

I bought you some perfume the other day but have not gotten around to mailing it. I hope you like it…. I never knew anyone as easy to please as you. I love you for it. I hope you always stay like that.

I still want you, Ann, for my wife. Nothing will ever change my mind. Whatever you say or do to hurt me, my feelings toward you will remain the same. In your next letter, please send me your ring size. Don't forget. I am going to send you a ring for Christmas.

Lovingly yours,
Herb

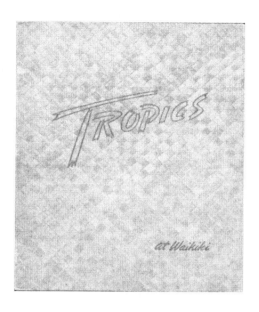

A 1940s menu from the Tropics on Kalakaua Avenue from Herb's collection. If the prices at Tropics—a restaurant that Herb frequented—compared with the Wagon Wheel's, a New York cut or T-bone steak there cost $1.35 in the early 1940s.

"Keep 'Em Flying"

Thanksgiving Day Dinner
Hickam Field, T. H.

Assorted Fruit Cocktail
Turkey Broth with Rice
Hearts of Celery   Ripe and Green Olives   Sweet Gherkins
Roast Tom Turkey, stuffed with Chestnuts
Giblet Gravy
Baked Southern Ham, Champagne Sauce
Dixie Candied Yams   Cream Whipped Potatoes
Green Fresh Peas
Head Lettuce with Asparagus Tips
Thousand Island Dressing
Parker House Rolls   Fruit Cake
Mince Pie, Hard Sauce   Pumpkin Pie
Cherry Pie a la Mode
Roquefort Cheese   Hard Crackers
Fresh Lemonade   Coffee
Fruits   Nuts   Bon Bons
Cigars   Cigarettes

COMPLIMENTS OF ADVERTISER PUBLISHING CO. LTD.

This menu, from Herb's collection, was for Thanksgiving dinner at Hickam, 1941. It is one of the few holidays Ann and Herb did not discuss, most likely because Herb was too busy to write about it.

November 14, 1941

Dear Herb,

How were the maneuvers? I'll bet it was thrilling flying to the other island in a plane. Are you still feeling depressed? I don't suppose you feel much better since they have repealed the Neutrality Act.

Back here, everyone is beginning to think about Christmas. I have been to the city several times lately, and I am going again tomorrow with Virginia. Do you remember her? She is the secretary at the Schwenksville High School….

I have not been doing much except that I have seen several movies. The last two were *You'll Never Get Rich*, with Fred Astaire and Rita Hayworth, and *A Yank in the R.A.F.*, with Tyrone Power and Betty Grable. Both were good. *You'll Never Get Rich* was a musical comedy about Army life, and the other was about an American flier who got to England by ferrying American planes there.

52

Herb, what would you like for Christmas?

Love, Ann

The Neutrality Acts, passed in the 1930s, sought to prevent the United States from getting involved in the European conflict as it had in World War I. But America's neutrality really ended with the Lend-Lease Act, and many provisions of the Neutrality Acts were repealed in November 1941.

As the country's relations with Japan eroded by late November 1941, U.S. forces in Hawaii went on alert. Aircraft were stowed in hangars or in open spaces nearby, and extra guards monitored aircraft and military installations. The military built protective fencing and installed floodlights where needed.

Although few officials doubted the imminence of hostilities, most thought they would take place in the Philippines—not Hawaii. Commanders in the Pacific received a dispatch to that effect:

> This dispatch is to be considered a war warning. An aggressive move by Japan is expected within the next few days. This will probably be an amphibious expedition against either the Philippines, the Thai or Kra Peninsulas, or possibly Borneo.

Nonetheless, the Hawaiian Department took steps to ready its forces for hostilities. On November 27, officials decided to send all aircraft carriers from Pearl Harbor out to sea and move half of the army's planes. In the week before December 7, the Hawaiian Department conducted a full-scale exercise. Army units from Schofield Barracks deployed, antiaircraft units drew ammunition and set up stations around the islands, and the Hawaiian Air Force armed aircraft and dispersed them to protective revetments. Fully operational, the Air Warning Service launched aircraft against simulated targets. On December 3, Herb's company went on maneuvers attached to the 24th Infantry Division of Schofield Barracks.

By Saturday, December 6, the Hawaiian Department had called off the alert. Herb's company packed up its gear, rolling up all its wire, stowing the switchboard, and loading radio and other equipment back into trucks, which headed in a convoy back to Hickam. The signalmen arrived at the base at 11 a.m. and unloaded the trucks, unconcerned about the alert, and carried on as usual. Airmen arrayed the bombers inspection style on the flight line. For hours, men lined up for passes to town and headed to Honolulu or Pearl Harbor to hear the "Battle of Music," a band contest.

With the entire exercise a success, the senior commanders on Oahu believed they would have plenty of warning to start long-range reconnaissance, set up communications between the army and navy, staff the Air Warning Service, and arm and disperse aircraft to fight the enemy. The Pacific Fleet would attack, and the Japanese would face a sky full of U.S. planes. On December 6, Frank Knox, Secretary of the Navy, announced, "The navy is ready to meet any threat."

On December 7, Ernest Galeassi, a private in Herb's company, got up, shaved, dressed, and went to mass in Hickam's gym, then to the chow hall for breakfast. He walked back to the barracks and sat down on its front steps, looking across the airfield. He soon spied planes almost grazing the barracks' roof, planes marked with the red rising sun of Japan, dubbed the "meatball" by the GIs. As the planes zoomed overhead, Galeassi yelled inside to those in the barracks, "We're being attacked!" He ran two blocks to the motor pool as an ear-splitting boom sounded from Pearl Harbor, the first target. Black smoke billowed over the naval base. Hickam's air raid siren blared.

While Galeassi sprinted to the motor pool to move the company's trucks under some palm trees, Herb worked teletype in Hickam's Bomber Command Signal Office in the Base Operations building—the centrally located nerve center of the base.* He relayed new developments from one headquarters to another and sent and took orders for the Commanding Generals. Only his helmet and the building protected him. Outside, dive bombers whined, machine-gun fire chattered, and bombs thundered.

Meanwhile, a lineman truck driver in Herb's company, Private Thomas J. Pillion, and another signalman drove a truck full of field wire, telephones, and other equipment to Base Ops. Japanese bombs hit the hangar line and hangars, whistling past Pillion and his colleague, Bill Kokosko, as they arrived at Base Ops and huddled under a palm tree. The air reeked of gunpowder.

Lt. Col. Guy N. Church, the ranking Signal Officer, drove up in his staff car and got out with his arms full of sporting guns. He handed Pillion and Kokosko each a shotgun but no ammunition. They left the guns at the message center. As the two signalmen exited Base Ops, Japanese planes splintered the Hawaiian Air Depot, hangars, and planes on the hangar line. Pillion and Kokosko ducked under the building where a grating had been removed. Minutes later, they headed to their company's supply building. Meanwhile, air force gunners manned the parade ground—without cover—and got mowed down like blades of grass, to be replaced by more gunners.

The bombing stopped for about 30 minutes. Ambulances began picking up the wounded. Then the bombers returned, blasting Hickam for another 15 minutes. This time, some Japanese planes exploded from antiaircraft fire. When an enemy plane blew

*Japanese intelligence mistakenly identified Base Ops as an officers' club, sparing the building.

55

up, everyone stood up and cheered as if at a baseball game. The enemy hammered supply buildings, the base chapel, Snake Ranch, and guard house. The sparkling, new consolidated barracks shook repeatedly with the force of the explosions, which splattered food, trays, and the bodies of men in the chow hall. Almost all of the 100 Japanese bombs dropped on Hickam hit a target. Reportedly the most heavily bombed building on Oahu, the consolidated barracks burned for four hours. Bodies lay everywhere.

Though at first some men at Hickam wandered about, panic stricken, most took heart and fought back, firing .50-caliber machine guns, Thompson submachine guns, Colt .45 automatic pistols, and even World War I-era bolt-action Springfield rifles. They may as well have thrown their guns at their attackers. Thirty-five AAF planes took flight, some engaging the enemy and others in pursuit, unaware that most of the Japanese planes had already left the area. Hawaiian Air Force fighter pilot and heir to the grape juice fortune George S. Welch shot down 4 of the 29 enemy planes destroyed that day, the first American to down a Japanese plane.

Pillion and his buddies spent most of the day running wire and supplying field telephones to bomb squads and headquarters groups. When Pillion and another signalman, Jim Bagot, drove back to Base Ops that night, they weaved to avoid craters in the parade ground and burning vehicles. At midnight, the air raid siren wailed. Spotlights beamed on more planes overhead, U.S. Navy planes. Trigger-happy, everyone with a weapon shot at them. The sky lit with red hot tracers, Pillion and Bagot dove for shelter under Base Ops. Feeling secure, they laughed, probably from nerves, and lit cigarettes. "Sgt. Herbert Gilmore"—Herb—told them to put out the smokes. "Go to hell," they replied.

This iconic photo shows Hickam's brand-new barracks in flames after the Japanese attack. The truck at the base of the flag pole belongs to Herb's company, members of which were fixing a damaged cable. The tattered flag in the photo later flew above the United Nations charter meeting in San Francisco, over the Big Three conference at Potsdam, and above the White House on August 14, 1945, when the Japanese surrendered. (Signal Corps photo from Herb's collection)

The spanking new barracks still burning after the attack, right, and two of the hangars burning, left. (Signal Corps photo from Herb's collection)

The Base Operations Building, where Herb and his Signal Company comrades worked on December 7, 1941. The crow's nest was hit that day, but the building, one of the oldest at Hickam, still stands. (Photo from Herb's collection)

Like Herb, men from all signal companies at Hickam stayed at their posts to radio, teletype, or phone messages at a moment's notice during the attack. Switchboard operators handled thousands of calls every hour. Linemen repaired severed or damaged lines. Those who stayed on duty in Base Ops, like Herb, should have received medals of recognition but did not, according to Pillion's oral history of the attack: "Everyone in the company performed the duties for which they were trained without question. I was proud to have served in the 324th Signal Company."

Oahu suffered horrifying carnage and wreckage: more than 2,300 servicemen died and 1,100 were wounded. AAF posts on Oahu lost more than 200 men, with 700 wounded. Though Hickam lost 121 men, with 274 wounded and 37 missing, the attack claimed no lives in Herb's company. Of the Hawaiian Air Force's 146 planes, 76 were lost; an additional 128 army planes were damaged island-wide. Forty explosions had rocked Honolulu, all but one the result of U.S. antiaircraft fire. Honolulu lost 48 civilians, 3 fire fighters, and 4 government employees.

During the attack, known in Hawaii as the "Blitz," untried troops responded as veterans. Silver stars and purple hearts decorated the chests of 233 men at Hickam afterwards. Two men in Herb's company, buddies of his, were cited: Joseph P. Miszczuk, of Nanticoke, Pennsylvania, and John S. Lopinsky, of Summerlee, West Virginia.* Lopinsky, an outstanding baseball player for the Hawaiian Air Force, played on a volleyball team with Herb.

The night of the Blitz, critical units headed for wooded areas beyond the base, on 24-hour alert. The bomber command moved to its forward post, which it used until the next day. Herb's

*I found the signatures of these men in one of my father's scrapbooks, among other names, home addresses, poems, and messages.

company sent enough signalmen along with the command to maintain 24-hour communications. The rest of the company stayed at Hickam to inspect and repair the signal equipment damaged by the raid. Except for one major cable out of service at Hickam, the attack did little damage to communications. Soldiers and civilians working during the second bombing wave had quickly patched all the important circuits in Hickam's cable, and the whole cable was restored the next day.

Like disaster evacuees, Hickam's men found shelter under trees or blankets that night or in pup tents, unlocked family quarters, or wherever they could sleep. Under a moonlit sky, a blackout cloaked all light on the ground to help thwart an invasion. Neighborhood wardens patrolled to see that residents shut off lights and covered windows with black cloth; those who failed to do so could be arrested.

Their company's barracks destroyed, Herb and his colleagues had to bunk elsewhere for three days. A Lord Elgin watch on which Ann had spent an entire month's wages disappeared, bombed into oblivion or looted. But Herb and his buddies had been spared. Herb wrote nothing to Ann about the Blitz immediately, probably because of censorship. But Pillion's account and a history of the 324th Signal Company substantiated that Herb was on duty during the attack.

Frenetic activity took place immediately after the Blitz. All important buildings in Hawaii received a coat of camouflage paint, including Hickam's majestic water tower and Honolulu's Aloha Tower, then the tallest structure in Hawaii. The military convinced 200 or so "lei women" to weave camouflage nets instead of leis. To prevent Japanese landings, the military strung barbed wire along the beaches. All paper money in the Territory was recalled and burned to prevent the misuse of U.S. currency if Hawaii was captured. As in World War I, people began planting vegetable gardens of eggplants, lettuce, carrots, sweet potatoes, and onions. Children started toting gas masks everywhere they went.

The consolidated barracks after the Blitz.
(Photo from Herb's collection)

Herb on the beach, now ringed with barbed wire.
(Photo from Herb's collection)

The military convinced the governor of Hawaii to declare martial law. The authorities arrested civilians, including 370 Japanese, 98 Germans, and 14 Italians, to prevent them from aiding the enemy. Martial law remained in effect for three years. Like grounded teenagers, the once light-hearted islands succumbed to curfews, rationing, and endless regulations.

Herb, like many Americans, viewed Japan's unannounced attack as sneaky. As the United States declared war on Japan on December 8, 1941, Americans rallied—none more than the airmen, soldiers, sailors, and marines on Oahu. They wanted revenge.

CHAPTER 3
MOBILIZING

The Kona wind blows softly now,
The palm trees whisper low,
But all America will remember
Whence came this dastard's blow.
Let the Nipponese remember this,
As they cringe beneath the sky,
At Hickam's flaming vengeance
For you, the first to die!
—Sgt. W. Joe Brimm, Hickam Field

The Japanese advanced to Hong Kong and Wake Island, the Netherlands East Indies, Philippines, and Singapore while GIs on Oahu hustled to rebuild. Air raid sirens blared, signaling drills. Everyone imagined sabotage afoot. Fighter planes stood ready to intercept enemy aircraft, and bombers flew endless search missions. Japanese subs lurked around the islands, shelling Maui and the "big island" of Hawaii and two smaller ones and sinking merchant ships. Military family members who wanted to leave Hawaii sailed to the mainland on the SS *Mariposa*.

Like the sun sinking under the horizon at Waikiki beach at dusk, Herb's hopes of a three-year stint vanished. His enlistment would far exceed the 33-month average for active-duty soldiers in the war. Dreading his indeterminate future in the army, he could bemoan his situation or resolve to do his bit.

December 13, 1941

Dear Ann,

I am still working at Fort Shafter on detached service. I seem to be getting along pretty well because I like it.

I have just come back from the showers and feel refreshed. Every time I take a shower, I stay for about an hour. I believe I could sleep while taking a shower.

I'm reading *Chad Hannah* by Walter D. Edwards. So far it is pretty good. It is about a boy who was reared in an orphanage. Later, he runs away and gets a job running a canal boat on the Erie Canal. I was lucky to get this book for the library is in bad condition.

The cookies you sent me were good except for one thing. There were not enough of them. The buddies I bunk with said, "They were damn good. Tell her to send some more." Ann, do you know what I would like and appreciate if you could send? Some homemade fudge. That's the trouble when you are a good cook. Don't be mad.

A beaded belt that I picked up in Honolulu is on its way to you. I hope you like it and wear it often because I like it. I hope it fits you.

> Yours truly, Love,
> Herb

On a day off in December, Herb hitched a ride to Honolulu rather than pay 15 cents for the bus or a quarter for a taxi. He left his ride at the Army and Navy YMCA on the corner of Hotel and Richards Streets. On the palm-tree shaded lawn of the Y, GIs slept off their drunks.

He passed the Black Cat Café on Hotel Street, where soldiers perched on barstools swigging beer from steins in the open air. The saloons and juke joints lent a carnival-like setting to the street. Concessions offered 10-cent hot dogs, 15-cent hamburgers, seafood, slot machines, and the like. The smell of grilled steak wafted from restaurants offering more substantial fare, where a Porterhouse steak with mushrooms cost $1 and a roast turkey dinner, 50 cents. Skinny boys in uniform wearing leis posed for photos in pictoriums with a "hula girl" for $1. Locals pedaled by on bicycles. Middle-aged women in shirtwaist dresses and sun hats, lei sellers, called out, "Lei, Mister? Only 25 cent."

Bill Hoagland (left), from
Bloomsburg, Pennsylvania, and
Herb striking a pose on the road
from Hickam to Waikiki.

Herb (center) and two buddies in civvies.

Herb and a friend on Hotel Street. (Photos from
Herb's collection)

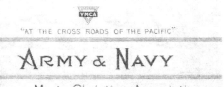

Herb must have gone to the Y at least once because he used stationery from there. On the left is the masthead of the stationery; at right, the graphic from the envelope. The Y housed United Service Organization (USO) activities and became known as the USO Army and Navy Club.

Herb ambled in and out of the shops, looking for a suitable gift for Ann and settling on the beaded belt. Returning to Hickam, he headed to the PX to look at engagement rings, picking out a white gold Art Deco-styled round diamond in a square setting surrounded by filigree. Its delicate design suited Ann's slender fingers, he thought, and he mailed it to her that day. On January 7, 1942, Ann announced their engagement.

While Herb shopped, the AAF reorganized to better wage war. It redesignated the Hawaiian Air Force the Seventh Air Force and the 18th Bombardment Wing, the VII Bomber Command, led by General Willis H. Hale. The Seventh Air Force would not only defend Hawaii but also train combat crews and modify aircraft for tactical units in the South Pacific. As the aerial striking force across the Central Pacific to Japan, its airmen would fly missions across that theater and make up combat units for the South Pacific theater. And Herb and his colleagues would follow them.

11 February 1942

Dearest Ann,

A letter has finally gotten here. I have been waiting a long time and have been so lonely. I feel as though I'm losing my mind—every day, the same routine. I thought I could get used to it, but I guess I can't take it.

It's going to be a very long time before I see you. It makes me sick to think about this. Sometimes I feel we are prisoners on an island, waiting for a boat that will never come. I used to blame what has happened to me on fate but cannot do so anymore. Forgive me for writing this way.

If you want to announce the engagement, go ahead. It will surprise people who know me for I always said I'm not the marrying kind. I guess I was talking through my hat.

Thanks for remembering me on Valentine's Day. I would send you a card, but I can't get a hold of one. I am remembering you not only on one day of the year but every day. Let's not discuss this damn war. So far I have not said anything about it and don't intend to. It would probably be censored anyway.

It will take a long time before you get this letter due to the boat schedules. Don't think that I don't write. What little time I have, I shall always write.

Always loving you,
Herb

Compounding Herb's frustration with the army, censors read his and other servicemen's letters to keep information, such as their location or their units' activities, from aiding the enemy. Officers also searched letters for signs of sinking morale among the troops, important during wartime.

An officer in Herb's unit, sometimes his company commander, censored his and his buddies' letters. At times a chaplain or dentist would do it. If a large part had to be cut, a censor would most likely confiscate the letter, not necessarily telling the soldier that his letter wasn't mailed. If a small section needed cutting, a censor would cut it out or obliterate it with ink. If a censor suspected espionage, he would apply special chemicals to check for invisible writing and confiscate the letter rather than return it to a serviceman. A censor would talk to a soldier whose letter needed cutting, viewing any infraction as carelessness—not an act of sabotage.*

February 19, 1942

Dear Ann,

Received your letter dated January 24. Did you receive the letters containing the money orders?

I am going to send you a turban and blouse to match. Do you think you would want it?

It looks as if the WACs are going to start relieving some of us fellas. Six hundred of them came here a couple of weeks ago. They are working at some post, probably office work. . . .

I am going to the University of Hawaii to inquire about an extension course. The Army is collaborating with the university to offer courses through a college back in the states. I am looking at catalogs, and it seems like a good deal. Commercial art will be my subject. This will occupy me above everything else. My time will be cramped, but it's such a good opportunity I want to take advantage of it. My first step is to go to the university and get the real degree. The Army is paying half of the fee; I pay the rest. I will let you know what college I choose. There are numerous ones to pick from.

*Censorship ended after World War II, although some letters in the early part of the Korean conflict were censored. By then, censoring mail took more time and effort than the military thought it was worth.

I am neglectful in my letter writing, but there is so much confusion here at times that I am lucky to write at all. Please be patient until you hear from me more often. I am glad you received your ring safely. I was not sure if you would because conditions were hot down here.

If the Japanese should ever come back, they would be surprised—met with such a comeback that they would leave quickly. We are well prepared for any invasion. The Japanese are far too clever to please me. They never fight in the open. They would rather stab you in the back without giving you a chance to protect yourself. They showed that on December 7, which I will never forget as long as I live.

It was kind of you to send me some cookies and candy, which were excellent. They were so good that my friend said he was going to write you saying that he is starving to death, and please send him something to eat before it's too late. . . .

Aloha,
Herb

March 8, 1942

Dear Herb,

I hope this letter finds you in better spirits than I'm in. The weekdays are enjoyable enough for the time passes quickly, but during the weekends, there isn't much to do since we must stay home to conserve tires and gas. . . .

Last night we saw *How Green Was My Valley* at the Norris. I enjoyed it very much, although I thought it too sad, but it deserved to win the Academy Award. I hope to read the book soon.

I understand they are broadcasting some of the programs we hear to Hawaii and the other islands. Have you heard any of them? I believe "Fibber Magee and Molly" and "Henry Aldrich" are two that are being broadcast.

Herb, I don't believe all my letters are reaching you. You wrote that you had been waiting so long for one from me. I have written a letter each week since January and you should have gotten one each week. I also sent cookies and candy that

69

should have reached you around St. Valentine's Day. Did you get them? Keep up your courage and spirits.

Love,

Ann

In alignment with the AAF's reorganization, the Seventh Air Force redesignated Herb's company the 400th Signal Company, Aviation, in March 1942, a change in number only. The staff of the company and its work remained the same. Weeks later, the company was attached to the Signal Section, Headquarters and Headquarters Squadron, VII Bomber Command. Herb's company handled communications, including messages to and from aircraft. A month later, the Seventh Air Force began operating under the control of the navy. It would work with navy, army, and Marine Corps forces on an island-hopping campaign to take certain Central Pacific islands in the drive toward Tokyo.

For months after the Blitz, the top brass of the Seventh Air Force asked the War Department for more airplanes to replace those destroyed. The year before, President Roosevelt had shocked the Congress when he proposed building 50,000 aircraft a year. Between 1939 and 1941, however, production facilities devoted to the AAF increased by 400 percent. Although most of that production went to Great Britain for defense aid under Lend-Lease agreements, it gave the U.S. military battle-tested planes. By the end of 1943, U.S. plants produced more than 7,000 planes a month. Ford's massive Willow Run bomber factory alone produced nearly one airplane an hour by early 1944.

April 13, 1942

Dear Ann,

Mother wrote that you gave her a plant for Easter. It was very kind of you.

I saw *How Green Was My Valley*, which was marvelous, but I like the book better for the picture doesn't have the detail the book did.

I read in the paper that the Army is starting a Woman's Auxiliary Corps, of which I do not approve. When a woman has to take orders from another woman, she is not going to like it. The women are going to have to take orders or punishment. I think the whole affair will be disastrous. I approve of women doing defense work but not joining this Woman's Auxiliary Corps, where they have almost the same duties a soldier does. I know the women who join will think they are doing the right thing for their country, but it is not going to be a bed of roses. If they really want to help win the war, they can get a defense job. How would you like to take orders 24 hours a day from someone who is not as intelligent or pretty as you? How would you like to ask permission for everything you want to do?

I have made another rating. They gave me a P.F.C., Private First Class, and a third grade technical rating, which isn't bad on the money side. I draw $65 per month. My address has been changed to A.P.O. #953, c/o Post Master, San Francisco, Cal. This applies to us in Foreign Service. If any of our mail gets into enemy hands, they would not be able to determine our post.

I agree 100% with George C. Marshall, Army Chief of Staff. He says now is the time for a strong offensive blow to the Axis. The Russian ambassador, Retvinov, says this also. Did you ever stop to think that if the Russians didn't stop Germany when they did, Hitler would probably be over here by now? The Russians have helped immensely in this war. The United States should help the Russians by giving them anything they ask for.

The Japanese claimed they would take Hawaii by April 15. If they are going to take it, they better start trying right now. If they come, they will have to use their entire fleet and all their armed forces and planes, which I don't think they can do now. They may try, but it will be a total loss for them. The situation in Bataan doesn't look good.

I went horseback riding the other day for the first time in about a year and a half. I still feel the results, mostly in my back. I am going again soon if I can get a pass. I go to probably the largest stables in Honolulu, with about 50 horses. It cost $1.50 an hour, but it is worth it for there is little recreation here besides swimming at Waikiki Beach and tennis. And as far as surfboard riding is concerned, I can't get my balance. I would like to learn, but it takes time and patience. I have not played tennis for a while for the master sergeant who used to play with me has left for the states.

Your bank is giving its employees bonuses and raises maybe because it thinks they are going to try to get defense jobs. It's easy to get such a job, where you can make more money, and the bank knows this. Ann, I will try to write every two weeks. This is the longest letter I've ever written in my life.

Yours truly,
Herb

Like many soldiers, Herb looked askance at the Woman's Auxiliary Corps (WAC), even though every working WAC freed a man to fight. Established in May 1942, WACs served as radio and telephone operators, photographers, lab personnel, finance specialists, and in other administrative posts. WACs, considered temporary employees who would not serve after the war, received less pay and fewer benefits than men in the army. On July 1, 1943, the WAC officially became part of the army. More than 100,000 served in the WAC at its peak. Contrary to Herb's notions, the WAC endured.

May 1, 1942

Dear Ann,
The Lieutenant I am working for feels proud to have been promoted to a Captain. A mass promotion of officers on

the whole island has meant that all of the lieutenants have been promoted to captain.

I mailed the last letter I wrote you (the four-page one) from town because my Company Commander asked me to condense it to one page. I did not like that and asked him why. The only reason he gave me was that it was too long and he did not want to read so long a letter. There is an order stating that we should write on one side of the paper to make the censoring easier for them, but it doesn't state how many pages we should write. Writing on one side of the paper during a paper shortage is stupid. This censoring business has its advantages and disadvantages. The only reason for censoring my letter was its length. After all, it is his job to read the letters. He should encourage, not discourage, letter writing.

The war looks fairly good for us (thanks to the Russians). If conditions keep going the way they have been, I think the war will be over by Christmas. The papers are saying that U.S. planes are bombing cities in Japan. It sounds good, but I don't believe it because Washington has not confirmed it yet.

Today is Lei Day here, a big event for the natives. Today, all the money from the sale of leis goes to buy war bonds and to the Army and Navy relief fund. I will mail this letter from town for I know this will never get past my Company Commander, but everything I wrote is true.

Love, yours truly,
Herb

As Herb mentioned in the preceding letter, Colonel James Doolittle led a bombing raid on Tokyo and three other Japanese cities on April 18. The pounding did little damage, but it revealed the weakness of Japan's defense of its homeland.

During the next several months, the Allies set up garrisons in India, Australia, New Zealand, and islands in the Pacific. Meanwhile on May 1, Hawaiians donned leis—symbols of affection—and kissed each other to celebrate Lei Day, a holiday of giving and receiving celebrated when flowers bloom all over the islands.*

May 17, 1942

Dear Ann,

I received three letters from you. Don't feel bad if I don't write as often as you, for I hardly get any time to myself anymore. The last couple of weeks have been rough. I can't get to sleep at night. Last night I went to bed at 8. But I was so restless, I had to get up and take a walk. I came back and finally got to sleep around 1 a.m.

Jack Benny's program is being broadcast over the radio, but the reception isn't at all good, too much static and interference.

It's getting hot down here now, and I do mean hot. I was thinking the other day if the war hadn't started, I would be on the sailing list to go home, but it wasn't in the cards for me to have such luck.

You asked me my opinion of your trying for a defense job. Would asking the bank for a raise help? This may scare them into thinking they might lose you. Try to make them think you have an opportunity for a defense job. It all depends on how you rate with them. I think you better stick to your present job. If you got a defense job, you would probably have to leave home and pay all your own expenses, which can cost a lot. Besides, even if you would make more money, after the war, you will be out of job. If you were not working now, then I would suggest getting a defense job, but as you say, your job is steady and will be so.

I read in the paper that they started that damn Women's Auxiliary Corps. The women who join will get $21 a month for their first four months. After that, they will get a $10 raise. This will be their monthly pay as long as they're in. They are not going to like it, and soon after joining, plenty of them will be squawking, just you wait and see.

---

*Hawaiians still celebrate Lei Day. In addition to strings of blossoms, leis can also consist of leaves, plants, shells, or feathers.

Mother writes and tells me who all is in the Army. There seem to be a lot of fellows I know from Norristown who are in the Army now. Some of them are not going to like it.

I don't take too seriously the notion that the war will last two or three years. If everyone does his bit and we start this offensive, it won't be long before the damn war is over. The Japanese have told so many damn lies—how they sank an aircraft carrier and numerous other ships—to lower the morale of the American people. I hope the people won't think the war is over yet. It's going to be a hard fight, but not a long one. According to [Secretary of State] Cordell Hull, the United Nations might achieve an earlier victory than was the case a few months ago. It took us a long time to get started, and we are still not doing all we really can. All we need are planes and more planes. We have plenty of fliers.

Merrill Gander's wife, Marge, the woman I wrote you about, is making a Hawaiian lei necklace for you. She goes up in the mountains and picks the seeds, from which she makes the necklaces in her spare time. They're very nice. She is also making Mother one. She had been knitting for the Red Cross but gave it up.

If it is not too expensive, will you send me some homemade cookies? I won't ask for any more.

As ever,
Herb

The Battle of the Coral Sea, fought in early May, marked the Allies' first successful strike against Japanese expansionism and gave Herb and other Americans a glimmer of hope about the war. Reflecting the sentiments of many in the military, he wrote, "The Battle of the Coral Sea showed how strong our navy is for it was its worst battle since the war started. It goes to show you what America can do once she starts."

The day after Herb wrote the preceding letter, May 18, the Seventh Air Force went on a special alert in anticipation of a Japanese strike on Midway or an air raid on Hawaii. By the end of

May, the Seventh had acquired more than 200 airplanes. More bombers arrived by June 10, answering the force's plea for more aircraft.

On May 30, 19 bomber and fighter planes from the Seventh flew 1,000 miles to take up temporary station on Midway, ending the alert as all available forces gathered to defend the island. The next day, the bombers flew missions extending for 600 miles in search of the enemy fleet, returning to Midway on June 1.

On June 3, search planes spied Japanese ships steaming toward Midway. Six B-17s from Herb's command took off to attack enemy ships 570 miles from Midway. The Battle of Midway blazed for the next two days as AAF and navy planes struck enemy vessels. The Japanese downed two AAF planes, one of which launched its torpedo before crashing. Two other AAF planes crash landed back at Midway riddled with holes. Extensive searches made by fliers on June 6 revealed no sign of the fleeing enemy.

B-17s flying over the Pacific Ocean in World War II.

Just six months after its drubbing at Pearl Harbor, the Seventh Air Force had its revenge at Midway, the first clear-cut victory over Japan's navy. Though the battle barely damaged the enemy's navy, it cut off part of its advance, proved the resolve of the Americans, and turned the tide of the war in the Pacific.

As the Battle of Midway wound down, the Commander of the Seventh Air Force, Major General Clarence L. Tinker, led a night bombing raid from Midway to Wake Island, hoping to catch retreating Japanese naval forces. Tinker's plane got lost and crashed, killing the general and all aboard. Their bodies and the plane were never recovered.*

June 9, 1942

Dearest Ann,

Received the pictures. The one I like best is of you and the lawn mower. You look healthy and as if you are getting skinnier. Are you? The orchard in the background looks wonderful. Of all the places I have seen, the orchard is as beautiful as any.

By the way, Ann, did I ever send you a Hawaiian towel? I think I sent you one, but I don't remember you saying you got it. Please let me know if you did. They are worth having. I am going to try to get some Hawaiian things for us. I hope you would like to have a room with Hawaiian decor.

Another thing, Ann, and this isn't as pleasant. After this damn war, I can't think of any steady job to go to, for I have learned no trade in the Army to help me get a job. I will not go back to the mill, for working there is the reason I left. I have been thinking about going to art school and taking up some reliable trade. I don't often plan ahead, but something like marriage should be thought of seriously.

I am saving some money and sending you a money order for $100 sometime in late July, which you may save for us for it will not do me any good here. I have no place to spend it.

The last few days I have been doing some drafting work—drawing maps. It's a change from what I have been doing, and I don't mind it. I may change my mind later. The work is okay, but I know I won't get along with my boss.

The boy I mentioned who asked for cookies has gone home. He has a touch of T.B., which is not serious, but if he stays here, the climate would not help him any. He looked bad and has been losing weight for the last few months. I guess they will send him to California for the duration. I miss him a

---

*An Oklahoman and member of the Osage Nation, Tinker was the highest ranking Native American officer in the U.S. Army. The Air Force named Tinker Air Force Base in Oklahoma City in his honor.

lot. He was the only honest guy in the company and the one guy I palled around with. As far as the rest of the men, I wouldn't give a 5-cent piece for any of them.

Even if the war ends by Christmas, my coming home is indefinite. The Japanese tried again to attack Hawaii but were halted at Midway. For the last couple of days, we were all looking for action for we are mad about Pearl Harbor and won't feel right if we don't get a crack at them. They realize they are barking up the wrong tree this time and believe they would sign a treaty if we would.

The only way to end this war is to destroy Germany and Japan by bombing and more bombing. The Battle of Midway proves that her navy is not strong. First, they tried Australia and failed, then Hawaii and failed. They are not completely destroyed, but their losses must have been greater than ours in both attacks. They have some confidence and are trying hard to win this war, but they lack initiative.

Aloha, as ever,
Herb

P.S. Give everyone my best wishes and tell your dad I don't think he will have to be in this war.

Herb's post script referred to the "old man's" draft registration, held on April 27, 1942, for men aged 45 to 64. Ann's 50-year-old father had filled out a draft registration form, required by a new Selective Service Act. The Fourth Registration, known as the "Old Man's Registration," collected information on the industrial capacity and skills of men born between April 27, 1877, and February 16, 1897. These men would not be drafted into military service, but Uncle Sam wanted to determine if their skills could be used in the war effort. The registration provided a complete inventory of manpower resources in the United States.

REGISTRATION CARD—(Men born on or after April 28, 1877 and on or before February 16, 1897)

SERIAL NUMBER	1. NAME (Print)		ORDER NUMBER
U. 512	William (First)	Fritz (Last)	

2. PLACE OF RESIDENCE (Print)

Skippack Twnp Monig Pa

(Number and street) (Town, township, village, or city) (County) (State)

[THE PLACE OF RESIDENCE GIVEN ON THE LINE ABOVE WILL DETERMINE LOCAL BOARD JURISDICTION; LINE 2 OF REGISTRATION CERTIFICATE WILL BE IDENTICAL]

3. MAILING ADDRESS

Schwenkville RD7 Pa.

[Mailing address if other than place indicated on line 2. If same insert word same]

4. TELEPHONE	5. AGE IN YEARS	6. PLACE OF BIRTH
none	50	Krasne (Town or county)
(Exchange) (Number)	DATE OF BIRTH June 22 1891 (Mo.) (Day) (Yr.)	Poland (State or country)

7. NAME AND ADDRESS OF PERSON WHO WILL ALWAYS KNOW YOUR ADDRESS

Mary Fritz Schwenksville RD1. Pa.

8. EMPLOYER'S NAME AND ADDRESS

Charles J. Muttart. Schwenksville Pa RD1

9. PLACE OF EMPLOYMENT OR BUSINESS

Sun Krestorchards Schwenksville Monty A

(Number and street or R. F. D. number) (Town) (County) (State)

I AFFIRM THAT I HAVE VERIFIED ABOVE ANSWERS AND THAT THEY ARE TRUE.

William Fritz

D. S. S. Form 1 (Revised 4-1-42) (over) 16—21630-2 (Registrant's signature)

A copy of part of the "old man's" draft registration record of Ann's father. He immigrated to the states from Poland in 1910. His name at birth was Ellias Firç.

June 17, 1942

Dear Ann,

Received two letters from you today. I think they were holding the mail during the Battle of Midway. They were not taking any chances during the crisis.

The cookies arrived, but you may as well stop sending them for it cost a lot and they were not in good condition. They are edible but tasted of gasoline and oil from the boats. They were probably in storage a long time. As much as I love them, it is not wise to mail them. Don't feel hurt; I know you would send them if I wanted them, but it is not worth the effort. (I love you for it.)

I received a letter today from a friend of mine back home who has been drafted. By the sound of his letter, he doesn't like it at all. I feel sorry for him; then, too, I feel sorry for myself. I tried to give him some advice on how to get along, but it will have little effect because he will not see the things that I mentioned until he has been in longer, and then it will be too late.

The beautiful sunset tonight made me feel lonely. Nonetheless, small things, such as scenery and music, give me joy; if it weren't for these, I don't believe I could keep on going.

Some of the native families are doing their best to help the morale of the soldiers and sailors by taking them to their homes and showing them a good time. The men meet at the "Y," and different Hawaiian families come around for them. Sometimes they accommodate as many as 10 men. I guess the fellows have a good time singing and doing the hula. Hawaiians are happy and friendly people. This has been more so since the war, but then, all the civilians have been friendlier than before the war, which is understandable.

The last couple of weeks, we had been getting up at 5:30 a.m. for exercise. This stopped when the war began, but it is starting again. Every day is the same, terribly monotonous. Some days I go in and work the whole day; other days I am idle all day, sitting around doing nothing. I'm tired of the whole thing. I can't think of anything as bad as this. Sometimes I wonder what I ever did to deserve this punishment. It's not that I am lazy; there is no work to keep me busy. Other people may like this sort of thing, but I can't see sitting around doing nothing. I read but get tired of this. They will not let me get out of where I am. I have tried to get other kind of work several times, but each time they have stopped and discouraged me. They have made me a Sergeant again, but this does not help any. I guess they think I'm supposed to rejoice, but I am not going to use any initiative for it does not help. There is too much professional jealousy to surmount. It is not worth the effort, and your work is not noticed.

Well, Ann, I hope this letter is not too morbid for you, and I will try to make my next letter more pleasant.

As ever,
Herb

81

P.S. In case you are interested; Honolulu means "fair haven" in the Hawaiian language. Incidentally, there are only 12 letters in the Hawaiian alphabet.*

The "Tired Fliers Program," to which Herb referred in the preceding letter, was instituted in May 1942 to relieve the exhaustion of fliers from hours on stand-by or patrol duty. Mostly wealthy private homeowners hosted the fliers, who rested, swam, ate, and relaxed in their homes for at least five days. Later on, submarine crews got the same treatment.

July 7, 1942

Dear Ann,

Received your letter of June 14, which took longer than usual due to this damn mail situation. I am sending two clippings from the *Honolulu Advertiser* concerning the mail. I am almost persuaded to believe what the second clipping says even if it was meant as a joke.

---

*Devised by Protestant missionaries in the 1820s, the Hawaiian alphabet consists of the letters a, e, h, i, k, l, m, n, o, p, u, and w.

A SAN FRANCISCO postal inspector disclaims responsibility for delayed mails to Hawaii. The Advertiser doesn't know who is to blame but some one is when it takes three weeks to get a letter by Clipper or steamer, mailed in Chicago or way stations, delivered in Honolulu.

Where Is The Mail?

The Great Mail Mystery becomes greater and more mysterious with each passing day, and as the plot thickens Hawaii grows more and more puzzled. This is one for the Crime Club, a whodunit thriller that holds the fascinated attention of every resident of the Territory. Is the mail in the dead letter office? Is it at the bottom of the sea? Is it lurking in some gloomy warehouse in the slums of Honolulu? The questions are something to keep us all awake at night. Who, in short, is the villain?

Thus far Hawaii has absolved the Honolulu postmaster, who is as mystified as anybody, if not more so. Ships are coming in from the Coast—though it's all a military secret. Have they no mail aboard? Even Sherlock Holmes would be baffled by that one.

After getting through a few more chapters we, as amateur detectives, are beginning to suspect some sinister scoundrel and his gang on the Pacific Coast of being the cause of it all. If Holmes can catch him soon, and shoot him, it'll be a great relief.

The other clipping almost tells you how I spent my Fourth of July. It also tells you what I wrote about: "Every day is the same." And it seems to be getting worse.

War Time Fourth Of July

Today, the Glorious Fourth commemorating the signing of America's Declaration of Independence 166 years ago, will be observed in embattled Hawaii by an increased determination to win the war by defeating an enemy which threatens our national way of life—a way of life established by the Founding Fathers. As they fought then, against tyranny and aggression, so we fight today, though on vaster fronts.

Unlike former years, there will be no special ceremonies to celebrate this occasion. Here in mid-Pacific we have agreed to devote the day to hard work so that the inevitable victory will come that much sooner. Hawaii is virtually alone in this "all-out work" program—for the first time in the history of America a small but vital part of it is passing up the traditional celebration of Independence Day in order that for generations to come Americans will be able to continue celebrating their independence.

The war still looks good for us. Germany has made her last offensive move; of course, she has made some headway. But from now on, she will be on the losing side. She has used up all her reserves. It is amazing how she can hold out; but she is going to be all washed out in the next few months (wait and see). If Japan attacks Russia, which I think it will shortly, Russia will prevail. I hope Japan does not realize this: The Russians are a marvelous people, and I wish some Americans would get some of Russia's fighting spirit.

Did you read in the paper that General Tinker of this field was killed in action? He led an air attack on Wake Island, and he and the crew are missing (killed). Five other men who raided Tokyo have been awarded a medal for valor. Yesterday, we had to stand in formation to show our respect. These men have every respect from me, for they are the ones who are actually winning this war for us, and it is an honor to salute them. They have a dangerous job and are living on borrowed time.

I just finished reading an excellent book, *Destination Chungking*, by Han Suyan, an autobiography of a Chinese girl, who tells of the war conditions in China and her and her lover's part in the war. If you get a chance, please read it. I would love to go to China someday.

I painted a picture of a bird dog. It is not quite finished, but when it is I will mail it to you.

It was sweet of you to send me a card, but you don't have to send cards to show your affection. I know you care for me, and you know how I feel about you. Ann, dear, you are the only person I am holding out and fighting for. I hope more than anything in the world to be with you so we can start our life together.

I love you,
Herb

84

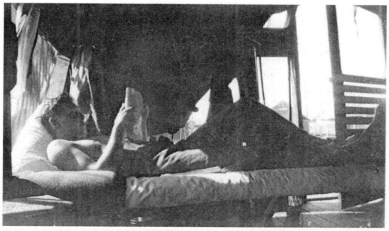
Herb, an avid reader, reading in his tent. (Photo from Herb's collection)

—★—

In a nod to the suspicion with which many Americans viewed Japanese Americans, Herb had written in the margin of the first news clipping enclosed, "Look at the names on the back of this article—all Jap names." When I turned over the article, I saw legal notices full of Japanese names.

Like most GIs in Hawaii, Herb, for the first time, lived in a place where he felt in the minority. More than one-third of Oahu's population was Japanese. Other Asian residents included Chinese, Filipinos, and Koreans. Such groups had deep roots in Hawaii, having immigrated since the mid-1800s to work on the sugar plantations. Portuguese and other Europeans had also come to work the plantations.*

—★—

---

*The Portuguese brought with them the ukulele, which became a fixture in Hawaiian music. "Ukulele" means "jumping flea" in Hawaiian; the natives likened the lively finger work involved in playing the instrument to the movements of a flea.

July 12, 1942, Saturday evening

Dear Ann,

The pictures are marvelous. You look grand. I notice you have a new hair style. Is that the new "Cut Militaire?" Whatever it is, it becomes you.

I am writing on a checkerboard because all the writing tables are occupied by the true soldiers, gambling. You see, it is two days after payday. This will go on for about five more days.

I sent you some of my favorite phonograph records. Did you receive them yet? I hope you like them as well as I. More are on the way.

Mother sent me pictures of your visit with them. Mother looks bad. She wrote me a sentimental letter, saying that when I went away, I took half her life away also. She felt terrible when I left, but she is mostly over it by now. She wants me to send her a professional photograph of me in uniform so she can put it in the paper on my birthday. I won't disappoint her, but it costs money, and anyway, this idea is silly. Who cares about my birthday? (But you know how mothers are.) She said she was proud of me, which I can't understand.

I still have some U.S. currency that I want to exchange for Hawaiian currency. The U.S. currency will be of no use after the 15th of this month. Don't hesitate to ask me for anything, Ann, and if it's here, I'll get it for you.

I put in for another transfer. Pray that I get it.

You better practice your tennis because I am getting good. I would hate to beat you when we play in the future (if there is a future; sometimes, I doubt it).

They had a squadron dance here last Sunday. It was horrible, and the women they hired to dance with us were the ugliest ones I have ever seen in my life. Some of them were Army nurses. Some guy (Cpl. Zeffzick) wants to know if Sara would write to him. (Between you and me, he is a dope.)

As ever,
Herb

86

Though Herb disdained gambling, it burned up some soldiers' paychecks. At the end of the month, the winners from Hickam and other bases on Oahu played for high stakes at Schofield Barracks.

Gambling proved only a temporary escape from the war, however. The Hawaiian Department held maneuvers on July 16 and 17. Herb's squadron drilled in practice tear gas attacks. Also that month, 35 B-17s from Herb's command flew to the South Pacific to operate on the eastern edge of the Japanese advance in the Solomon Islands and beyond. Leading up to the invasion of Guadalcanal, the bombers raided the island, conducted search missions, and shot reconnaissance photos of it and Tulagi.

This Hickam soldier models the gas mask used during gas attack drills Herb endured. (Photo courtesy of the U.S. Army Museum of Hawaii)

On August 7, Allied forces—mostly American—landed on Guadalcanal, Tulagi, and Florida in the southern Solomons. They quickly captured the airfield on Guadalcanal. In the ensuing days, the marines held on through vicious land attacks and naval bombardments. The battle not only yielded the first air base, Henderson Field, captured from the enemy but also slowed Japan's buildup of troops. The fighting on Guadalcanal would go on for six months.

August 18, 1942

Dear Ann,

The reports from the Solomon Islands have been good. I hope they are true and that they keep up the good work.

It has been the same here; the temperature is rising to a point where you can't stand it in the sun. The nights, however, are marvelous; in fact, you can't find more beautiful nights anywhere.

How is the sugar shortage affecting people back there? Does your family find it hard getting along with ½ a pound a week? The people here are fortunate not to have to ration sugar. There is plenty. On both sides of the road, from here into Honolulu, all you see is sugar cane. Last summer I tasted some sugar stalks, which didn't taste bad at all; in fact, some of the natives make a meal of it. Gasoline and tires seem to be the biggest problem right now.

Do you get enough gas to get to work? It must be hard to watch the gas tank every time you drive. Maybe it's for the best for people will get tired of rationing and want to see action and end this damn war.

We cannot mail any more letters through the civilian post office. We have to mail them through the military for censorship. Also, as you may have noticed, we have to write on only one side of the paper, making our letters as brief as possible. I hate it because it discourages letter writing to the point that one doesn't feel like writing at all. Please try to understand why my letters will not be as interesting and long as they have been.

As ever,
Herb

While the war in the Pacific heated up, Ann and Herb, along with all Americans, did their bit for the war effort. Ann wrote, "Nylon stockings are hard to come by and if you find out when the mills have them for sale, you line up for hours to get your three pairs allowed." The U.S. economy shifted to war production almost overnight when the war began, and consumer goods ceased to be a top priority. Shortages began almost immediately, with the rationing of tires on December 27, 1941. Rationing ensured that everyone got a fair share of goods in short supply.

Food rationing started in spring 1942, when the Office of Price Administration (OPA) issued each family member—including babies—ration books. These books contained stamps and specified the amounts of certain types of food allowed. The stamp program, administered through local banks, covered food, fuel oil, gasoline, and shoes. The OPA rationed foods such as sugar—the first food item to be rationed—coffee, red meat, dairy products, and fat.* Another rationing program required applicants to appeal to a local ration board before they could buy tires, automobiles, typewriters, bicycles, rubber footwear, and kitchen appliances.

The government also asked citizens to turn in old tires, raincoats, gloves, garden hoses, and rubber shoes for recycling. To save rubber, the government asked Americans to reduce their driving, and to save gas, to drive more slowly and share rides. By December 1942, gasoline was rationed nationwide.

In addition to rubber and gas, Americans recycled scrap metal, with schools and local groups holding scrap metal drives countrywide. Women saved waste fat and grease and returned them to butchers, who paid for the fat and sold it to rendering plants for processing into explosives. Scrap paper was also

---

*Most rationing endured until August 1945, with tire rationing ending on December 31, 1945. Sugar rationing continued in some parts of the country until 1947.

89

collected, needed for packing weapons and equipment for shipping overseas.

A gasoline ration card (both sides) that belonged to my grandfather, William Fritz.

August 29, 1942

Dear Ann,

I knew you would like the Strauss waltzes and am glad they got there unbroken. I sent them because they were starting to warp. The guy who had the record player has been transferred, so I could not play them anymore.

When you mentioned how odd it is that "this war may change things," I don't know if you mean change individuals or the world. The war is showing how the world would be if we lost. But some people don't seem to realize that we are fighting countries that have prepared for years, unlike the U.S. Most people are too optimistic. At first, I was, too, but most Americans are not united. Brotherly love is a thing of the past. It's me first; you after me, especially in the Army. I have stopped trying for the corruption is too great, and it all boils down to not being worth it.

Mother wrote and mentioned that you brought her some gladiolus, which she loves. Thank you for your kindness. She also mentioned that you have asked her up to your house when the peaches are ripe. Do you think she is worrying too much? I ask because she looks awful in the pictures she sent. Of course, I did not tell her this.

You have many, many pictures of me. What are you doing—starting a Rogue's Gallery? You may get tired of looking at my mug. But, if you want a picture of me in uniform, you will get it. This has become quite the style down here: Everyone is wearing a uniform. I am afraid I don't look like a good soldier boy, for you know how I feel about the Army.

Aloha,
Herb

The head shot that Ann asked Herb
to have taken. (Photo from Herb's
collection)

September 5, 1942

Dear Ann,

Finally, I got around to mailing my paintings. I guess you
thought I had forgotten.

It's okay that you started a joint account. I guess by this
time you got the other money I sent.

My friends, the Ganders, told me last Sunday that they
are going back home in the near future. They hate to leave the
islands, but Merrill's company is sending them back. They got
accustomed to life here. Marge Gander has bought you a nice
evening handkerchief with an orchid on it with which she is
going to introduce herself to you, I think. She was working in a
store here to occupy her time. I bought some fabric from her
there that I think she sent you. Maybe you could make a
housecoat out of it. The girls here are wearing that type of
thing and it is quite nice. I also sent you some Hawaiian soap,
which I hope you like.

We have new blackout hours, 35 minutes earlier than
before, making conditions worse. It's been so long since I've
seen lighted rooms that it will be a treat to see them again.
Every month I buy new batteries for the flashlight, which is the

only thing we may use—with blue blackout paper over the bulb. One would never believe that we are living in a civilization, period. Once the war began, we had a shortage of flashlight batteries for a long time. Most of the guys were going around feeling their way here and there.

Right now, we have a potato shortage and eat rice instead. I am beginning to look and feel like a Japanese or Chinese. We cannot get the most common food, though we are not starving or going hungry. Of the food we do get there is plenty, but it's the same stuff, so much starch. I had to buy vitamin pills to get proper food balance.

The weather has been the same, always welcome for tennis. We are using these victory tennis balls, which have no crude rubber in them. They are fair but stubborn and clumsy, so we make the best of it. Have you tried any? I have been over here two years and about three weeks, a long time wasted. My looks are beginning to change and I am ready to leave as soon as they let me. I've had enough.

Here is something a little silly but nice. Please kiss your next letter at the signature. If you put lipstick on a little heavier, it will leave a print, which will remind me of how your lips are. Crazy idea, I know, but do it.

Aloha,
Herb

Marge Gander and Herb (left), who were friends from back home. Herb (right), on the lawn of the Ganders's home on Oahu. He was lucky to have friends in Hawaii to visit, though they returned to Pennsylvania in 1942. (Photos from Herb's collection)

September 18, 1942

Dear Ann,

I'm glad you like the outrigger canoe; it's lots of fun to ride in a real one.

Don't feel too bad about the broken records; they can always be replaced, and I didn't pack them that well. It's too bad that "Lovely Hula Hands" got broken. It's a nice number and I wanted you to hear it.

Pictures I took to be developed at the PX have been there for three weeks. The stores here really don't care whether they do business. They know if you really want something, you are willing to wait as long as it takes.

We still have no potatoes, likewise milk. We have been eating rice and more rice and drinking powdered milk, which isn't good. I'm not complaining; in fact, I think it is good. It gives us the feeling of being at war and getting it over with.

I had hoped to be with you at Christmastime, but I have given that up as a dream. The war is too big, but many people don't realize this. My opinion of the American people has diminished. As I said before, there is too much graft, hatred, and jealousy, which has to be taken care of to win this war.

I do hope you like the bracelet.

As ever,
Herb

September 29, 1942

Dear Ann,

Glad you had a good time at Cape May. I wish I was there now. Thanks a million for the salt water taffy and Fanny Farmer candy, which arrived in good condition.

Quite a few guys are getting yellow jaundice down here. There are 30 cases of it on my post. They are discovering that it comes from the yellow fever shots they have been giving us.

A rumor went around that the Army would hire women to do clerical work, but nothing ever came of it. In a way, hiring civilians to do clerical work is not wise because men like me can do it just as well as they. This saves money for the

U.S. because civilians doing such work make $150 to $250 a month. We can do it for $70 and $85 a month.

Have you met my brother's wife? If so, what sort of girl is she? My sister and Mother each wrote saying they don't care for her, but they don't stop to think about how John is. Do you think there is lasting love and marriage there?

Mother and Dad had a swell time at your house. I thank you very much for your kindness.

Aloha,

Herb

—★—

When I asked Mother about my father's relationship with his brother, John, whom she called a "dullard," she told me the following story: One Sunday before he joined the army, Herb went to a dance in a converted one-room schoolhouse. He danced a few numbers. But all of a sudden, his father barged in and grabbed Herb by his ear.

"You don't dance on Sunday. It's the Lord's day," he scolded. Humiliated in front of his friends, Herb stumbled out of the dance while his father held onto his ear. Out of jealousy, spite, or to curry favor with their father, Herb's brother John had ratted Herb out. Their father, a straight-laced Methodist, forbade dancing on Sundays. Stung by his brother's betrayal, Herb didn't speak to John for years after that but eventually forgave him.

The story explained my father's quarrel with John but made me wonder about his relationship with his father. Though he wrote to his mother during the war and referred to her often, he hardly mentioned his father in his letters. According to Mother, their relationship was never strained. But surely my father had modeled his strict parenting style after his father's, which in the 1930s, consisted of harsh and quick discipline to keep kids on the straight and narrow.

One summer day when I was 9, Mother took me shopping with her to Lit Brothers department store. I admired a birthstone

95

ring, an oval-shaped aquamarine set in silver, while passing the jewelry counter. Not wanting to hear Mother's favorite refrain, "We can't afford it," I didn't ask her for it. I just slipped it in my pocket when no one was looking.

"Where did you get that?" Mother asked later on when she spied the ring on my finger. I couldn't lie. She and my father discussed the matter and decided I had to return it to the store. He drove me there. The cool air from the air conditioning chilled me as we entered the store.

When we got about 20 feet from the jewelry counter, he said, "Just go to the lady at the counter and tell her you took the ring and are returning it." He watched as I approached the counter alone, trying to make myself small, inconspicuous, as I always did around Daddy but even more so in this instance.

"I took this and I'm returning it," I said softly, putting the ring in her palm. The saleslady looked at me, kindly but wincing.

"Thank you," she said. I turned back to my father and we drove home.

The following Christmas, I unwrapped a small box and quickly closed the lid: my parents had bought me the ring I'd stolen. I didn't wear it, though, because it reminded me of the shame and embarrassment I felt about the theft. I never stole again.

—★—

October 11, 1942

Dear Herb,

Did you buy out the whole store to make up that package for me? I was thrilled with the fork and spoon salad set. And, of course, I adore the necklaces and the two brooches, which are novel. And the perfume is out of this world. I think I can make a pin out of the carved fish on the keychain. And the coasters, ash trays, and napkin rings (that's what they are, aren't they?) are all useful additions to my hope chest. You're sweet to send me all those beautiful things.

I had your painting framed at Bussa's, and I think they did a good job. The frame is a combination of light brown- and beige-colored wood. Everyone at the bank thought your painting was wonderful.

Today was one of those lovely warm fall days, and Sara Garges and I went for a long walk. It was too bad the weather wasn't nice last week when your family was here. By the way, has your friend, Wendall Armor, written to Sara yet? She has not received any letters from him.

The snapshots were interesting, particularly the one of the couple in the fond embrace. Are they friends of yours?

Herb, I cannot give you an opinion of your brother John's wife. I have only met her on two occasions and then only for a short time. She is a lively, spirited girl, and they seem to care for each other.

It frightened me to learn of the yellow jaundice cases down there. I hope you are all right.

Your letters have been coming regularly lately. I'm anxious to get those pictures.

Love,
Ann

Herb suspected his brother John's wife, Jesse, of being an "Allotment Annie," a woman who married a GI to get the monthly allotment deducted from his paycheck for a wife or family. John met Jesse, according to Mother, when he served on an army post down South. After they married, she came to live with Herb's and John's parents in their Norristown row house. Jesse, a chubby girl with a round face, dark hair, and a Southern drawl, didn't work or offer to help with the household chores. My grandparents considered her a freeloader. John's marriage to Jesse would not last.

October 9, 1942

Dear Ann,

I received the V-mail on September 29. I don't think it is any faster than other mail. By spring, I think the war will come to an end.

Right now, the elections interest people more than anything else. One of the delegates here, Sam King, has declined his nomination and accepted a position in the Navy, changing things.* I read that Washington was dissatisfied with the election returns here, with the Japanese in office. The Japanese make up 36 percent of the population here, and with this many, one doesn't know what to expect from them. Of course, there are good ones but just as many bad ones.

Writing letters has become a problem. I can't concentrate because the only place we have to write letters is a day room, where it is more like Pandemonium.

Your mention of weddings has raised a question in my mind: What sort of wedding would you like? It would be marvelous to have our wedding as soon as possible when I come home, would it not? By that time, we will have enough money, but then what? It sure is a problem, which we have to think about and discuss.

You can send me an electric razor if you want. I really could use one as we have electric, but sometimes we have no hot water, and shaving in cold water is uncomfortable.

For your Christmas present, I am sending you some Hawaiian dishes that I think are beautiful and I know you will think so. I will try to send you more later. Right now their price is high. I am hoping it will go lower. If not, I will buy more anyway and mail them about five days from today. I think they will get there by Christmas.

I sure would like to get more painting to my credit. I am becoming slack under these conditions, finding it impossible to paint the way I want. I want to go to school to study more and think it's best. I haven't learned a thing in this Army.

*The Territory of Hawaii elected a single nonvoting delegate to the U.S. Congress.

Your letters—in fact, only yours—have helped me with my morale. Thanks. But as far as forgetting this time, that will never happen for one can never forget how horrible it is. I am as well as I can be, physically.

By the way, how did you make out sleeping with the wedding cake? Who did you dream of—crumbs? It was a sweet thing to do. Write soon.

Aloha,

Herb

On the first wedding anniversary of her friends, Thelma and Elmer Swenson, Ann went to the freezer and pulled out a piece of their wedding cake, which she had saved in wax paper. Inspired by a tradition dating to the 18th century, she placed it under her pillow that night. The cake would evoke dreams of her future husband, according to the tradition.

November 6, 1942

Dear Ann,

The hills and scenery are still as beautiful as ever. I would like to get a job here when the war is over. It's a great place to live. One has to be here to really feel it for oneself. It's going to be quite a place after the war and will offer grand opportunities to get ahead.

The picture of the "fond embrace," as you called it, is a scene from Sacred Falls, one of the most beautiful places here. The subjects are two guys who came over with me. The picture is one of the first shots I took here. I was surprised that the censor passed it, as I tried to send a similar shot and it did not go through.

A lot of Christmas presents arrived today, making the fellows happy.

My work seems to be going okay. I still find it interesting. The last couple of days have kept me busy and the time passes quickly but half of it is wasted. We finish work at 4 o'clock, and it stays light for only an hour and a half, giving me little time to do anything I want. The summer gives me more time.

I will be going to the dentist shortly. I have a cavity and want to get it taken care of. Some people think teeth go bad faster down here due to the water, which lacks the proper minerals.

As ever, Herb

To get to Sacred Falls, Herb and his friends hiked a 2-mile trail on Oahu's north shore. There, they swam in the clear, cool plunge pool at the base of a pristine 1,100-foot waterfall nestled at the end of a narrow canyon. From their spot near the plunge pool, Herb and his buddies could see the last 80 feet of the falls.*

Herb (far left) and three buddies at Sacred Falls. Bill Hoagland is facing the camera, center. Next to him (the "huggee" is a friend only identified as "Oakley." The other friends are unknown. (Photo from Herb's collection)

Another favorite spot of Herb's, the Nuuanu Pali, a traversable pass, wound through the Koolau Mountains at the

*This is now Sacred Falls State Park.

head of the Nuuanu Valley. The Pali, which means "cliff" in Hawaiian, led to a lookout. From there, Herb and his buddies could see in all directions as if at the top of the world. Brisk winds funneled through the valley, blasting their faces. A vista of rolling meadows and rugged mountain peaks veiled with mist surrounded the men as they smelled a mixture of rain, ferns, and damp earth. In the height-cooled air, the mountains steepened quickly, ending in a breath-taking drop of 1,000 feet of rock.

Herb (top) with friends at the Pali, "Oakley" is in the center. Other friends are unknown.

Some of Herb's friends at the Pali. "Oakley" is in the center, front; Bill Hoagland is behind him and Joseph Ferrick is on the far right. The friend on the far left is unknown.

Another view fromthePali,1940s. (Photos from Herb's collection)

A caption on one of Herb's pictures of the Pali reflects a sinister side of the scenery: "Suicide Cliff." Here 18th-century soldiers fought Hawaii's pivotal Battle of Nuuanu. Kamehameha I sailed from his home island of Hawaii to Oahu with an army of 10,000 warriors in 1795. In the final battle for Oahu, Kamehameha drove its defenders up into the valley, trapping them above the cliff. With no place to go, Oahu's defenders fought desperately against spears, stones, and bullets. But the invaders prevailed, forcing hundreds of warriors over the cliff to their deaths 1,000 feet below.*

*A hundred years later, workers building the highway over the Pali to connect the windward side of Oahu with Honolulu found 800 human skulls believed to be the remains of those ancient warriors.

102

King Kamehameha statue outside of
the Iolani Palace in Honolulu, 1940s.
Photo from Herb's collection)

November 24, 1942

Dear Ann,

The ring arrived. I love it. It's marvelous—one of the
swankiest and neatest looking I have ever seen. You couldn't
have gotten me anything that I would appreciate more. Is it a
Sardonyx ring? I hope you like the dishes as much as I like this
ring. Spending Christmas with you would be the best
Christmas present for me. Christmas is one of the nicest
holidays—not only the gayness of it but its meaning. I am in
good spirits.

If only we would live by the thought, "It's better to give
than receive," this world would be a more peaceful place. But
such a thing is impossible. Half the people don't know the true
meaning of Christmas. I will not feel jubilant at Christmas—
more or less the opposite. I guess I am becoming a morbid
individual, though I have my reasons.

Mother wrote that Mrs. Gander is home. Has she been in the bank to see you yet? Before she left, she told me she would locate you. They were lucky to get home for Christmas. Before they left, they called me on the phone to say good-by. Of course, I didn't feel so well because I got a kick out of going to their house and getting away from all this. I miss them.

So much is happening, but I can say little due to the censorship. I wrote Mother that I am saving money and that we have about $150 saved. She thought this was grand and told me that I would never regret it and the first $100 is the hardest to save.

How would you like to live here after we get married? It's quite a life down here, away from the Army. Something lovely gets into your blood here, though this place will never be like it was before the war. Ann, I will close now with *Ma Ke Aloha Pau Ole*—My Love for You Shall Never End.

As ever,
Herb

November 28, 1942

Dear Ann,

The show you mentioned must have been good. Irving Berlin wrote the music for it, didn't he? All the movie stars and songwriters are helping boost morale. I give them credit for trying; it's a hard job.

The Russians are doing marvelous work and will keep on doing it. Our greatest problem now is taking care of the Japs. Things seem stark for them now. They are piling up losses. As for any more action here, I think it's through. Japan is holding what little it has, and its' attacking here again seems hopeless. They are active in Burma now, which is more important to them than this place.

I bought some canvas and a few brushes to paint your portrait when I come home. In the meantime, I am going to send them to you for safekeeping. If this is asking too much, let me know, and I will send them home. I bought them because they were a bargain but I haven't anyplace to keep them....

I think the pictures that you will get soon are the best snaps I have had taken. As for having room for pictures of you, I'll always have room for them; after all, Ann, they're not large, are they?

The paper on which I am writing is a gift from the church, likewise, the envelopes. Wish your parents a "Merry Christmas" for me.

Until I hear from you again, I remain

As ever,
Herb

December 6, 1942

Dearest Ann,

A year ago today, I didn't know whether I would be killed or captured by the Japs. It was great tumult and quite a feeling and an experience I hope I never have again. Since then, there have been many changes for the better.

I'm sure that I will be out of here by this time next year. My prospects for staying alive for the duration are brighter than the last time I wrote.

The mail is getting slow again due to the Christmas rush. With so many priorities and necessities here, mail is of little importance.

Fresh meats and vegetables are impossible to have. The civilians are starting their Victory Gardens, but they are hardly noticeable. The farmers here plant mostly sugar cane or something on a large scale, such as pineapples, and hardly have time and space for their gardens. Most anything you put in the ground here grows with a little care.

All the fellows are getting Christmas boxes with lots of good things to eat, and they share them willingly. Of course, when one of these boxes comes, we don't go to the mess hall for the boxes contain much better things to eat.

We had a peaceful Thanksgiving; in fact, if the calendar didn't remind us that it was Thanksgiving Day, it would have probably gone by unnoticed.

The Japanese had a fountain here at Kapiolani Park, but

it has become a scrap pile.* It seems that the civilian population protested its being there. Much more dangerous, some centers of Japanese propaganda have been temporarily suspended but not eliminated. The Japanese press was closed down at the outbreak of the war but not on this island because the island-born Japanese cannot read English. All the Japanese schools have closed down; there were quite a few of them. These schools taught no English at all—strictly Japanese.

Well, Ann, keep hoping for the best for us. We deserve all the breaks we will get.

As ever,
Herb

On Saturday night, December 19, Herb headed to Honolulu to dine with his friend, George. Leaving his ride, he walked toward Chinatown, where soldiers socialized, drank, shopped, or visited the brothels on River Street—the "Street of Dreams." Servicemen lined up to spend $3 for about three minutes with a white prostitute at The Modern Rooms, Senator Hotel, the Bronx, or another of 20 or so brothels approved and inspected by the army. Herb wondered at the business they brought in, all together about $1 million a month. His buddies and he heard twice yearly sex hygiene talks by their commanding officer, medical officer, and chaplain. Still, GIs headed to town to get "stewed, screwed, and tattooed."

He met George at the corner of Hotel and Manunakea Streets in Chinatown. Though they could choose from several Chinese restaurants, including Lau Yee Chai in Waikiki or the Kau Kau Korner, Herb and George chose Wo Fat. A good restaurant with a pagoda-style roof, Wo Fat stood next to the red-light district, one of the first Chinese restaurants in the United States, dating to 1882.

---

*The Phoenix Fountain, erected in 1919, commemorated the ascendancy of Japan's Emperor Taisho and had been funded by contributions of $1 from each Japanese household in Hawaii.

Rebuilt twice after fires and then later remodeled in 1938 atop the old building, the restaurant issued free dining coupons to servicemen during the war and continued to honor the coupons decades later.

Inside the restaurant, the smell of soy sauce, onions, and garlic made Herb's mouth water. George and Herb wound their way past red columns to a square table covered with a fresh linen tablecloth. They sat down in front of napkins folded like arrows pointing skyward and ordered eight courses, including chicken à la Canton, crisp duck, fried noodles, pork with vegetables, sour ribs, egg fu yung, and fried taro. Herb savored the tender meat. After tasting the sweetly spiced jasmine tea, he told George, "I love this tea." George, "a well-educated Chinese" and apparently gracious man whom Herb had met on Oahu told him, "I'll send some to your fiancée if you want."

December 20, 1942

Dear Ann,

You can uncross your fingers now. I am definitely staying here for the duration.

Rarely is anyone indispensable. Don't worry about the predicament you will leave the bank in if you quit. I am sure if they wanted to fire you or lay you off, they would not feel the loyalty you do about quitting. Have you asked for a raise? What was their reaction? They should return your loyalty and show you some appreciation. Find yourself a good prospect, such as office work in a defense plant or airplane factory, which will pay more. Make sure you have a good chance for a new job and then state the facts to your employer. A lot of people are making plenty of money in this war. I wish I could make some of it. At home, you can take advantage of such opportunities, which smart people are doing. After this war, things are going to be worse than people think. Ann, if you can get a better job, go and get it. Look out for yourself because no one else is going to.

Five more days until Christmas—it's unbelievable. A few stores in town have skimpy Christmas decorations. The spirit among the soldiers is low, and I don't see much spirit in the civilians, either.

People here have gone 100 percent for buying war bonds. In a three-day drive, or I'll say spree, people here bought over $4,000,000 worth of bonds. It's incredible, but true. The tax revenue for 1942 was $29,662,418.55 on this island alone.*

I ate a delicious eight-course Chinese dinner in town recently. Afterwards, my friend, George, offered to send you some tea. I mentioned that I really liked this tea, so he was happy to help someone else appreciate it also.

Well, Ann, I guess I'll close this letter, so the censors won't complain about writing so much.

As ever,
Herb

Christmas in Honolulu, 1940s. (Photo from Herb's collection.)

*Hawaii's per capita purchases of war bonds topped any state's.

Yau Lee Chai restaurant in Waikiki in the 1940s. (Photo from Herb's collection.)

Days after Herb and George ate their Chinese dinner, Herb's command launched the AAF's longest massed flight to date: 4,300 nautical miles. A few nights before Christmas 1942, 26 "Liberators"—B-24s—left Oahu and stopped at Midway, an Allied staging base. From there, the bombers, along with navy forces, raided Wake Island. The strike surprised the enemy as the bombers faced neither searchlights nor antiaircraft fire until after the attack had begun. All planes returned safely, with only slight damage to two, in the first air attack on enemy bases in the Central Pacific.

December 26, 1942

Dear Ann,

I guess your letter of December 6 was meant as my Christmas present because it came the day before Christmas; nothing could have been better.

I had a quiet Christmas. I didn't mind working alone in the office; after work, I went swimming. In the evening, I listened to some Christmas music transcribed from San Francisco. This, my dear, was my Christmas.

The Christmas holidays hardly affect the civilians here or us. A liquor shortage has gone on for two months, which makes some people gripe. This is a fast place, Ann, dear. I never saw so much liquor in one small place in all my life. They can

109

easily get along for a while without liquor. Christmas here was truly "hot and dry."

I heard the news that Jean Darlan was murdered. Why can't they get Hitler? Someone will get him sooner or later.

I received the oil paints, which are marvelous. I shall use them when I paint you. They are too nice to use yet, and, anyway, I want to paint something worthwhile with them.

I need a new tennis racket now that my old one needs new strings. This will cost about 12 dollars—expensive or what? I think it's worth it because playing tennis is the only thing I do in my spare time. Without that, there is nothing. It's going to take a long time, too; they probably will have to send it back to the mainland. No one here has time to bother with restringing a tennis racket.

Did you receive the money in my last letter to you? We don't have much but enough for a honeymoon. I wonder how I would do as a farmer. I was thinking seriously of becoming one.

As ever,
Herb

Headlines worldwide announced the assassination of Jean L.X.F. Darlan, whom Herb referred to in the preceding letter. Admiral and minister of the French navy turned supreme commander of all French forces in the pro-German Vichy regime, Darlan had cooperated with Hitler against Britain. He was killed by a Vichy-hating follower of Charles de Gaulle.

January 4, 1943

Dear Ann,

Thought I may as well start this New Year out right and couldn't think of a better way than writing to you. What a glorious and happy new year I had. First of all, I was on duty all day. Later, I decided I would enjoy a swim after work. About 2 o'clock, it started to rain. The rain spoiled not only swimming but also tennis, so towards the end of the day, I was

110

getting mad. At 4:30, I went to get some chow, after which I took a shower, read a little, and finally slept the New Year in.

The candy came today. Thanks a million. I love you and your thoughtfulness. I received a card from Mary and a box of nuts from her and your mother. The nuts were good and fresh; please tell them I really appreciate this. I didn't send any cards this year and hope they didn't mind. Write and tell me how you spent the holidays.

Love,
Herb

January 10, 1943

Dear Ann,

We had a lot of rain here the last couple of weeks and more than normal rainfall for the year, which is 3 inches. I wasn't allowed to mention this while it was raining, but now the papers have confirmed it, so there's no harm in telling you: A few small towns were flooded, and everything was very muddy. It seldom rains here. When it does, it's uncomfortable—not at all refreshing—and everything gets muddy.

Last Friday, we had to attend a training film on Identification of Friendly and Enemy Aircraft. We saw another film about what to do and say in case we are ever taken as prisoners of war.

Yesterday, I had a chance to play tennis. In the evening I went to the post theatre and saw *I Married an Angel*, starring Nelson E. and Jeanette MacDonald. (Good.) I had some time to read. The books I have just read were *Kindred of the Dust*, by Peter B. Kyne, and *The Modern Hero*, by Louis Bramfield. Both are good and I enjoyed them because I hadn't read for so long and, I guess, anything seemed good. Both are novels, which I wanted to read for a change.

Well, Sweetheart, I guess this is all the news for now, so until I hear from you, I am

Yours truly,
Herb

January 17, 1943

Dearest Ann,

I received your letter of December 22 today, although I had given up on getting a letter from you because of the uncertainty of the shipping. We now have to get special permission to receive any packages from home.

I went into town yesterday and had another Chinese dinner. No one has really tasted good food until they've had a regular eight-course Chinese dinner.

I went to the amateur boxing matches in the gym the other day to pass the time. Some of the boys really went into the ring for blood. Somehow, boxing doesn't much interest me, but every man to his taste.

Marge Gander wrote saying she misses this place and wishes she were here. She lives in Philadelphia and would like to have you and Mother down to her house for dinner. She gets lonesome, with the job her husband has, which doesn't give them much time together. She also mentioned that she met you and you are very sweet.

Artie Shaw and Joe E. Brown are here entertaining the Armed Forces. I have not seen either one and really don't care to because the crowd (defense workers, soldiers, sailors) and everything else one has to put up with makes it not worth the effort. Joe E. Brown came here at his own expense. His son was killed in combat service, according to the paper.

Yours truly,

Herb

P.S. I received a letter from the friend I wrote you about who went back to the states with T.B. He has married and is stationed on the West Coast. He seems very happy and has invited you and me to Thanksgiving dinner next year. I told him we will be glad to spend it with him and his wife if possible. That is really planning for the future, isn't it?

Boxing and other sports played a major role in the Hawaiian Department. Soldiers assigned to teams at Hickam played their respective sport several times a week during duty hours. Units competed in basketball, boxing, touch football, cross-country, track, softball, bowling, and baseball. Even non-team members were expected to attend sporting events, which figured prominently in the *Hickam News* and then the *Hickam Highlights*.

January 24, 1943

Dear Ann,

More and more people are coming here for defense jobs. There are too many people here now, and if more come, I don't see where they are going to live. Living costs are terribly expensive. Some of the workers have as many as 11 in a house suitable for 5, sleeping in kitchens and even bathtubs. The situation is serious during blackouts, what with poor ventilation and fumes from all sorts of gases. A decent house with only four rooms rents for $75 a month. Of course, you wouldn't want more than that; it keeps you from the elements. It never gets cold enough for a fire, and people here never heard of fires in the house to keep warm. I guess the only maintenance needed for such houses is painting due to the salt air, which is hard on them. Also, termites are plentiful here; likewise, rats and mice.

The military government is getting more lenient, allowing people to stay out on the streets till 10 o'clock (before it was 8 o'clock). Movie houses are staying open till 9 p.m. However, the blackout is still going strong, and, therefore, with people crowding and bumping into each other while entering a theatre, almost anything can happen. One has to wait hours in line to see a second-rate picture. It's not worth it.

I am sending you some more records.

I love you,
Herb

In January, the Seventh Air Force started photo reconnaissance and bombing raids of the Gilbert and Marshall Islands. On January 25, bombers from Herb's command staged a photo reconnaissance mission to Wake Island from Oahu through Midway. They also dropped bombs, 53 of which hit the island. After completing the photo runs, several Japanese planes intercepted the bombers, which downed at least one enemy fighter. Three bombers from the command were hit but not shot down.

Herb worked long hours during the last week in January and the first in February. After work, he dragged himself into the shower and hit his bunk. One night, he outlined the following letter using his flashlight. He found this arrangement comfortable and conducive to thinking, even though the glare from the flashlight hurt his eyes. As he wrote, soft Hawaiian music played.

February 12, 1943

Dear Ann,

Remember me? I'm the guy who used to write to you. Honestly, Ann, I have been busy for three weeks and am still working hard—4:30 a.m. to 7:30 p.m.

I asked Armour—the guy who wrote Sara—if he'd heard from her. He said he wrote her but never received an answer. Maybe her letter was lost. I don't think he will write again. He is now going around with a Chinese girl and doesn't have time for anything else.

I had a fairly good tan about three weeks ago, but since this "boom" [at work], I have become sickly looking and can't get enough sleep. It is 8:30 now, and I'm beginning to feel sleepy, but I am writing for your sake and mine.

Fifteen hundred Japanese men have enlisted in the service and will be trained back in the states. Having a trained army of Japanese here would not be wise, with the thousands of civilian Japanese; sabotage would be too easily encouraged. They have not started to draft Japanese yet.

I love you,
Herb

Many Japanese in Hawaii referred to themselves as Americans of Japanese Ancestry and identified with the United States rather than Japan. When the army dropped its ban on the enlistment of Japanese Americans in 1943, second-generation Japanese Americans from Hawaii and the mainland enlisted even as the government interned 1,441 of their relatives. Their unit, the 442nd Regimental Combat Team, is the most decorated infantry regiment in U.S. Army history and launched the career of Hawaii's long-serving senator, Daniel Inouye.

February 14, 1943

Dear Ann,

I'm glad that you received the tea. Don't you think it has an oriental taste to it?

Ann, don't feel bad about not sending me anything. It's too much trouble to receive anything now. I love to get packages, but it seems all lovely things have been taken from me, and one more doesn't make much difference. Ann, I will be so damn glad when this war is over. I think I will cry with joy. But I won't be satisfied until Germany and Japan are completely bombed off the map, never to rise again in power, at least in our day.

The war is getting on as you probably know. I wonder if Russia will get the credit she deserves after this mess is over. The outlook in the Pacific is much better than it was a few months ago and will get better as time goes on. . . .

It's still a little chilly here, and I have to sleep with two blankets to keep warm. After the sun goes down, it gets colder and the trade winds blow in through the windows of our barracks. It sometimes reminds me of the winter winds back home.

Aloha,
Herb

March 9, 1943

Dear Ann,

Your letters are coming regularly. I hope you understand how difficult it is for me to answer; this is the first letter I've written in three weeks. I'm writing when I really should be doing my work, which never seems to end anymore.

I am awaiting the arrival of my first correspondence course and am anxious to see how good it is. Some of the correspondence courses are not worth the effort one puts into them, but the one I am trying is from the Massachusetts Department of Education. My next problem is finding enough time to do my duties and the course. I will probably have to work late into the evening.

You wrote about the women taking over the teller's job in the bank. I think women could do this sort of work as well as men. During wartime, women can do numerous jobs as well as men. They have proven it.

I will be glad to cheer up anyone who is lonely, so tell your friend Peggy to write her brother or find out exactly where he is, and I'll see what I can do. Until then, I love you, Ann.

Aloha, Herb

The day after Herb wrote the preceding letter—the tenth day of the month—was payday at Hickam in early 1943. Herb and the rest of the men in his company marched up to the day room.

"Company, HALT," commanded the sergeant. "Parade, REST." Spreading their feet slightly but keeping them straight without locking their knees, the men rested the weight of their bodies equally on the heels and balls of their feet. They placed their hands at the small of their backs, centered on their belts. They kept the fingers of both hands extended and joined, interlocking the thumbs so that the palms of the right hands faced outward. They held their head and eyes at "attention" and remained silent, moving nothing unless otherwise directed. The first sergeant sat

116

with the pay officer at a desk and called out each soldier's name. When Herb heard his name, he stepped up to the desk, saluted the pay officer, repeated his name, received his pay in cash, saluted again, did an about face, and left the room. The rest of the men did likewise until each man got paid. After receiving his pay, Herb, like most of the men, had the day off.

CHAPTER 4
WAITING FOR A WEDDING

I have always wanted a church wedding and would rather like to be married in your church. I even have my attendants picked out, Virginia as my maid of honor and Sis and Sarah as bridesmaids.
—Ann Fritz

In early 1943, Japan planned for its next moves as the Allies debated the best use of their resources, split between Europe and the Pacific. The Allies chose a two-pronged advance in the Pacific, one of which involved island hopping through the Solomon Islands and New Guinea to cut off Japanese positions. The other advance, involving Herb and his colleagues in the VII Bomber Command, would charge through the Central Pacific by amphibious invasion starting in mid-1943.

While the military made its plans, Herb planned for the short and long term. He looked forward to a long-awaited furlough, his wedding, and life after the service.

March 31, 1943

Dearest Ann,

I know it's been a long time since you've heard from me. Not a day that goes by that I don't think of you. We shall have our day. Ann, maybe in my next letter I can tell you if I am going to get a furlough of about six days in the next few months. (I have mentioned this to no one and hope to keep it secret as I don't want anyone to get worked up about my coming home.)

If fate is with us, I would like to get married while on furlough and bring you here if possible. If you want this, we will have to think of the disadvantages and do lots of planning to make things as easy as possible. You would have to get a war job doing secretarial work and probably have to live in town in an apartment. I know the job will not be hard to achieve but the apartment will. It's fairly safe here and not prone to another attack. Good jobs are plentiful and the money I make will keep you going. I hate to take chances but this seems to be the only way. Let me know what you think of these plans.

My studies have not come yet. Whatever they send me, I will take seriously. I hope my time will not be too cramped, what with my Army duties, formations, gas and rifle drills, and whatever else befalls my overburdened shoulders. I am planning to study with Commercial Illustrating and will try to get work at one of the large stores here. Of course, all this will have to wait until this damn war ends. I haven't looked into the prospect of a job yet—these are more or less dreams.

Let's hope your boss will go on another trip to New York so you can have it easy again. The same thing sometimes happens to my coworker, Bill, and me. We take turns to get some sleep or play tennis or whatever we deserve whenever our boss decides to "take a break," a commonly used phrase in the Army. When the cat's away, the mice will play, and believe me, we both take advantage of this break, which happens about twice weekly.

The sun is starting to get much warmer, reminding me that summer is on its way. You will be welcoming spring soon, and I hope the winter has not been too bad. There is nothing drearier than long winter nights with nothing to do, especially in the country.

I have seen the broadcast of the ["Hawaii Calls"] radio program that you mentioned. Do you have any trouble hearing it? The performers stand along the beach underneath a banyan tree, which are the queerest trees I have ever seen—their roots grow down from the branches. The scenery suits the program perfectly, though, and the passersby view the broadcast as an everyday occurrence.*

Ann, dear, I must stop writing. Let's pray for the best for us.

I love you.
Herb

Herb's coworker, Bill Hoagland, and Herb (right) in front of the Royal Hawaiian Hotel, where soldiers could get a beer or a room for 25 cents a night. The military used the hotel as a rest and recuperation center once the war broke out. (Photo from Herb's collection)

*The Moana Hotel's Banyan Court featured a massive, ancient banyan tree, which faced the ocean. From there, Webley Edwards hosted the "Hawaii Calls" radio show, which helped lure snowbound mainlanders to Hawaii.

April 10, 1943

Dearest,

Ann, I know it's hard not to feel neglected but try to understand. My hours are still as long as before, but I am getting used to them now and don't mind half as much as I did.

I can't say definitely about my furlough, but my chances are looking better every day. I will probably fly from here to San Francisco, but if I am lucky I can get a hop from there to the east. My 15 days will start when I reach San Francisco, allowing me a few days to spend at home and with <u>you</u>.

Your raise isn't much, but, Ann, it's something and maybe as you suggested you'll get another raise in a few months. Why don't you stick it out and wait? Even if it is only $10 more, it's better to have this permanent job than a temporary job, which most defense jobs are. A lot of people are going to want work after the war. God only knows where they are going to get it.

Shoes are also being rationed here, but I have had two pair for a long time and I can still get along well with these and am willing to sacrifice if it would make this war end one day earlier. Mentioning rationing of clothing, in Australia and some other places, the merchants are not allowed to advertise clothing, merchandise, or bargain sales of any kind, which is good as it won't alarm everyone about buying clothing. . . .

I saw Walt Disney's *Fantasia* and found the cartoon characters boring. The music was superb, but I don't think such beautiful music goes with the silly actions *Fantasia* portrays. A little of this cartoon stuff goes a long way with me. I am satisfied with the regular short cartoons; to sit through a whole feature is too much.

I love you,
Herb

[undated but written in mid-April 1943]

Dear Herb,

I'm keeping my fingers crossed about your furlough. I have a feeling you will get it but hope you will be allowed 15 days at home instead of 15 days from the time you reach San Francisco. Don't you think they might give extra time if you told them you plan to be married? Anyway, if you only get home for six days, it will be wonderful, and I will be thankful for it.

As I said in my letter of last week, it would be swell if we could get married while you are on furlough, and I think we could do so even if you only stay five or six days. We probably couldn't get married much before your last day because of the planning involved. I have been doing a lot of planning.

I received the two money orders amounting to $110 with your letter and have deposited them. The balance is now $508.

I have been thinking that it would be great if I could go back with you after we got married. It would be easier for you to have me there with you. It would be a wonderful trip for me, and I could be with you for I have missed you so much.

> With all my love,
> Ann

Though planning her wedding tempted fate, Ann couldn't resist doing so. All-girl and world-class shopper, she loved well-made clothing and goods, having learned to sew, embroider, and do other fancy work from her mother. Though Norristown, where she worked, offered linens, hand-carved furniture, and imported china—the best quality of merchandise—she thought, "I'll shop in Philadelphia for my gown."

While Ann dreamed of her wedding, bombers from Herb's command got their first crack at the Japanese. The bombers flew southwest on April 20, 1943, from Hawaii to Funafuti, in the Ellice Islands (now called Tuvalu). After refueling, they headed northwest to Nauru Island, an enemy stronghold important for its rich phosphate reserves used for making gunpowder. Despite heavy antiaircraft fire, the bombers destroyed oil supplies on the runway. The mission was the longest over-water mission in AAF history.

The Japanese bombed the air field at Funafuti the next day, hitting two bombers, one of which had a payload of 3,000 pounds. It exploded, damaging five other airplanes. On April 23, bombers from Herb's command raided Tarawa, surprising the enemy at its main air base in the Gilbert Islands and hitting the gas storage and barracks areas.

April 28, 1943

Dear Ann,

The good news is that I will get my furlough, but I will have to wait my turn as quite a few fellows are entitled to one before I am.

Things are about the same for me. (Incidentally, I am now a Sgt.) I'm getting a tooth filled and another, extracted. I haven't been to a dentist for a year. It's costing $8, which is expensive but the best I can do. Doctors and dentists are in demand—so few doctors and yet so many people need medical and dental care. I had to wait seven weeks for a half-hour appointment, and the dentist was far from good. One doctor told me many islanders have some kind of tropical skin disease, but half of them don't realize it and don't know they need a doctor.

A medical officer told me that Honolulu has 20 cases of infantile paralysis. He also advised me to avoid public swimming pools and overcrowded beaches. You have to watch something as serious as this with the utmost care, especially on an island. I read an article on a cure for infantile paralysis by an Australian nurse who believes in massaging or some similar method.

By this time, I guess you received the batik blouse, and I hope you like it. Did you have any trouble arranging the turban, which is really the thing to wear with such a blouse, and is, I think, smart looking. (Incidentally, it came from India.)

I wired your Mother a corsage of spring flowers for Mother's Day. I hope it reached her in time. Ann, give everyone my late and best regards for the Easter holiday and a special one to you.

I received a letter from my friend, Andrew Beyer, who, by the way, is to be our best man at the wedding. He's a swell guy and one of my intimate friends. He is anxious to take part and wants me as best man at his wedding in the near future and is waiting for my return. I have neglected my correspondence—not only to Andrew, but to so many other friends. I think one should write letters only on important occasions, not for just the sake of saying, "Hello, I'm fine and hope you are the same." But some people don't understand me and feel hurt if they don't hear from me. They don't realize that if any matter of importance came my way, I would let them know as soon as possible. To tell of my experiences is too much trouble, and half of them would not believe me.

Aloha,

Herb

—★—

While at the Montgomery County Historical Society on my trip to Norristown, I had wound through microfilmed war-era editions of *The Times Herald*, the local newspaper, which ran stories on local boys in the service. I spied a blurb and photo of my father's friend, Andrew M. Beyer, who had joined the Marine Corps. His family had sent a photo to the paper to note his birthday, a common practice when parents wondered if their sons would survive the war. I photocopied the page and put it with my notes.

When I got home and read the blurb again, for some reason, the home address of Andy's parents resonated with me: 318 James Street, Norristown. I got out the plastic bin of family records Mother had given me, thanking her mentally for saving them. I sorted through copies of old birth and death certificates; little prayer cards from family members' funerals printed with the 23rd Psalm, which I handled reverently; and yellowed letters and photos. I tried to avoid seeing the card from the funeral of my

125

sister, April, the loss of whom still stung after four years. From the bin wafted that familiar smell—of my old relatives—who'd held tightly to those prayer cards, crying with grief.

I found an envelope with the return address of 318 James Street, the same address as Andy Beyer's parents. Inside was a letter to Mother from my Aunt Edna, the second wife of Daddy's brother John. My heart almost stopped: It had to be—Edna was Andy Beyer's sister. Uncle John had married the sister of Daddy's best friend. Astounded, I wondered if Andy was still alive. If so, could I ask him about my father?

I searched for the phone number of my cousin Paul, the son of Aunt Edna and Uncle John. Paul practiced dentistry, and calling his office would be an imposition, I thought. But I couldn't contain my excitement. I phoned the office, and he took my call.

"Is Andy Beyer your uncle?" I asked Paul, trying to sound calm.

"Oh, yeah, ol' Uncle Andy. . . . He and his wife moved out to California after the war. He became a professional clown and he's listed in the *Guinness Book of World Records* for being the world's oldest clown. He's an icon out there in L.A."

"Is he still alive?"

"Yeah, and he's doing pretty well the last I heard."

"Do you know how to reach him?"

"Sure."

Pressing the phone to my ear, I jumped up and down, like an ebullient child on a trampoline. I regaled Paul with how I connected Andy and Aunt Edna.

"I'll call you back with Andy's phone number and address," he said.

As soon as he did, I wrote "Uncle Andy" a letter, deciding a phone call might unsettle a nonagenarian. I enclosed a photocopy of a letter Andy had written my father during the war as evidence of my identity and copies of photos of Andy with other old friends of Daddy's, hoping he could identify them.

After high school, Andy went to what was then Drexel Institute, according to the newspaper clipping. Afterwards, he joined the Marine Corps and went to boot camp at Parris Island, South Carolina, and on to Corpus Christi, Texas, where he graduated from radio school. By March 1945, Andy was a Staff Sergeant stationed at Cherry Point, North Carolina. He married a Philadelphia girl in 1944. (Unfortunately for my parents' wedding plans, the marines had designs on Andy.)

I waited a couple of weeks for a reply to my letter. When it came, I snatched the letter from the mailbox and read what Andy's wife, Margaret, had written:

> Dear Liz,
> . . . I know this is not the answer you hoped for. Andy is 94
> and has dementia. . . . His memory is poor. . . . He wasn't
> able to recall anything about Herb, even though he
> remembered his name. . . . And he did not recognize
> anyone in the pictures you sent. . . .

Crestfallen, I reread the letter looking for what I knew wasn't there. I read the copy of the page from the 2004 *Guinness Book* recognizing Andy as the world's oldest performing clown at age 86, which Margaret had enclosed. For decades, Andy had delighted audiences as Bumbo the Clown at birthday parties, picnics, baby showers, and his own dinner table. Gratified to have received the letter, I folded it up and put it with my other research material, wishing I had started this project sooner. By now, most if not all of my father's friends had died and I stood little chance of finding any of them. But the letter only spurred my determination to understand my father. Like a toddler with a security blanket, I was not letting go or giving up on my quest.

—★—

May 8, 1943

Dear Ann,

Received your letters of March 21 and 28. I'm trying to
write once a week and may do so but find it hard.

You mentioned seeing *Random Harvest*. I liked the book,
but it's far from the best. It must be hard to have someone
forget you as though you never existed. I am reading a very
good book now, *The Sun Is My Undoing*, by Marguerite Stein.
Read it when you get a chance. She is a marvelous writer. The
book deals with the early slave trade and abolitionists in
Europe. I only get to read at night when I'm in bed.

I'm sure I'll be home in five or six months. The prospect
of getting married looks good, but I don't think you can return
with me for reasons I will explain later. I would like to get
married, though, and as soon as I am sure about when I'm
coming home, I will let you know so you can plan whatever
kind of wedding you wish. We just have to be patient and wait
for my turn, but my name is already on the eligibility list. No
one knows when the sailing orders are being published.

Ann, don't think me stupid, but I bought another
engagement ring, which is far prettier and better than the one
you have. It's a set, and the rings match perfectly. The moment I
saw it, I admired it and wasn't satisfied until I bought it. This
one has our initials in it, and I shall bring it along when I come
home.

Love,
Herb

A week after Herb wrote the preceding letter, 18 planes from
his command took off from Midway to blast water targets on
Wake Island. With Japanese planes attacking the bombers from all
directions, only seven bombers hit the targets. The bomber pilots
zigzagged, climbed and fell, and ducked in and out of clouds to
evade the enemy.

128

One Liberator failed to stay in formation and fell prey to eight enemy planes, losing its second engine when cannon fire pierced and burst inside of it. The crew lacked the fuel to return to Midway so threw all nose and waist guns overboard and prepared to ditch. Completely stalled, the plane dove toward the sea with the pilot and copilot strapped in their seats, the engineer between the copilot's seat and the armor plate, padded with cushions. The seven other airmen wedged into the middle of the plane, braced by parachutes and other padding. The plane plunged into a dead calm sea but broke into three pieces, killing the bombardier. Four and a half hours later, a sub chaser picked up the survivors, waiting in two life rafts. The plane was the first B-24 in Herb's command lost to enemy action.

By mid-May some of the men in Herb's company had left on furlough, boosting his confidence about going home. As he wrote the following letter, he listened to a transcribed St. Patrick's Day program on the radio. "All the radio programs are two and some three months old," he wrote.

May 17, 1943

Dear Ann,

Your letters are coming faster than before. I'm surprised to learn that you have been crying over not getting letters from me. Please don't. You know if I get time, I always write and think of you every day.

I saw *Casablanca* and enjoyed it. It is one of the best pictures I have seen this year.

I'm busy as usual but am used to it now and wouldn't know what to do with time on my hands. When one is occupied with work, time goes by faster than when idle. Before we got this busy, I used to think too much and it started to work on my mind.

I am getting along nicely with my course and enjoying it. I have sent my first drawings to be graded; I'm anxious to know how I made out.

My coming home looks brighter. Things are going along smoothly. Just be a little more patient. I'm trying not to be overanxious, but it's hard. My name is being submitted in June, and it should only take a couple of months. I'm sure of this, so be patient and don't get too optimistic because plenty can happen in the meantime. I told the family of the possibility of my furlough and know they will get anxious.

I'm sending you some swell recordings of Irving Berlin and Andre Kostelanitz. I hope you like them. Well, Ann, let's not do anymore crying and remember I'm always thinking of you.

Aloha,
Herb

On Saturday night, May 29, Ann went to visit Herb's parents. They had set the record player up in the living room. As Ann settled into an easy chair, Herb's father placed the stylus onto a record and they listened to a scratchy audio greeting from Herb.

"And to you, Ann, I miss you more than words can say and can't wait to see you again and make you my wife." When Ann heard Herb's voice, she felt as if he were sitting beside her. She wiped her tears away with a hankie. From the record, Herb's overjoyed parents learned that he was coming home on furlough.

June 1, 1943

Dearest,

I received three letters last week. It was very good of you. Since you've written me about your furlough, the days do not seem so long, and I have been happier, with much to look forward to.

I'm glad you saw *Casablanca*. I liked it very much. I read *The Sun Is My Undoing* last winter. It took me several months to finish it, but I enjoyed it because it was so different. Miss Stein

130

must have a vivid imagination. Have you read *Benjamin Blake*? It has the same basic background as The *Sun Is My Undoing* and also devotes a good part of the story to life on a South Sea Isle. I forget who wrote it, but the movie *Son of Fury* was based on the story, although the book was supposed to have been better.

About our plans, of course, you know best whether I should go back with you. Anything you decide will be fine with me.

I suppose you won't know much ahead just when you will be coming, so if you will have about 15 or 20 days at home, we will have a few days together to make our wedding plans. I'd rather wait till you are here and can plan with me. We won't have a large wedding, so I think we can arrange everything in a few days.

No, darling, I do not think you are stupid for buying another ring. I'm sure I will like the set if you like it. I am proud of your excellent taste. I have temporarily set my vacation for the latter part of August but can change it if you should come earlier.

All my love,
Ann

When Ann felt certain of Herb's furlough, she bought her wedding dress at Strawbridge and Clothier in Philadelphia for $29.95. The ivory gown of slipper satin with a sweetheart neckline embroidered with seed pearls flattered her figure and the short train suited her. Ann also got a veil at the same store for $19 and found bridesmaid gowns in the style of her dress—aqua for the bridesmaids and dusty rose for her maid of honor. She chose her best friend, Ginny, as her maid of honor, and her sister, Mary, and friend, Sara, as bridesmaids. Herb would pick the groomsmen from the few men he knew still at home.

—★—

When I asked Mother about her wedding, she said, "A big fuss would have been unseemly during wartime. . . . I wanted to be married in Herb's church and assumed he would, too." The uncertain date of Herb's arrival, war, and Mother's practical nature, I realized, had trumped any grand wedding plans.

—★—

June 7, 1943

Dear Ann,

You ask me how I spent my Easter. Frankly, it was terrible. I don't know what I did that day, but it was no different from any other day. Although Christmas is my favorite holiday, commercialization is ruining it, like all holidays. Since the war, people seem uninterested in holidays, especially here, which can be expected.

I'm still working hard, and it is getting more interesting. It's one of the best jobs I ever had. I only wish it was out of the Army.

I met Walter Krieger, whom I used to go to school with in Norristown. Seeing him brought back some memories (and I'm sure I don't want to live in Norristown when I come home). He told me news about people I know. So the last few days have been a little different for me. He said that I have changed somewhat, but my feelings are the same; I just keep them hidden as much as possible. He is a bore but means well.

The flower I sent you is to be worn as a clip or on a necklace. It is a hibiscus—the flower of the island. They grow in many colors, and it's about the prettiest flower I've ever seen. I tried to press one to send to you, but it didn't pass the inspectors. Things such as flowers, coconuts, and the like have germs on them that they don't want coming into the U.S. The hibiscus only blooms for 24 hours and has no fragrance; some of them look like orchids. Well, I better stop before I run off the paper.

I love you,
Herb

P.S. Walter Krieger is a very stupid person.

July 2-4, 1943

Dear Ann,

    I had been working from 4 to 12. Now I am working from 8 to 4:30 and have even less time to myself. My time is pretty cramped again.

    For the first time in about a month, I played tennis tonight after work. I played doubles with some of the fellows in the squadron. Two were Filipino boys who are not bad players and are very fast. We played four sets; scores were two sets each.

    Walter K. came over to my barracks tonight; he just left. I was hoping he would leave earlier so I could start this letter before it got late and my mind got too foggy. I was wondering today if I could get home by September. Only four replacements came in June. I can't understand why they are keeping so many men in the states. They have about half of the U.S. Army there yet. We will never win a war by staying home.

    I got a blister on the bottom of my left foot. It is sore. I guess I won't be playing tennis until it heals.

    Today was a quiet 4th of July, much different than what the day used to be. Have you been taking any pictures? I would like to see a few of you. We are not allowed to take a picture on the post—against military regulations.

As ever,
Herb

On July 4, Herb reminisced about a happier July—of 1939—when he accompanied Ann and her parents on a trip to the New York World's Fair. He shot a picture that day of Ann in a dress of green, her favorite color. Walking the fairgrounds tired all of them; by the end of the day, their legs and feet felt as if they were stiffened with concrete. Ann, too, thought about that July of four years ago and looked at the old snapshots.

"What a great time we had," she thought. "I'll probably wear that green dress again when Herb comes home."

Herb and Ann at the 1939 World's
Fair, New York. (Photo from Herb's
collection)

During July, Army, navy, marine, and AAF forces began
their charge across the Central Pacific when the Joint Chiefs of
Staff ordered an amphibious assault against the Gilbert Islands.
Marking the end of the Seventh Air Force's main role as defender
of Hawaii, the force prepared to send its planes hundreds and
even thousands of miles beyond Oahu.

July 11, 1943

Dear Herb,

I'm spending a warm Sunday evening answering letters. I
guess my letters are more interesting to you since they are
arriving more quickly. My news is stale when my letters reach
you a month later. . . .

I hope you can get home by September. For one thing,
chances are it won't be so hot then, and too, it would be nice if
we could celebrate our birthdays together this year, especially
since it will be my 21st. I hope we can spend a few days at the

shore. Herb, perhaps we could spend our honeymoon there. September is a nice month at the shore. . .

We took some snapshots last week, and maybe I can send some of them. I've been hoarding a film or two for the furlough. I even found one of the new color films, which are scarcer than rubber tires. Until next time, Herb—

All my love,
Ann

While Ann and her family took photos, Herb's command continued photo reconnaissance and bombing raids of Wake staged through Midway, the last of which took place in July. On one mission in that month, a B-24 from the command crashed into the ocean after a mid-air collision with an enemy fighter. Bomber crew members continued to fire until the plane crashed, killing them all.

July 20, 1943

Dear Herb,

I'm really slipping up on my correspondence. My last letter to you was dated July 4. There isn't anything important to write about. I've been working and playing tennis in the evenings. And on Sundays I daydream and plan for your homecoming in between. Darling, I'm looking forward to it so much.

I hope everything goes all right so that we can get married. I think we can make most of the arrangements when you arrive. And I'm so anxious to see the ring. It will be a real thrill to have you put it on my finger yourself. I'm making this letter a bit short as it may not reach you before you start home.

I'm sending along the snaps I mentioned in my last letter. The group picture was taken the other Sunday when we spent the day at the park. I go back and forth to work with three of the girls. Sara (next to me) and Bea (on the end) are vacationing at the shore this week, so Vivian and I are traveling alone to work. Vivian and Virginia Detwiler want me to spend part of my vacation at the shore with them, and I have told

them that I'll try but not about our plans and your furlough.
Will they be surprised when they find out I intend going to the
shore but with you instead of them.

Well, Darling, that's really all since I don't know exactly
when you will be starting home. I'll send my wishes for your
safe homecoming now, and I'll be praying for you. Until next
time, remember

I love you,
Ann

Ann (left) with friends Sara Garges and Bea Hillas. (Family photo)

While Ann relaxed in the park, Herb and his buddies hiked
up hills with 40 pounds of gear on their backs. On August 6,
military officials on Oahu got orders to form and train forces for
the assault on the Ellice, Gilbert, and Nauru Islands. To toughen
the men for field service, the Hawaiian Department started a
conditioning program. Herb and the others in his company had to
hike approximately 8 miles along trails and across country in the
mountain ranges of Oahu. Those chosen for a hike left the
company at 6:45 a.m. by truck. When the truck got to the foothills,
the men formed columns and started climbing and walking on

trails and roads, through hillside fields and woods, taking a rest when needed.

Saturday night
August 14, 1943

Ann Dear,

Please try to understand how hard it was to write you informing you of the furlough situation. I wrote to Mother on Wednesday explaining it to the best of my knowledge. I'm afraid for her sake that my letter was discouraging. I mentioned that I wasn't getting my furlough until a later date and told her not to get overly optimistic (which she is). There was some question about whether I would be reassigned or furloughed. My spirits had sunk, and I was worried, mostly hoping for the best. Since then, I have had good news and think this time it's final and definite. Things look much brighter now. The First Sgt. told me that I would probably leave in early September.

I received your V-mail and know you are optimistic also. I can say now that I will be with you 4 weeks from today. If anything happens this time, I will be the most disappointed and disgusted guy in the Army. Before I forget, it will be a 15-day furlough, starting with my landing in California. I will leave here by airplane and, as I mentioned before, will have only 5 days at home. This is better than nothing. I'm taking it while I have a chance.

Trying to get rail transportation from California to Pennsylvania is going to be a problem from what I understand. I'm hoping that I can make it home from California by train in 3 and no later than 4 days. I think servicemen have a priority for train transportation. You should have time to answer this letter if you want, and I will let you know the latest developments, if any. I shall write once more before I leave and send you a telegram if I can while in California.

I'll write Mother in a few days. She's probably telling everyone in Norristown that I'm coming home. It's wrong to do this because she doesn't realize what can happen.

If you want to get married in the few days I am home, we will; it's entirely up to you. I am perfectly willing to wait to be married until the whole damn affair is over. I shall always love you. You must understand that this is war and after coming back from furlough there is a possibility of my moving farther into the South Pacific. I can tell you more about it when I see you.

Walter K. gets clippings from the hometown paper, and he comes over to my barracks every Sunday to show them to me. Some are interesting. He takes the cake and I still think he is stupid. He talks so much of his girl and the good times they had at Fry's, which happens to be one of the worst dives in Norristown—at least when I was there. He glorifies the dump (shows how much sense he has).

Ann, I will write again before leaving.

I love you always,
Herb

Herb finally left Honolulu on Wednesday, September 1, for his furlough, his first trip home in 3 years and 3 months. He spent a few days at his parents' home, reuniting with Ann and friends.

On the warm Thursday evening of September 9, he donned his dress uniform and, along with his family, made his way to Norristown's Haws Avenue Methodist Church. The sun hung low in the late summer sky as the wedding party and guests gathered for my parents' wedding at 7 o'clock. That night, Norristown was Paris.

Haws Avenue Methodist Church as it looked in the 1940s. The church still stands in Norristown at the corner of Haws Avenue and Marshall Street. Andrew Carnegie gave $1,300 toward the purchase of the church's pipe organ. The original curved solid-oak pews still grace the sanctuary. (Photo from my parents' collection)

As organist Catherine Morgan played music the couple had chosen, the ushers escorted the few guests down the aisle of the sanctuary to the first rows. Holding their bouquets, Ann's bridesmaids waited for their cue in the narthex, filling it with the smell of roses and perfume. Then, escorted by Herb's groomsmen, including his brother John, they proceeded down the aisle at their prescribed intervals. They took their places at the altar before Reverend William C. Skeath. A hush signaled everyone's attention.

"Here Comes the Bride" resounded in the 47-year-old stone church as the guests rose. Ann slipped her hand through her father's left elbow. A sylph in satin and tulle, she walked with her father as the train of her gown glided behind her, a shimmery wake. As luminous as the pearls around her neck, she smiled beneath her veil as she approached the altar. Ann's bouquet of gardenias fragranced the altar as she took her place next to Herb after her father gave her away. Gazing at each other, the couple exchanged vows and rings. Herb gently pulled half of Ann's veil over her head and placed it against her back. They kissed, now husband and wife.

The wedding party from left to right: Mary Fritz, Sara Garges, Virginia Detwiler, Ann and Herb, John F. Gilmore, Archie Erwin, and Bobby Dougherty (Herb's nephew). (Photo from my parents' collection)

As they strolled up the aisle, Ann's hand now tucked into Herb's elbow, they beamed at their well-wishers, whom they received in the narthex. Ann kissed her guests; Herb kissed his mother, new mother-in-law, sisters, and bridesmaids and shook hands with everyone else. Then the bridal party headed to Bussa's, the best photography studio in Norristown, and posed for the wedding pictures.

The wedding party and guests drove to the reception at Schwenksville's Spring Mountain House, a rustic resort in

Montgomery County dating to 1883. Because of the wedding's hasty arrangement, only friends in the bridal party and family attended. But that didn't dampen anyone's spirits. Happy to escape the doldrums of war, the wedding goers raised their champagne flutes as the best man toasted, "Here's to Ann and Herb." Glasses clinked and champagne bubbles fizzed.

After the reception, Ann's father drove his family, new son-in-law, and Ann's bridesmaid, Sara, back toward the orchard in Ann's Chevy. When they arrived at Sara's home, next to the orchard, the darkness of the night prompted Herb to whisper to Ann, "Should I walk her to the door?" Ann shook her head. She wanted Herb all to herself. Hitching up her skirt, Sara trudged up to her front door alone.

At her parents' bungalow, Ann prepared for her wedding night in the same bedroom she usually shared with her sister. She removed her veil and glasses as Herb slipped 33 tiny, satin-covered buttons out of their buttonholes in the back of Ann's wedding gown. They made love for the first time. As the wooden bed creaked, Ann thought, "I hope Mary and my parents can't hear it." It was the first of only three nights that the couple spent together in 1943 and most of 1944.

CHAPTER 5
HOLDING PATTERN

Mail Call is one formation that everyone meets promptly. If you get a letter, everything is jim-dandy. If you don't, it's tough, brother, tough.

—7th AAF *Brief Magazine*, March 21, 1944

On the Sunday after the wedding, Ann got up, bathed, and put on the new blue dress she had bought for Herb's visit. She painted her lips, used some lipstick to color her cheeks, and tamed her curly hair. Bacon, frying in the kitchen, made Herb's mouth water.

"Do you need help packing?" she asked him.

"No, that's okay. I don't have much to pack."

Ann's long coat and hat staved off the morning's chill as her parents drove the couple to Philadelphia's 30th Street Station. The perfume she wore settled in as they drove, replacing the car's usual smell of stale smoke from her father's stogies.

Under the train station's columned porte-cochere, Ann and Herb got out, shut the Chevy's doors with a thump, and bid her parents good bye. The newlyweds entered the station and sat in the lobby, its marble walls conveying a staid elegance.

"Isn't this place beautiful?" Ann said as she looked up at the gold-, red-, and cream-colored coffered ceiling. Herb nodded. After a while, they headed for the platform and boarded the train for Chicago, as far as Ann would go.

After they parted in Chicago, Ann clutched her coat closer against her as she walked down a windy street to a drug store for some Kleenex to dry her eyes. She took "The Admiral," to Philadelphia at 1:30 p.m., thinking, "I'm lucky I got a reclining seat." She watched the scenery through the window for about five hours until dusk, her tears blurring the view at times. The gentle rocking motion of the train lulled her to sleep, numbing her loneliness. Back in Philadelphia, she took a local train, arriving in Norristown at about 7 in the morning. She stopped at her mother-in-law's and had a cup of coffee with her, telling her about the train ride.

"Do you want to take the clothes and other things Herb left here with you?" Herb's mother asked her.

"Yes," she said. "I'm happy to have them."

When she got home later that morning, Ann sat at the kitchen table, her head in her hands.

"I miss him so much," she cried while her mother patted her shoulders to console her. She headed for the bath, knowing a warm tub could wash away the blues. After another day off, Ann, like a kid returning to school after summer vacation, grudgingly went back to work.

Meanwhile, in its push toward Tokyo, the United States planned to take the Mariana Islands to establish air bases for operations across the Central Pacific to the Philippines and into Japan. To accomplish this, the military chose the Gilbert Islands—2,400 miles southwest of Hawaii—as the bomber base for weakening Japan's defense of the Marianas. And the Seventh Air Force prepared to play its role in the first American offensive in the Central Pacific: the seizure of the Gilberts.

While Herb enjoyed his furlough, units of the Seventh Air Force had begun support operations to control air approaches to the Gilberts. U.S. occupation forces and engineers went ashore at Baker Island, almost due east of Tarawa, to develop air facilities for its base there.

September 14, 1943

My Darling Herb,

There is something heartbreaking about watching a train move farther away, knowing all of your heart and half of your being is on that train and wishing so hard it hurts that you could have gone along. But I'm so happy you took me to Chicago with you for each extra minute I could be with you was precious. I was glad you found your friend Ed for at least you wouldn't be quite as lonely.

A bunch of GIs sat in front of me on the train and "made merry with spirits" most of the way home. Two of the fellows had their wives with them, and the wives acted worse than the husbands. But their carryings on didn't bother me too much.

Darling, will you promise to take care of yourself for me? You said you had made up your mind to make the best of the situation until the war ends. When you get disgusted, remember that this war can't last forever. Remember the wonderful six days we've just had and think of the good times ahead. When you are back home, you will get the break you deserve. I know you will make a success of whatever you decide to do. And if we both try hard, it won't be long before we have that home we want so much.

My prayers and wishes for your safety and our being together again soon go with you always. Until next time, Herb,

I love you very much.

Ann

Herb arrived at Hamilton Field in San Francisco at 1:30 p.m. on September 18 and learned that he would leave for Hawaii at 5 p.m. the next day. He got a pass into town, where he saw *For Whom the Bell Tolls*. Afterwards, he returned to the base and went to bed.

The next day, planes crisscrossed the sky above Sun Krest Orchard, their white contrails slanting through the blue—sharp at first and then blurry, reminding Ann of Herb's flight back to Hawaii. In the afternoon, Ann rode her bicycle down to Ginny's home and played three sets of tennis and walked six miles, her thoughts drifting skyward.

While Ann imagined Herb's flight to Hawaii, bomb squadrons from Herb's command, along with navy and Marine Corps fliers, attacked Tarawa to neutralize the airfield there. General Truman H. Landon, Commander of the VII Bomber Command, piloted the *Pacific Tramp*, a Liberator that would gain fame roaming the Pacific bombing Japanese strongholds.* In more than 200 sorties, the airmen dropped 30 tons of bombs and gathered complete photo reconnaissance of Tarawa. Japan fought back with antiaircraft fire and interception, holding on. Though the photos would help the Allies, the persistence of the Japanese would prove troublesome.

September 23, 1943 [postmark]

Dearest Ann,

After waiting around here since the 18th, I'm finally leaving in one hour. One of the motors of our plane had to be changed.

Three fellows that came over here together have gotten married; one of the guys lives in Oakland, California, so he had a good time—better than the rest of us.

They are having a tear gas attack test here and everyone with a gas mask is wearing it. So far, I have not smelled any of the fumes and don't want to. None of us waiting for a flight has a gas mask. I wouldn't want to be crying around here.

I was told to get ready to take off, so this letter will have to be mailed soon. We have already gotten our baggage weighed and our lift belts. So I'll sign off and start in again when I get to

---

*Bomber crews gave their planes colorful names such as *Pacific Tramp, Bodacious Idjut, Battlin' Bitch,* and *Memphis Belle.*

Honolulu. The time is 9 o'clock; we expect to get there at 7:30 tonight. I'll always think of and love you.

> Your loving husband,
> Herb

September 22, 1943

Dearest Ann,

I arrived here safely at 11 p.m. yesterday. Your letter came today. I forgot to put a stamp on my letter that I wrote you in such a rush. I gave it to someone to mail just before I got on the plane. . . .

Some of the fellows already knew about my getting married while on furlough. It seems that Walter K.'s girl, Mildred [Freese], wrote and told him, and he told the other guys. I'm glad you didn't say anything when we parted in Chicago. I'll remember you as smiling but slightly teary eyed. I would not want it any other way, Dear. I love you. Being home was living a dream for me, and being with you was one of the best times I ever had in my life. It has spoiled me for I have a greater yearning to be back.

When you wrote of GIs on the train with you, that is only one example of what they're like from Chicago to San Francisco. Often, they're worse and more numerous. I hope you understood now why I didn't take you to San Francisco. I have respect for my wife, and taking you would be a poor way of showing it.

> Your loving husband,
> Herb

September 30, 1943

Dearest Ann,

I've been trying to get started on this letter since 7 o'clock, but Walter K. came over and talked and talked, preventing me from starting. He received a picture of Mildred and wanted me to see it. He said he was going to write a letter about the picture, that it was enough to make him commit hari-kari.

If possible, Ann, will you send me a couple pairs of tennis shoes? They are impossible to buy down here. My size is 8-½

147

but if this is going to cause trouble because of rationing, don't bother. My last pair has worn down to where I'm playing on bare feet. I tried to buy a pair when I was in San Francisco, but I couldn't get any. They must be hard to get.

I just came from visiting a friend of mine in the hospital who had an operation to remove a tattoo on his arm. To do this, they cut skin from his leg and graphed it onto his arm, where they also had to cut. It was a painful operation and a long time will pass before he is better.

Did I tell you I saw the play, *Macbeth*, starring Judith Anderson and Maurice Evans?* The performance was marvelous. These two are about the best. Judith Anderson had been here for four months during which time she and Evans performed *Macbeth* on different parts of the island. I really have to give her credit because I imagine it's not easy to play such a role for a group of GIs. I had been given a free ticket as a lot of other servicemen had.

We have been working overtime at the office. Sometimes it's 9 o'clock before I get finished.

Yours always,
Herb

September 24, 1943

My Dearest Herb,

I have been so happy all day. Mother phoned me at work this morning and said I got a letter from you. Your letter from San Francisco thrilled me yesterday, and reading "your loving husband" was especially sweet. I've been so happy these last few weeks since my birthday and I know (may God hear my prayers) when you come home to me, the rest of our years together will be happy ones. Herb, I miss you so much and hope with all my heart this war soon comes to a victorious and quick ending. Of

---

*Englishman Maurice Evans, a captain in the Army and noted Shakespearean actor, headed the Army's Special Services in the Central Pacific. He and Judith Anderson had performed on Broadway together in the past. The production of *Macbeth* that Herb saw took seven curtain calls on opening night.

course, if you listen to the radio news commentators, the war is practically over except for the shouting. Why can't they be content with reporting the actual happenings as they occur instead of building up everyone's hopes with their own opinions? I shouldn't listen to them. . . .

Please take good care of yourself, and let me know if you find out anything more about being sent elsewhere.

Your little wife,
Ann

September 29, 1943

Dearest Herb,

I had a swell day today.

Do you remember the girl I wrote about last year, Thelma Swenson, who gave me a piece of her wedding cake to sleep on when she got married? When she worked in Norristown, I used to eat lunch every day with her, her sister, Marie; Mary Casey; and Mildred Traister. So at luncheon today, they had a wedding shower for me. Mildred and Marie each gave us a yellow and green bath towel set, and Thelma and Elmer gave us a nice luncheon cloth. We also got a pair of good-looking metal bookends. We spent half the time asking and answering each other's questions about our husbands in the service.

And to make my day perfect, your letter of September 22 was here when I got home this evening. I hadn't expected to hear from you until next week. And the second letter you wrote from California came without a stamp. It was marked "FREE." Servicemen have free postage here in the states.

And, oh yes, the album of records came yesterday, and none was chipped or broken. I like them very much.

Darling, I miss you so much, but after seeing how much happiness I had in six short days, I know our life together will make up for the time we've been separated. Try to believe that, Herb, and I think you will feel a little better.

I love you always,
Ann

149

Wartime wives knew how it felt to be alone. The husband of Ann's friend, Thelma Swenson, served at Ft. Bragg, North Carolina. The husbands of two more of Ann's friends working in the bank's trust department served in the army, one of whom was stationed in Nebraska and bound for overseas.

Meanwhile, on a cloudy October 4 on Oahu's Windward Coast, Herb's company held a party to celebrate Organization Day—the second anniversary of the activation of the 400th Signal Company, Aviation. A skeleton shift stayed behind to work as the rest of the company went to Lanikai, where they played games, went swimming, and ate dinner. The unit's historian wrote, "Everyone's morale and conduct were excellent."

October 6, 1943

Dearest Ann,

Gardner [Wagoner] was over to see me last night, and he asked me to go to town sometime with him. He is doing different work from what he was before the furlough. As you remember, he was a Mess Sergeant, and I think, dissatisfied, but he says his job now is a lot better. A Mess Sergeant's job is not an easy one. He mentioned that he was sorry he didn't get married while he was home. He is discontented, but who isn't down here? There is so much complaining about everything. Certain guys live from day to day just for a letter, and when it doesn't come, they feel sad. A little thing such as a letter means so much.

I'm expecting Walter K. to come over here almost any moment. He reads all of his girlfriend's letters to me. Although I appear interested, I am bored for that is something I can hardly endure—listening to someone read his letters out loud.

I'm still working hard; this seems to be the only way to keep my mind occupied and free of daydreams. I hope I never have to wait for furlough as long as I did the first time. If this is so, I don't see how I can stand it.

The Army is no place for a person with an artistic temperament. There's no end to what you have to contend with.

150

It gets me thinking about what I am thankful for. We try to make the best of it, but it is hard as you have to please a lot of people. There is no human understanding. It's all routine. If there were more recreation or places to go to ease your mind, it would help a lot. It's no use in my rambling on about this as if you could do something about it. The people who could don't give a damn. A decent guy's life could be ruined forever.

I'm thinking now of the wedding gown buttons. That incident amuses me. Next time, I suggest a zipper. It is much easier and faster.

I started to save your letters. It will be fun to read our letters together some day. I took out a dependent's allotment for you, but before it takes effect you will have to send in a duplicate copy of our marriage certificate to the address on the enclosed. You may use this letter and send in the certificate. Try to take care of this as soon as possible.

Your loving husband,
Herb

As an army wife, Ann now received an allotment deducted from Herb's paycheck. Like all soldiers, Herb also endured deductions for a life insurance policy, which GIs were strongly encouraged to buy. Another 25 cents went to the Old Soldiers Home and $1.75 went for the laundry. For a private, whose monthly pay was $21, this added up. In addition, if a soldier lost or damaged a piece of equipment or incurred expenses at the PX, the army docked his pay. The army also urged soldiers to buy war bonds, which enlisted men bought in multiples of $1.75. The bonds, redeemable with interest, helped to pay for the war.

On a Wednesday night in early October, Ann's friends, Thelma and Marie, came to see Ann's wedding gifts and the tokens Herb had sent from Hawaii. When Ann showed them the wedding pictures, which she'd picked up that day, Thelma said, "They're good pictures."

While Ann entertained her friends, Herb wrote a V-mail, or piece of Victory mail, to her parents, apologizing in case they thought he'd neglected them while home. Developed to save shipping space for mail, a V-mail was a one-page sheet, a combination letter and envelope. Although a V-mail offered brief space to write, it sufficed for Herb's purpose. After writing in the space provided, a GI added the name and address of the recipient, folded the sheet, added postage, if necessary, and mailed the letter. The letter then went to a photographic lab, which collected and microfilmed all mail bound for a certain location, reducing a letter to thumb-nail size. From the lab, the film containing many V-mails then went by the fastest route possible to a receiving station near the destination. Finally, individual facsimiles of the V-mails were reproduced and the mail delivered to the addressees.

Herb and his buddies complained about the small size of the V-mails, but they saved an enormous amount of tonnage on mail ships and planes during the war, space needed for war supplies. A single mail sack, for example, replaced 37 mail bags required to carry 150,000 one-page letters, reducing the weight of that amount of mail from 2,575 pounds to 45 pounds.

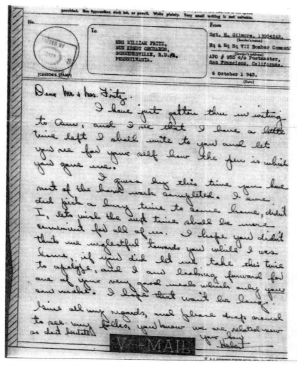

Herb's V-mail to Ann's parents.

On October 12, two officers and 13 enlisted men from Herb's company went on detached service with a provisional unit at Kahuku Army Base on Oahu. A week later, they left by landing ship tank for Nanomea Island—just south of the Gilbert Islands—to install, operate, and maintain signal communications with the navy and marine units stationed on the island. A plane bearing the company's captain crashed off Palmyra Island, killing all aboard.

October 16, 1943

Dearest Ann,

This week has been exceptionally busy as much is happening, but I can mention none of it. It's all new to me as it is to other people; no one seems to know what's ahead.

Payday came; I drew the large sum of $21.* It is enough to get by; it seemed sort of strange to get it as I always drew at least $60. I think I will have to borrow some cash to buy Christmas gifts.

I just got through work and it's 8:30, Saturday night. I haven't had a chance to play tennis, although I will on Wednesday when I finish work.

A friend of mine suggested a swim in the pool the other night at 9 o'clock. I enjoyed the swim, under a full moon, and the pool was practically deserted. The water felt warm, but the air was cool, and we had forgotten to take towels to dry off with after swimming. I now have a slight cold. But the swim was well worth it. I rarely go to the pool here on the post as it is not very clean, but at night you don't see any dirt so it's easy to enjoy.

Walter K. came over one night this week feeling "tight" and acted worse than a child. He is bad enough sober. He said he was tired of lying around doing nothing. He suggested that we go downtown and get drunk sometime. Of course, this is out of my line, and he soon saw that I wanted him to go and left a little peeved. A couple of nights later, he came and apologized.

Your husband,
Herb

*Though Herb was still a sergeant, his pay reflected the deduction for Ann's allotment.

This training photo was shot at Hickam's pool, christened by Esther Williams in 1944. It is still in use today. Herb is on the far left. The identity of the others is unknown. (Signal Corps photo from Herb's collection.)

Sunday evening, October 17, 1943

Dearest Herb,

We got another nice wedding gift today. One of our neighbors sent over a beautiful linen tablecloth, the fifth one I've gotten. Thelma Swenson tells me an old saying goes, "the number of tablecloths one gets for wedding presents means one will have that many children." I hadn't counted on <u>that</u> many. Maybe I shouldn't mind getting five tablecloths as wedding gifts for I know of one girl who got 14!

I keep wishing and praying that the war ends soon and we can be together again. War is so horrible, and people all over the world are suffering terribly. You remarked about the small flags hanging in the windows of homes in Norristown with the appropriate number of stars on them to represent each child in the service. Some of them had three or even four stars on them. What a happy day it will be when the word "Peace" comes, and those children come home, but not all of them will. Even though we won't be able to be together immediately afterwards, at least the suffering of many will cease, and the future will begin to brighten once more. Here's hoping that day comes soon. It will be fun to reread our letters together. I have saved every letter you ever wrote me in a small chest.

Mother and I went to apply for Ration Book #4 at the local school the other night. One thing about rationing is that it is fairly simple to secure a ration book, but the headaches start when one goes to use the book.

After we got the books, we decided to see if we could find tennis shoes for you. We found a store that had two pair. One pair is size 8, the other, size 9. Probably neither pair will be fit you perfectly, but I couldn't find size 8-½ like you requested.

Take care of yourself, Herb, and keep on daydreaming (as long as it doesn't interfere with your work) for daydreams take away—or at least help us forget for a while—the harsh realities. Just as dreams come true, our daydreams will come true—wait and see. I love you, Herb,

As ever,
Ann

October 21, 1943

Dear Ann,

I wish I could have some of the lovely weather you are having. There is nothing more refreshing than an autumn day. It makes me homesick just thinking about it—a beautiful thought, though.

We haven't given children much thought, have we? We can't do much about that now—much to my regret. Having children is up to you, and I am willing if you are. Two children would be nice, don't you think? I hope nothing of this sort is happening now, is it? I was a little hesitant, as I didn't want anything to happen. (You probably knew this.)

I am not overworked, but I keep occupied and plan ahead to spend what free time I have in some constructive way. I get tired of lying around, and I start thinking of things that make me lonely. I have to be doing something to make me forget.

Mrs. Roosevelt was here when I came back. She was inspecting military camps and, according to the paper, pleased with the conditions here. I really don't know what she saw but don't think her observations are valid.

The censor returned this letter to me. I mentioned an incident from the paper that he told me to rewrite. Now to do this, I will have to word it differently and I will probably face the same outcome, so I won't mention it. . . .

> Your loving husband,
> Herb

October 28, 1943

Dear Ann,

I have just finished work; it's 8:30.

It would be nice if you could go see Marge. I imagine life is pretty dull for her at times. She gets lonesome with Merrill's traveling so much. I appreciated the kindness she and Merrill showed me when they were here.

I just received the marriage certificate and will probably need it at times. You probably have taken care of your allotment by this time. You will only get it for one month as I was promoted to Staff Sergeant yesterday, and the allotment is automatically canceled. I shall take out an allotment for you for fifty dollars a month. The prior allotment is only for those under the grade of S/Sgt.

You mention that one of the two fellows who came back there on furlough from working in the shipyard at Pearl Harbor married a wahine here.* I would like to know where he found her—more power to him. I was surprised to hear that he likes it here. Generally, the defense workers dislike it and want to get back home as soon as possible. I can see their point of view as living expenses are high and finding a decent home, almost impossible.

I'm glad you like the wedding pictures and wish I could see them. Are you going to send me the small one?

I am listening to "Hour of Charm," and they are playing one of my favorite tunes, "In a Little Spanish Town." Do you remember it?§

---

* "Wahine" is Hawaiian for "native woman."

§One of Herb's favorite programs, "Hour of Charm," featured the All-Girl Orchestra

Payday is near, and if I get enough cash I am going to take a day off and go to town. Don't get worried if you don't hear from me for a while as I am going to be very busy.

Your loving husband,
Herb

Sunday afternoon
October 31, 1943

Dearest Herb,

Several commentators I've heard sound optimistic about a near victory over Germany but not so optimistic about the war in the Pacific. One person went so far as to say the war with Japan won't end until 1949. It seems that if the war on one front ended and all forces could be focused on one area, it shouldn't take so long to end the war entirely. Anyway, I hope all that activity you spoke of develops into something that will end it all soon.

I stopped to see [your] Mother after work yesterday. She is well, although she worries about Grandpop. He isn't at all well. I went up to see him briefly, but he didn't recognize me at first. When he knew who I was, he tried to talk to me. It seemed to be an effort for him, and I could not understand all he said. I do not think he will last long, and I think he realizes this, also.

From all indications, we won't become parents until the war is over. I hope the possibility of this happening now hasn't worried you. If it has, you can stop worrying. I understand how you felt about it when you were home and felt the same way. But the trip was such an ordeal for you, and we had so little time that I wanted to please you in every way and felt you should have whatever you wanted. So I left this decision up to you. I know I have a lot to learn—about the subject I just wrote of—and other aspects of marriage. You will have to be patient with me. In fact,

and Choir with Evelyn Kaye and her Magic Violin and Vivien (a soprano actually named Hollace Shaw). More than 1,000 female musicians from all over the United States auditioned for the orchestra. The women signed contracts requiring them to wear their hair long and flowing and keep their weight under 120 pounds. They rehearsed from early morning until evening until they memorized every note.

158

I guess there is much for us both to learn, but we are intelligent enough to be broadminded and understanding.

I guess this will do for tonight; I'll write again tomorrow.

I love you, Herb,

Ann

As Herb wrote the following letter, his radio played the angelic warbling of opera star, Gladys Swarthout, singing "Night and Day." The music, like a sedative, soothed him and suited the moment, as he did think of Ann night and day.*

October 31, 1943

Dear Ann,

I have to be careful with what I write from now on or my letters will be censored. If you have any questions, I shall try to answer them and stay within the limits of censorship.

I am going into town on Tuesday to buy your Christmas present. You know as much as I what I intend to send you. I am patiently waiting for my Christmas box and am sorry I asked you to send me sneakers for I won't need them anymore for tennis. But I can use them for some other purpose.

I received a toilet kit from the Norristown Chamber of Commerce. This was a surprise because it was the first time I'd heard from them since joining the Army.

We had some excitement in the barracks last night. Someone was caught stealing money from another man's trouser pockets while he was sleeping. The person who caught him is a

---

* During the war, major American radio networks produced and provided pressed-vinyl transcription recordings of shows to the U.S. Armed Forces Radio Service (AFRS). AFRS distributed the shows worldwide for rebroadcast to troops in the field. It accessed network lines and recorded its own shows or distributed the networks' original discs or tapes. AFRS edited out commercials and current events pieces by dubbing them to another master disc or tape. The transcriptions, as government property, were supposed to be destroyed after they had served their purpose. Thousands of them were simply dumped, however, ending up in the hands of collectors. These discs are the only form in which the broadcasts survive, and their existence explains why such recordings are still available today.

boxer, and he didn't spare any punches. The thief was yelling loudly, and in a short while everyone awoke wondering what was going on. We soon overcame our drowsiness, and many of the fellows took a punch at the thief. He was beaten up seriously and is now in the hospital. I have no patience or sympathy for anyone who steals from other soldiers, especially when we are living in the same barracks where you expect to trust others. This stealing has been going on for a long time, and I think they finally caught the real thief. But we also know of another one whom we keep a close watch on. In fact, he was caught robbing someone in the Post Exchange, which put him in the guard house for 6 months.

Our food is the same and one has to be pretty hungry to enjoy it. We have a good baker in the squadron, and his pastries are a treat. The cooks are poor and all they do is open a lot of tin cans, occasionally even scorching this food. I'm sorry now that I didn't take advantage of the food at your house and mine. I really enjoyed that last meal at your house, and when I think about it, it makes me hungry again. Your mother is one of the best cooks I know.

Yours always,
Herb

What the censors kept Herb from writing about—-the deployment of squadrons for the island-hopping campaign—had begun. While Seventh Air Force fighters already guarded Canton and Baker Island, squadrons from Herb's command flew to the Ellice Islands as a striking force in November 1943. Other men—three officers and 80 enlisted men from Herb's squadron—sailed southwest for 2,244 nautical miles to Funafuti on the transport ship, *President Tyler*, as part of a provisional unit.

By November 6, the Seventh Air Force had established its advanced headquarters on Funafuti. Squadrons from the command's bombardment groups moved to bases in the Ellice Islands. By now, Seventh Air Force squadrons spanned five islands,

160

occupying an area approximately 480 miles from Funafuti on the south to Baker Island on the north and approximately 740 miles from Canton on the east to Nanomea on the west.

The mission of the Seventh Air Force in the campaigns for both the Gilberts and the Marshalls was the same and continuous: its squadrons would attack the enemy's air bases to deny the use of its planes, help to defend friendly air bases, perform search and photo reconnaissance, and provide air transport among bases. Specific targets in the Marshalls included enemy air facilities on Mille, Jaluit, Roi, Wotje, Taroa, Kwajalein, and Kusaie.

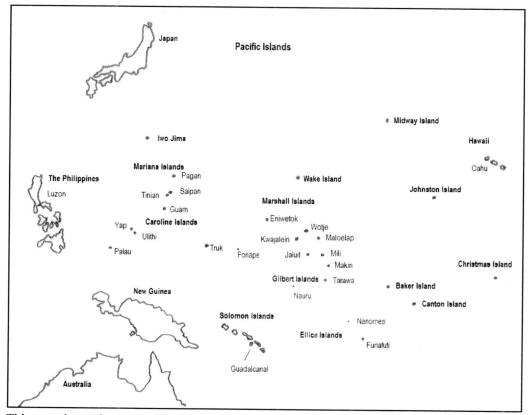

This map shows the some of the islands to which the Seventh Air Force sent men or aircraft. (Map by the author)

November 3, 1943

Dearest Ann,

Received your letters of October 15 and 18 today.

When I come home, I do not want to live with either of our parents (no hard feelings on either side), but we are married now and should be living alone. A small apartment will have to do until we get something better. I would like to start buying a house as soon as possible and, if our money holds out, I expect to have at least $2,000 at the end of the war. . . .

We had a slight tidal wave today. At 12 noon, the winds blew fiercely, stirring up dust for a while, but then it rained, which curbed the dust. But the mud is so thick—I don't know which is worse, mud or dust. Some of the surrounding islands had an earthquake this morning, causing the rainstorms. Right now, everything is peaceful, and the stars and a pretty moon are shining. I guess everything is complete but having you here. . . .

I'll love you always,
Your loving husband,
Herb

P.S. Your letters smell so lovely.

Thursday evening
November 4, 1943

Dearest Herb,

I just got your letter of the 28th, and I'm glad to hear about your promotion to Staff Sergeant. I'm so proud and know that you worked hard and gained this rank through your own efforts.

Herb, your letter has started me wondering. Were you trying to tell me that you are being sent elsewhere soon as you suspected? I hope I am wrong. I have always felt that you would be safe if you stayed where you are. But I know this is all up to someone else. Anyway, dearest, if you are sent somewhere else, I realize it will be for duty in a more active area, and I know your responsibilities will be much greater. So you're not to worry about me—I'll be all right. And no matter what happens—I'll always love you. And until you come back to me, I'll be waiting

162

for you. No matter where you go, my love and prayers go with you. . . .

Here's the best of luck to you, dear, and Godspeed to you. May He watch over you and keep you safe wherever you may be. I love you, Herb.

Yours always,
Ann

November 7, 1943

Dearest Ann,

It seems like weeks since I last wrote you due to the same old reason—I am working too much. I am behind schedule in everything.

There have been so many changes around here that a guy feels lost amongst all of these new men, some of whom are very stupid. In fact, we need a new man in our office and not one of them is satisfactory. Not one has an IQ of 100. They are the worst that ever came over here, and it is rumored that most of them are 4-Fs and are limited service.[*] These are the kind of men who will live through the war and go home to brag of their victory. It's cause for griping because most likely they will stay here, and the experienced men will be sent someplace else. It would be just as well to send the new men to a new location and start them off that way. But it's the Army's way of doing things, and we are not supposed to ask why. Yes, indeed, Ann, you have little conception of what some of us are going through. One just has to get a good hold of oneself and learn to take it. I don't expect anything from the Army. Take things as they come and try to make the best of it is the only solution.

---

[*]Registrants for the draft were excluded from service mainly for muscular and bone malformations, hearing or circulatory ailments, mental deficiency or disease, hernias, and syphilis. Thirty percent of registrants nationwide were rejected for physical defects and dubbed "4-Fs." For some women, a 4-F was not worth dating.

My friend who is in the hospital for the tattoo operation is a good example of how Army life changes one. He is thinking too much, and if he doesn't snap out of it, he will lose his mind. I went to see him last night, and he told me he was awake all night with pain in his head and different parts of his body. He wanted to scream out loud but could not make a sound. He looked to me because he had a horrible night and needs mental care. But the sad part about it is no one cares, and there are so many who are going the same way he is. I can't help him much because all I can do is listen. He would be much better off if he could get out of the Army, which would also be best for the Army. But to the Army, he is just another man and does not count for much.

Sunday night
November 8

Today was one of the busiest Sundays that I can remember. Usually Sundays are quieter than weekdays, but it seems we did more today than we did all week.

Early Friday morning a Negro soldier got into the nurse's quarters. He gave one of them quite a scare. This was the second time it has happened. We don't know if it is the same Negro. She had time to get her gun and scared him off before he did any damage. She chased him about two blocks, then lost track of him. Now, they have a guard around the quarters all the time. It surprises me that there is not more of this going on. Perhaps we don't hear about it. The Negroes seem to like this place a lot. The climate agrees with them. Some of them are forward in such a way that it makes you put them in their place. They have the attitude that this is their war also and take advantage by doing things to show that they are as good as others. No doubt some of them have sacrificed as much as others. But a great majority of them more or less feel, "White boy, I'm just as good as you, and if you don't like it, go to Hell." I think they should stay to themselves, and I leave them alone. But it's hard to do this. They seem to like to mingle with the whites.

I think in about a month when you hear from me you will know what is happening. Rumors are becoming realities.

I can't say much about it. I'm still here, yet, for how long, no one seems to know.

I love you,
Your Herb

Between January 1942 and June 1943, the AAF grew faster than ever, expanding its ranks by 52 percent. The procurement program swelled the AAF with men, mostly, whose skills, backgrounds, mental abilities, education, and training varied greatly. With 500 Military Occupational Specialties, the AAF found suitable work for them, even though Herb considered them "very stupid."

Some of the AAF's new GIs were black and they started appearing in Honolulu in 1942. Herb and many other white soldiers had never interacted with blacks before. His attitude reflected the norm for the times.

—★—

I interviewed my sister, April, about my father the year before her death. The eldest of us sisters, she knew him longer than my other sisters or I.

"Daddy was popular with the ladies and always tried to make people laugh," she said. "He played games with me as a young girl and took me to parades and other activities."

April remembered one parade in particular, a Fourth of July parade, when she was 5 years old, her blonde hair in braids. The parade route ran through Morton, a black area that bordered my parents' first house. As April and my father watched the parade from the roadside, she let go of his hand and moved up to the front row for a better view. Forgetting that she'd left Daddy behind, April reached for his hand but instead grabbed a black man's hand. When April looked up and saw whose hand she held, the man reassured her: "It's OK, honey." Afraid that she'd lost Daddy, April looked back to find him. He also smiled reassuringly.

Years later, Mother wrote about my father's attitude toward our black neighbors: "The events at Little Rock, Arkansas, had taken place, and Herb and I had many a fight over the fact that the black children who lived with their grandparents in the house that adjoined our lot in Morton wanted to come in our yard to play. I saw no harm because they were 'just children' but he saw it differently."

—★—

Monday evening
November 8, 1943

Dear Herb,

From what you have been writing, my suspicions about your being sent out are right. I had hoped it was only a rumor. I'm not worrying since you asked me not to, just wondering. Probably as you say, everything will come out okay.

The excitement in your barracks you wrote about must have really been something and, unpleasant as it was, I suppose it eased your minds to know the thief was caught. It seems a shame this goes on among servicemen, for most of the enlisted men are more or less on the same financial basis. Why should one man steal from his comrades who are all working equally hard for what they get? But I guess it takes all kinds to make a world, and the Army has some of the bad ones, too.

What you said about the Army cooks amused me, although it's not funny to you soldiers. From my viewpoint, it's a good thing the Army cooks aren't too good: My cooking won't seem bad when you come home. Mother was pleased to hear you like her cooking. I haven't anything else, so I'll sign off with—

All my love,
Ann

November 9, 1943

Dearest Ann,

Received your letter dated October 25 today; this was faster than usual. This is good time with the Christmas mail starting to pile up.

Speaking of the war's ending, some people in England think the war between England and Germany will end by New Year's. It's hard to say anything about Japan. I believe it is our strongest enemy. I also think the war will not last until 1949 as some people say. Of course, it's best not to get optimistic, but 1949 seems a long time away, and people are going to wonder why it's taking so long. The war in this area has only begun. In a few months, the South Pacific will see a lot of excitement.

I haven't seen Walter K. for about 10 days. I don't know what's the matter with him. He generally comes over to see me three times a week. I'm sure I didn't say anything to make him mad or hurt his feelings, although I thought a lot about it. The last time he was over he said he was recommended for P.F.C., but his recommendation was disapproved. I shall go over to his place tomorrow night and see what the trouble is.

We got finished early today for a change. I took advantage of the daylight left and you can guess what I did—played tennis. This was the first time in two weeks. You know to be a half-decent player, you should get in at least 1 hour a day.

Did I tell you that Gordon Hibbard got a letter from Sara?* By the way, he is not here anymore, but his A.P.O. is still the same. He wrote to Sara before he left for "down under." I miss him more than the rest as he slept next to me in the barracks. He was a friendly guy. . . .

Your loving husband,
Herb

*Herb's friend, Gordon Hibbard, and his older brother, Gerald, both served in Herb's command. Gerald flew combat in the *Pacific Tramp*, and Gordon worked as an engineer on the ground crew of that aircraft. The Hibbard brothers hoped to return to their father's farm in New York after the war.

November 12, 1943

Dearest Ann,

Don't forget to tell me what you desire for Christmas as the gifts I am sending you are all I could afford when my cash was low. Please don't have me arrested for non-support.

Things are as usual at the office, once again running smoothly. I could stand it this way for a long time because I need the rest. . . .

Mother isn't writing as often as you. I hope she isn't worrying too much about Grandpop. She seems to get satisfaction out of worrying about people. I wish my brother and sisters would help her more than they do; she is easily hurt, and they can't understand her. I'm sure the happiest she ever was in her life was when I came home. I try to write her as much as I can.

Now that the allotment has been approved, you should have received your first payment. You may only get it for one more month as I wrote in my last letter. I will make you out an allotment for 45 dollars a month. I shall continue to buy bonds for three more months and then start sending you 85 dollars a month. I'm hoping this can last for about a year, notwithstanding the war's ending, for which it would be worth losing the money. But if I can keep this up, we will have a good start by the time I come home.

Your husband,
Herb

Sunday night
November 14, 1943

My dearest Herb,

I'm not surprised at what you say about the type of men now coming in. The Army has had to lower its requirements to secure enough men to fill the ranks; most of the really physically fit men were taken long ago, and the Army can't be as fussy.

Looking at the pictures you sent in yesterday's letter (November 9), I sympathize with you on the loss of your friends. Losing comrades and friends must be the grimmest part of war.

On Friday night, I went to the city to see Marge and Merrill Gander. Merrill was home between trips, so I finally met him. Marge showed me all the things she brought back from Hawaii—scrapbooks of snapshots, souvenirs, and clippings, all of which I enjoyed. They also introduced me to the game "Battleship," with which they used to entertain you. I had lots of fun. Marge is swell, and they are a nice couple. They were both glad to hear about your promotion, and Merrill said he wished he had been home while you were here or that you two could have met while in San Francisco. He was there around the time you were.

I feel sorry that your friend in the hospital is suffering mentally, as you say. Doesn't he have a wife or girl in whom he is interested enough to make it worthwhile to stick out his time in the Army? I don't suppose there is much you or anyone else can do.

I sure give that nurse credit for scaring away the Negro intruder. As you remarked, the Negroes' importance in society has advanced, and a lot of them imagine themselves on an equal basis with white people. You may have read in the papers a while back about an incident in Detroit that started with a fistfight between a white man and a Negro and developed into a riot. And in Philadelphia recently, an alarming number of women have been attacked by Negroes. But since "freedom for all regardless of color, race or creed" is the byword of America, not much could be done to suppress the Negroes' growing importance.

You wanted me to tell you what to send me. I would like either a blouse or handbag such as you sent me before, but I will be pleased with what you've already gotten me. As for Dad and Mother, they would be pleased with anything you choose, especially something typical of the Islands. All the things you've given me have been lovely. You have wonderful taste, really. Good night, dearest.

I love you,
Ann

169

November 17, 1943

Dearest Ann,

I wanted to answer your latest letters last night, but Walter K. came over and stayed until the lights went out. So my night was a boring one (poor Mildred).

I have received my Christmas box. I thought I may as well open it, hoping the sneakers might be inside. I am glad I did because today I played tennis in them. I did not open the rest of the small packages, although I'm greatly tempted to do so. I know I will like whatever is in them, and if things get worse down here and I have to move, I will open them before Christmas. But the way things look, I will still be here until Christmas at least.

Work has returned to normal at last. Today was an easy day. I took full advantage of it and didn't do much all day. Most of the guys have moved on, making the barracks quieter than usual. I miss some of them; others, not at all.

It is pretty tough down there, much worse than here. Some of the boys there are writing to guys here, and they complain of rats, malaria, and the heat. Many of them can't stand it and have come back. It's nothing pleasant to look forward to. I think I could take it for a while, but after 6 months, I would be ready to come back. Sleeping with rats and contracting malaria must be hell. I am sure I will be going after Christmas. If you read on the back of page 5 of the long letter I wrote you, you will see something written near the top.

I love you much too much.

Yours always, Herb

"The back of page 5 of the long letter" had a faintly penciled (and misspelled) clue, inconspicuous to the censor but clear to anyone who knew where to look for it: FUNA-FUTI. After three months of waiting, Herb expected to be sent to the advance headquarters of the Seventh Air Force at Funafuti in the Ellice Islands.

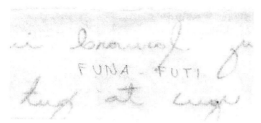

Herb's clue to Ann about where he'd be going.

In their preinvasion bombing of the Gilberts, the heavy bombers from Herb's command had completed 141 sorties to the islands. Navy fliers pounded Tarawa and Makin even harder from carrier-based aircraft.

Nevertheless, marine and army forces waded ashore on Tarawa under fire from 4,500 well supplied and prepared Japanese defenders on November 21, 1943. Though prior amphibious landings of U.S. forces in the war had met little or no initial resistance, they battled for 76 bloody hours on Tarawa before subduing the enemy. Afterwards, American corpses lined the beach and bobbed like buoys in the surf. One-third of the marines perished or suffered wounds as nearly 6,000 Japanese and Americans died fighting on the tiny island. Army forces invading Makin the same day lost 186 men.

In the final weeks of November, squadrons from Herb's command blasted sites in the Marshalls to soften them up and support base development in the Gilberts. Before the end of the month, plans for U.S. air forces to advance into the Gilberts had begun. By November 24, some officers and 35 enlisted men from Herb's squadron helped occupy the Gilbert Islands in support of the bomber command. Another 66 men from Herb's squadron headed for Funafuti, but Herb was not among them.

Sunday night
November 21, 1943

Dearest Herb,

    I'm sorry I haven't written for 5 days, but I didn't have anything to write about. Last Saturday we saw a very uninteresting movie, *First Comes Courage*. I find these propaganda-packed movies boring and even disgusting.

    Two of my friends were pleasantly surprised this week. Do you remember the dark-haired Italian girl I introduced you to— Gisella Battista? Her boyfriend, Joe Bearoff, is from Bridgeport and says he knows you. Do you know him? He's your brother John's age. Joe is in the Navy and had been in Detroit going to advanced school. He had just finished and expected to go to the West Coast and to sea duty. Luckily, he was assigned to an aircraft carrier, and his home base is Philadelphia. The ship hasn't been commissioned yet, so for the next few months, he'll be coming home every other night and each weekend. Gisella has been overjoyed.

    The other friend who had good luck was Sara. Her Charlie Giambrone, who had been in Florida for the past few months, came home Tuesday on a 10-day furlough. Charlie says he remembers you—his younger brother, Joe, and you were classmates, and he asked about you. So Sara has been in the clouds, too. She seems really interested in him, although her parents object because of his religion [Catholic] and Italian background. I am curious about what she will decide to do.

    Did I say I'd be having a vacation while my boss recuperates? It's far from a vacation. I'm doing a good bit of his work and my own, too. It surely will be simple when I'm a mere secretary again.

    I hope you are all right, and I'm still praying that you won't be sent out.

I love you, Ann

Friday night

November 26, 1943

Dearest Herb,

I just got your letter of the 17th. I was glad to hear from you and to know you are well and still on the Islands.

The bank had its dinner dance on Wednesday night at Palumbo's in the city.* I went with Gisella and her boyfriend, Joe, and had a good time. Naturally, I wished you could have been with me. But we'll go when you come home.

Yesterday was Thanksgiving. We all missed you when we sat down to dinner. Because you couldn't be here, things weren't complete for me. Sis was home, and the food was wonderful, but I had no enthusiasm for the holiday.

I never would have found the message in your letter if you hadn't called it to my attention. I didn't realize what it meant until Sis said maybe it was the name of an island. I went to get a map, and sure enough, we saw it on a sketch of the Gilberts and surrounding islands. I hope telling me didn't get you in trouble. I imagined when the news of the attack on the Gilbert Islands broke that this was where the men from Hawaii had been sent. I suppose you can take consolation in the fact that these islands are neither as far away from the mainland as New Guinea or the Solomons nor as close to Japan as the Marshall Islands or Wake.

Malaria seems to be one of the diseases affecting a large number of men in this war. I had believed man had virtually conquered malaria through medicine and research. From what you write, to exist on these islands must be nearly unbearable.

You close your letter by saying you hope I am happy. Yes, darling, I am happy. I'm happy because you love me and I am the wife of someone wonderful. I only hope I can make you as happy as you deserve to be when you come home.

I love you, Ann

*Palumbo's, one of South Philadelphia's best known restaurants, was owned by Frank Palumbo, who also ran three night clubs, all venues for the heyday of Philly's popular music scene in the 1940s and 1950s. Palumbo's and the clubs showcased Frank Sinatra, Sergio Franchi, Louis Prima, Louis Armstrong, the Clooney Sisters, and Jimmy Durante, among other acts.

November 30, 1943

Dearest Ann,

You are getting the drift of what I'm trying to tell you, but it is nothing to get alarmed about.

Tomorrow I happen to have off. I plan to play tennis in the morning and go into town in the afternoon and see a show. This is the first time I've had off in six weeks.

The temptation too great for me, I opened all the Christmas gifts. Who knows? I may not even be here on Christmas. A friend and I got a kick out of opening them. The fruitcake you baked was the best I ever tasted. Did you really bake it? Did you put rum in it? A couple of guys had a small piece. Their comments were, "Your wife sure does know how to bake." The wallet is swell. I thought the small package might be the wedding picture. I love it and you look beautiful. I don't like how I look, but pictures don't lie, so I guess it's the best the photographer could do. Your beauty makes up for the lack of mine. You're sweet for sending it, and the case is just perfect. Thanks a lot for all the other gifts and your thoughtfulness.

Mother's Christmas package came—in bad condition; the sides were bulging out and the string was just hanging on. I opened it and was not surprised with what I found. It was a cake cut in three pieces and turning green with mildew. I could not eat it without getting sick in the stomach, perhaps ending it all. However, the candy that she sent was wrapped better and I could eat that.

I am not in a writing mood tonight, Ann, so will you please pardon this poor excuse of a letter until my mood improves in that regard?

Your loving husband,
Herb

Wednesday night
December 1, 1943

Dearest Herb,

I guess your Thanksgiving was rather dismal, being so far from home. But I felt the same way as you did. . . .

I'll be glad to get back into the routine of taking and transcribing notes, filing, and all the rest that had seemed monotonous before my boss got sick. I have been working much harder these last four weeks than I ever did. He's coming in mornings next week, so things will gradually get back to normal. I have found, though, it really doesn't pay to exhaust yourself at your job for no one notices or acknowledges your achievement. One gets just as far accomplishing only what is expected of him and what he is capable of doing without exerting special energy. I guess you have found this to be especially true in the Army. You are wise deciding not to work too hard. I'm sure you accomplish more than what they expect of you. . . .

Sorry this turned out to be a discourse. I'll write a newsier letter next time.

I love you,
Ann

P.S. Here's a moron joke to end all moron jokes: Have you heard about the moron who put a skirt around his bureau so his drawers wouldn't show? I'm sorry. I promise not to tell another one unless it's better than that.

During December 1943, Herb's command advanced in the Central Pacific. Bomb squadrons based on the Ellice Islands and Canton continued raiding sites in the Marshalls, halfway between Hawaii and Australia. Others flew to the Gilberts as soon as airfields there became available. Tarawa, the most important new base, began operating as a staging and bomber base for the command. It also served as the headquarters and forward echelon of the Seventh Air Force, which moved from Funafuti as 1944 dawned to help seize and occupy the Marshall Islands.

3 December '43

Dearest Ann,
I love the snaps and think they are the best pictures I have of you. Thanks for sending them. I really like your hair this way. It makes you look beautiful. . . .

175

My friend who had the tattoo removal operation left the hospital, and I gave him some of the fruitcake you sent. He said it was the best he ever tasted. He is going to have an ugly scar on his right arm below the elbow and another scar on his leg where they had to take skin to graph it onto his arm. He said it was a very painful operation. I can understand this as they didn't give him any ether or anything to deaden the pain. . . .

Do you know this fellow [Donald Mayberry] in the clipping, who married one of the gals down here? She is a very ugly girl. Give my regards to all.

Your husband, Herb

December 5, 1943

Dearest Herb,

Here it is, Sunday night again. The war seemed particularly prominent today since it is the second Sunday anniversary (though it's a sacrilege to call it an "anniversary") of Pearl Harbor—December 7, 1941. Today was similar to that Sunday, though it was a bright and lovely day compared with the hazy day of two years ago. The temperature was about the same, though—not very cold—about 45°, and as on that afternoon, Sara and I went walking.

That walk did me a world of good (we covered about 4 miles). Sara has a keen mind, and we always enjoy our talks when the two of us get together.

Sara and I were great friends during my last year in high school and business school, and we were always together. After a series of whirlwind courtships, she has made up her mind that Charlie Giambrone is the one for her. Charlie is a nice guy, and they make a good match. I hope the four of us can get together after the war.

I got home around 9 and went to the dance at the high school with Ginny, a boring affair mostly attended by the high school jitterbugs and staid middle-aged married couples, but I went to please Ginny. I saw Boots Elliott's wife, Catherine, at the dance, and she says Boots is in Italy. She hears from him frequently, and he is all right. He's in the Air Force, too—a

176

personnel clerk, I think.

We got another wedding gift tonight from one of my friends, Dot Gebert Sacks, who used to ride to work with Sara and me. Dot got married February a year ago and she and her husband went to housekeeping, but about six months later, he was drafted. She got a job at the Jacobs plant in Pottstown and has kept up the house all this time. I admire her spirit.

I have an application for a new "B" gasoline ration book to make out tonight, dear, so I'll sign off.

I love you,
Ann

6 December 1943

Dearest Ann,

The trade winds are starting to come in and will continue 'til about April. In the morning, I like to take a short walk at 6 o'clock, when the winds are the strongest and I can see the beautiful sunrise as if at an Easter sunrise service.

I thought you may have heard or read about this incident in the paper (the editorial about General Patton). I think Patton was wrong; if he can't control his emotions better than this, he shouldn't have so much responsibility. There is no excuse for such an act from an officer as high as he. One with so much rank does so little work and gets the credit. He should stand trial and let the people decide. There is no doubt he hit the soldier. It has been covered up for as long as possible, but such a thing cannot be hushed up. If the soldier would have hit Patton, he would have gone to the guard house.

We may still be moving. After thinking it over, I decided not to take it so badly; it's possible there are worse places than where we may be sent, so I have to count my blessings.

In the last couple of months, I can actually see myself doing my bit in getting this damn war over with.

Your loving husband,
Herb

—★—

When I pulled the preceding letter from its envelope, out came a frail clipping of an editorial titled "Gen. Patton's Offense" from the *Honolulu Star-Bulletin*. The editorial harshly criticized General George S. Patton and the military. Early in August 1943, General Patton slapped and insulted two army soldiers who were recovering at evacuation hospitals while under his command during the Sicily Campaign. The military covered up the incident until *Washington Post* columnist Drew Pearson broke the story. The two soldiers Patton slapped suffered from "battle fatigue," known also as "shell shock" or "battle stress." Today, doctors recognize this condition as post-traumatic stress disorder, resulting from prolonged severe exposure to traumatic events, such as death and destruction.

—★—

Wednesday night
December 8, 1943

Dearest Herb,

I'm so glad you liked the Christmas boxes. Yes, I really did bake the fruitcake, all by myself, and "doctored" it with brandy. Most of the fun I had this Christmas was packing and sending those gifs to you. . . .

Yesterday, I received a wedding gift from Andy Beyer—a set of pure linen table napkins (no tablecloth this time). They're really lovely. I'm going to send him a Christmas card and thank him for both of us. . . .

Well, dear, I do hope you have a pleasant Christmas—at least have a good dinner, even if you must go out and buy it. I hope we will spend next Christmas together, and I'm still hoping you won't be sent out. . . .

God bless you and keep you safe,

Ann

8 December 1943

Dearest Ann,

Received your letter of November 16 today. The other

package came yesterday. Everything you sent was packed neatly, and nothing was spoiled.

I finally got my watch from the jeweler's after nine months. I wish I had the one you gave me as it was much better one than this one. I will get you a blouse and a purse as you requested as soon as I go into town. I hope you like the earrings. Do you ever wear them? I like to see girls wear them, and you are the only one whom I want to see wearing them. . . .

Each time I look at your pictures, I admire them more. I hope you don't hesitate to go and get whatever you need or want. Don't deprive yourself in any way. I appreciate your thoughtfulness in saving your nice things for me. I like a well-dressed woman. You're going to be this woman.

Your husband,
Herb

December 9, 1943

Dearest Herb,

The clipping you sent was interesting. Donald Mayberry was in my class in high school. He was one of the fellows I wrote you about a while ago. Remember? He and another fellow from town, Stewart Sands, were home about a month after you were.

No, Donald's wife is no beauty, but neither is he (far from it). I saw him when he was home, and he was surprised to hear I had married. He was due in San Francisco by October 18, and the wedding was on November 18, so he didn't waste much time when he got back. I'm willing to bet it was a "shotgun wedding." When he was home, he talked of staying in San Francisco and not returning to the Islands. He made every effort to remain here but was ordered to return, in which case I suppose he thought he might as well marry the girl. She is only 16 and someone said she also has a 2-year-old child. I guess she is as bad as he. Donald was never an angel and was in quite a few scrapes here at home. One would think his travels would have made him a little wiser, but evidently they haven't. I do not feel a bit sorry for him, but I do feel sorry for his parents. They're nice people.

I have heard that the other fellow from Schwenksville who is in Pearl Harbor and was best man at Donald's wedding— Stewart Sands—is to marry a native girl. If you come across the clipping and picture of the bride, I'd appreciate it if you'd send it to me.

I wonder about these marriages: what will these fellows do when the war is over? They won't want to bring these girls to their homes in the states, and they will be tired of living out there. I don't suppose many of them look that far ahead.

All my love,
Ann

December 14, 1943

Dearest Ann,

Today has been a tiring day. Everything seemed to go wrong. Right now, I am getting a sore throat and have just gargled. So far, it has not been effective. I feel as if I could sleep a long, long time. To be home for a short time would be so wonderful. We are going to make good use of those cocktail glasses that your friends gave us. I wish I was there mixing a few right now.

"I'm wishing for us to be together this Christmas" is just another saying to me. People can't get along by wishing; we just have to wait. I get so damn sick of people wishing for this and that. It makes me mad to spend the best years of my life as the worst years. The last three years of my life are entirely wasted (all but a few days, and you know the few days I'm referring to).

I received a letter from the minister, but I am in no mood to write to such a person. In fact, although it is just 7 o'clock now, after writing this morbid letter to you, I am going to bed, hoping I will feel better tomorrow. Ann, if you only knew what this sort of life is like. Sorry if I'm making you feel bad, but telling you that I'm not happy unless I am with you should help.

Your loving husband,
Herb

Thursday night
December 16, 1943

Dearest Herb,

I received the Christmas package. The luncheon mat set is pretty and, of course, differs from what one would find here. And the earrings are really nice. I'll wear them constantly. I'm going to try to be the well-dressed woman you like (providing our means can afford it). I have always liked pretty and expensive clothes, but since we were never wealthy, I have had to be practical and economical. This is a good thing, after all, for if one has money it is not hard to learn to spend it. On the other hand, if one has been accustomed to wealth and is suddenly deprived of it, it is hard to learn to be thrifty.

I was interested in the Patton incident you mentioned. We heard the [Drew] Pearson program in which he disclosed the news, and I wondered what would come of it. I feel as you and a lot of people do that he should be relieved of his position. But from the latest news, the Senate investigation has been dropped, and the General will in fact receive the permanent promotion for which he had been recommended before this fuss.

I went Christmas shopping with the girls last night. What a time! The streets and shops were jammed. I didn't do much buying—two hankies, a scarf, a pair of skating socks for Sis, and some ribbon. We ate at Kugler's on Chestnut Street and then waited for the Carol Sing at Wanamaker's. I enjoyed both.

We're having zero weather, and I mean that literally—it was 0° this morning. And the ice is getting good for skating—I'll be out on it Sunday afternoon if it doesn't snow between now and then. In spite of the cold weather, the house hasn't been too cold, though. We're cautiously watching the coal pile dwindle. Coal is scarce. We're fortunate, though, for we can easily get wood when the coal is gone.

Herb, I wish so much you could be home on Christmas. I'm going to miss you so much. This is the fourth Christmas we've spent thousands of miles apart. How many more do you suppose we'll spend this way before we start counting the other way? Do you think the good times that are to come for us will

181

make up for these past 3 years? I guess we must be patient a while longer and we will be rewarded. I'm so grateful for the six days we had. I'm so glad we're married and proud to be your wife. Maybe next year this time we'll be together, or at least the end of the war may be in sight. Until the next time,

I love you,

Ann

While Herb felt ill and homesick, Ann took in two of Philadelphia's time-worn cultural institutions. She and her friends dined at Kugler's, considered the city's largest and most beautifully appointed restaurant in the early 1900s. They chose from distinctively local menu items such as chicken salad with fried oysters, snapper soup, terrapin, hundreds of shellfish dishes, game, and, of all things, catfish and waffles.

After eating, Ann and her friends joined other holiday shoppers in a beloved 25-year-old Philadelphia tradition: the Carol Sing in the seven-story Grand Court at Wanamaker's accompanied by the world's largest pipe organ.* As Ann and her friends unbuttoned their coats, store clerks closed the registers, handed out songbooks, and invited shoppers to sing carols. The organist pushed buttons from a device at the organ's console to project the page number of each carol onto the marble wall of the Grand Court. The throng of shoppers stuffed their gloves into their coat pockets, opened songbooks, and raised their voices in song, happy for a respite from war weariness. Facing another Christmas without Herb, Ann sang out with gusto despite the lump in her throat.

*Today, the organ still accompanies the Carol Sing (though Wanamaker's is now Macy's) and is the largest operational pipe organ in the world, with 28,000 pipes.

December 17, 1943

Dearest Ann,

Today has been a more peaceful day than usual. I am in a better mood than the last time I wrote you. My cold is better; a good night's sleep is all I needed.

They are having a prize fight in the gym. I've seen several fights, and they don't interest me much. A few of the boxers are good and have boxed professionally. But I am taking advantage of the quietness around here since most of the fellows went to the fight.

One of the boys has a skin disease that is common here.* He has had it for 3 months, and the doctors can't seem to cure him. He is going to the hospital tomorrow, which makes him happy. He is under the impression that he is going there to rest. If this doesn't cure him, they told him that he has to be sent to a cooler climate. It is a queer disease, which makes him break out with water blisters that later form red spots on different parts of his body. Some doctors say it comes from the salt water; others say from dampness. No one really knows. I have been fortunate so far but have been cautious and kept my distance from those who have it.

Loving you always,
Herb

Wednesday night
December 22, 1943

My dearest Herb,

Flying in those big Army planes must be an experience. However, I'm thankful you aren't a pilot. I'd be a nervous wreck visualizing you flying a plane in this war. It's a vital job, but I'm satisfied that you are part of the ground crew that keeps them flying.

---

*"Jungle rot," a skin infection affecting GIs, stemmed from germs entering through chafed spots or the tiniest skin wound. Scratching a bug bite, for example, could cause it. The only treatment, an antibacterial liquid, just limited the spread of infection. In rare cases, GIs with the condition were evacuated.

We had quite an experience Saturday. Dad stopped to get gas for the car and discovered the ration book wasn't in the glove compartment. He came home and we searched the house—no ration book. We were ready to go to the Board to try to get another. Yesterday, we got a letter from a partner in a trucking concern in West Chester enclosing the book, owner's card, and tire inspection record, saying it had been found near the college on Saturday by one of his truckers. He could easily have thrown away the other cards and used the ration book himself. The incident did a lot to renew my faith in human beings.

So sorry I wrote "wishing" we could be together at Christmas. You're right—wishing doesn't do much good. But, my dearest, wishing is like daydreaming—a little once in a while won't hurt anyone, and it helps one forget (for the moment at least) things that are too real and of which we are altogether too conscious. Have you heard the old lyric, "if you wish long enough and strong enough, your wish will come true?" I have found this to be true. I can't think of many things I have wished for that I didn't get. Maybe that is why I'm "spoiled" as you said when you were home—I've always had everything I wanted. Anyway, I'm trying hard to get over being "spoiled" by the time you get home.

Hope you soon felt better than you did when you wrote on the 14th. As you said, "the picture isn't complete without you." It won't be complete until we are together always. But each passing day brings that day closer. Until then, I'll keep on missing you very much.

All my love,
Ann

Ann had good reason to be thankful Herb wasn't a pilot. More than 88,000 AAF airmen died either from battle, wounds, accidents, or in some other way or were declared missing in the war. A bomber crewman in the Pacific had a 50 percent chance of finishing the 30 combat missions constituting a tour of duty without losing his life.* Aware of these odds, some pilots protected themselves by wearing steel army helmets. Gunners in some cases dragged sheets of steel on board their planes on which to stand or sit to protect the family jewels.

Christmas Eve 1943

Dearest Ann,

One of the fellows has a 12-inch-tall wooden Christmas tree with a few candles on it, painted green with painted dots as balls. From the light of this small tree, I am writing this letter to you.

It would be normal to feel sad on such a night and go get drunk to forget. But I feel like doing neither of these. I am getting hardened to such things. Some of the men are really sad tonight, and it's hard not to ignore them. A few are trying to act cheerful, but it's no use. We can't escape as we've got to face the facts. Sometimes, it's worse than a prison. When you are in prison, you know what is what, but being free yet under these circumstances, it's hard to take.

Today I learned that I should be around here longer than I thought. I am not anxious or requesting to go as some men are. I'm plenty mad at this damn war and can't see why it's taking so long. Some of these poor excuses for leaders could really do more than merely talk and predict when the war will be over.

I have been busy again, which is the only reason I haven't been writing as regularly. I have to work tomorrow but don't expect to be busy. Just being there is bad enough, and I'd rather be busy.

Just this minute, my friend, the baker, brought me a piece of pumpkin pie. He said when he gets home, he will teach you how to make it. It smells delicious. I have it here beside me and can hardly wait until I taste it. Pause. It sure was good. . . .

Your loving husband,
Herb

---

*Later in the war, a tour consisted of 40 missions for aircrews.

Sunday night
December 26, 1943

Dearest Herb,

Another Christmas has passed and become a memory. It was one of the nicest ones in the past several years. We spent Christmas Eve helping Mother get the ducks ready for the oven and putting the finishing touches on the decorations. We opened our gifts Christmas morning after breakfast and everyone was pleased with them. I got lovely things. But of all, I love the earrings you sent best. The bank gave me $15 and a wedding gift of $17.

The Christmas dinner of duck and the usual Christmas dishes were scrumptious. We had the best Sherry wine, too, but I'm no expert on wines. But we all missed you when we sat down to dinner—you'd have thoroughly enjoyed it. After dinner, I went ice skating with Ginny.

I went to church with your mother this morning and enjoyed the service, especially the music. I had lunch with your Mother and Dad but the weather got bad, so I came home in the middle of the afternoon. I have been taking it easy since then. It's raining now and it will probably freeze, making the roads miserable. But it's to be expected in December.

I felt differently this Christmas from last year, and I think others did too. Last year, we celebrated Christmas but everyone doubted the future—it all seemed so uncertain. We have at last taken some strides toward ending this war. For the first time, I have a glimmer of the end in sight.

While writing, I've been listening to a program called "One Man's Family," a discussion of the outcome of the wars. The consensus seems to be that both the European and Asiatic wars will be "unconditional surrenders," and the war in Europe will end around the end of 1944 and the war with Japan a year later. Peacetime will return to this country in 1948. Though the end is still far off, we are progressing at last.

I don't know how to lift your spirits for the only thing to really cheer you is the end of war, which is what I live for from day to day. But dearest, don't ever give up hope if for nothing

186

else than for my sake. For I love you so much and pray for our life together. I know both our prayers will be answered.

> All my love,
> Ann

> Wednesday night
> December 29, 1943

Dearest Herb,

I got your letter of December 17 yesterday—it was a bit slower than usual getting here—most likely due to the Christmas mail.

Speaking of Christmas gifts, Bea (the hairdresser who cried because she was so happy when we told her we were getting married, remember?) got a gorgeous five-skin Kolinsky fur neckpiece from her boyfriend. She's been in the clouds for the past two weeks. And, best of all, he had a six-day leave over Christmas, so they had a grand time. Sara got a lovely housecoat from Charlie, although he wasn't lucky enough to get home for the holidays.

Today I received notice of the new Class-E allotment of $80 to start as of November 1. I haven't received the checks yet. I'll let you know when they start. . . .

I saw a good movie last night, *Lassie Come Home*. The picture was unusual and reminded me in several scenes of *How Green Was My Valley*, but it wasn't as good. It was the story of a boy and his dog and was in Technicolor. Have you seen it?

Darling, it's late and I'm awfully sleepy, so please excuse me for tonight.

> I love you,
> Ann

> December 29, 1943

Dearest Ann,

The mail situation is bad; however, I did receive your letter dated December 5, the first in seven days.

I worked on Christmas until noon. After eating a fairly good dinner, I played tennis for only a few minutes because rain

187

made it impossible to go on. That made us mad—of all days, just when we had the afternoon off. After this, I came back to the barracks, took a shower, and had a well needed sleep. . . .

On Christmas Eve, I wrote you a letter, which you probably have received by this time. I wasn't in a good humor as you have noticed, but tonight seems to find me a little better but still mad at things in general. . . .

This has been the first letter I have written in five days; I haven't written to Mother in two weeks and need to get started on a letter to her. . . .

Your loving husband,
Herb

The SS *Matsonia*, which brought mail, among other things, to the servicemen in Hawaii. (Photo from Herb's collection)

New Year's Eve, 10 p.m.
December 31, 1943

Dearest Herb,

New Year's Eve—another year passed. It hardly seems possible that a whole year has gone by since everyone was saying, "Well, here's 1943 and things are going to happen this year." Now here's 1944 and everyone's saying the same thing. "We'll see great things happen in 1944. The war in Europe will end in 1944, a history-making year, etc." The war must end sometime, and it might happen in 1944, but I won't be surprised when New Year's Day 1945 rolls around and we'll hear the same prediction. Probably the next year will go quickly, too, and we will be closer to ending this war and to seeing see each other again. Maybe you'll have another furlough. Who knows what the year has in store for us? Anyway, here's hoping it's something good and that it will be a happier year for everyone, everywhere.

We had some news at the bank. Mr. Berger, the Treasurer—the guy who is so stingy with the raises and salaries—has resigned as of the end of January. He has taken a position with a woolen concern in South America. When I wanted to quit to better myself, he just grunted, but when he is concerned, it's a different story. I don't begrudge him—I wish him success as long as he doesn't come back to the bank. I only hope his successor is more generous. I rather envy him going to South America. . . .

I miss you, Dear, especially tonight, and I'm thinking about our three days of married life and hoping we can soon continue where we left off. Until next year, I love you.

Your loving wife,
Ann

New Year's Eve
December 31, 1943

Dearest Ann,

The mail situation is still a sad affair. Though I haven't heard from you for a long time, I shall try to write a decent letter. One of these days your letters will all come at once, making it hard for me to answer them all. But a letter is always welcome—the more letters, the happier I am.

A friend and I have gotten a quart of southern whiskey to celebrate this evening, so I better get this letter off to you while still sober. We intend to get drunk and forget. It's a high price to pay, but it's worth it once in a while. . . .

Our tennis friend, the one who sent you the tea, presented us with the whiskey, which is as precious as gold here. No doubt I will have a big headache and be sorry for this. I'll let you know the ill effects, if any. Just this minute, my friend, smiling broadly, is coming in the door with the spirits under his arm. I shall stop this letter for now. I hope you understand and please forgive me. My first drink will be to you, a beautiful creature and loving wife, and to your happiness during this new year. So, good night, my dear, until I can continue this letter. It's 9 o'clock, 3 hours before the New Year.

January 1, 1944

I awoke this morning not feeling well; I was still a little drunk. I had a fairly good time and don't regret it.

Of all days at work, this seemed to be one of the busiest that I remember. I just got finished about one hour ago. I'm tired and a little sick to my stomach. Now I know I can't drink so much. . . .

And—all the edibles were eaten; nothing was wasted. The fruitcake went over best of all. . . .

Yours always and
forever, Herb

While Herb girded for combat duty, squadrons of Liberators from his command softened up Kwajalein for the invasion of the Marshall Islands. The bombers faced fierce enemy opposition over Kwajalein, Mille, Wotje, and Maloelap. One squad lost 17 planes.

Wednesday night
January 12, 1944

Dearest Herb,

I've gotten two letters from you this week—the one written New Year's Eve and the other dated the 5th. Thank you for the toast, my dear, a lovely sentiment.

My New Year started out with a bang. I went skating with Sis on the creek near the house, and while skating backwards tripped over a piece of protruding old ice, falling flat on my back and hitting my head. I wasn't knocked out, but almost. I went home and napped with an ice bag on the bump. Later I washed my hair, bathed, and went to bed, and this morning woke up feeling fine, and the bump is almost gone.

Last Thursday, I received the third allotment check, this one for $80 and marked drawn for November '43. Today I received another $80 check. Is there some mistake? I won't deposit it yet.

I don't know what to expect about your leaving the Islands. In one recent letter you said you expected to be there longer, but you're not as hopeful in your letter of January 5.

I'm still disgusted with my salary of $23 a week, but it is enough to exist on while I'm living at home. I will try to put all the money you send into the account. I wish I could save more, but there's always something to buy. Last month it was Christmas gifts and now I'll have to start saving for income tax. This shouldn't amount to much, but I do not want to withdraw money from the bank at the last minute. Our little pile will go so fast when you come home and we start getting all the things we need. We'll be thankful then for what we've saved.

About buying a home—we'll probably have to work a year or two for that. The F.H.A. is an answer to small investors like us and probably will be our solution. . . .

It's time to say good night, darling, and if you were here you'd see my love for you shining in my eyes, or I'd tell you how much I love you with a kiss. But we're 6,000 miles apart, so you'll have to imagine the love in my eyes and instead I'll say, my husband,

I love you,
Ann

Ann in her ice skating outfit. (Family photo)

January 23, 1944

Dearest Ann,

Don't be fooled by my happy look on the pictures I send you; as you know, looks can be deceiving; however, I'm glad you like them. How about some recent ones of you?

I, too, believe if you wish long and hard enough, you will probably get your wish with a little work. I'm sorry if I sounded too harsh. I find it doesn't pay to wish too much. I've learned to take things as they come and be prepared for anything. I've also learned not to put too much faith in human beings. I believe in getting the job done myself.

I received your letters dated December 20 and 22 on Wednesday of this week—as if Christmas had not yet come. . . .

We have been very busy at the office.

I expect to be moved and am ready for anything. It will not be the place you have in mind but where the Marines recently landed. (Look at the same place as in the other letter.) I have nothing good to look forward to, and as I said, it may be two months or two weeks. I'm not jubilant about it because the shape of some of the fellows coming back is not good. But someone has to go, and a few men must sacrifice before we win this damn war. One of my best friends is leaving next week and is not anxious to go at all. We are going to have dinner in town tomorrow night, and this will probably be his last one for a long time and maybe his final one, who knows? He's being sent to replace someone who has malaria—not a pleasant thought, is it? So please, don't be surprised to learn of my leaving, and don't worry, I'll get by. If I learn anything definite, I shall write and let you know somehow.

I have a lingering cold, making me feel sleepy and lazy. Everyone here either has a cold or is getting rid of one. I finished at the office early today and went to the barracks to rest. At 3:30, we had to attend rifle instruction to practice stripping the rifle from all its parts. This has been a monthly occurrence since I have been back, even though we can do it blindfolded by now. Well, Ann, this isn't an encouraging letter, is it? But what's the use of trying to kid ourselves?

Your loving husband,
Herb

"Where the marines recently landed" had to be Tarawa. Herb's clue had eluded the censor again.

January 27, 1944

Dearest Ann,

My cold has developed into something more serious. I have not been to work today, spent the day so far partly sleeping and resting in bed, where I still am. All the fellows think I have dengue fever, but so far I have little fever. I am actually cold, even though I am wearing a sweat shirt and have two army blankets on. The temperature is 87°. It seems impossible that I could be cold. I have a good idea what dengue and malaria are like. I want to get into physical shape as soon as possible to be better able to fight disease. If I stay in bed the rest of the day, I'll probably be okay tomorrow.

This is a perfect opportunity to get caught up with my

correspondence. Since the 24th, the mail from the mainland has been pouring in, and I have received your letter dated January 3. So for me to get even with you, I better start pushing on this pen!

I received a letter from Mother. She sounds as if I have already moved to someplace else. I wish she wouldn't think that way. If I go, no one back there should do anything or worry about it.

The dangerous part about it is disease, and I am going to be more than careful about what I eat and do when I get there. Many are coming back because of malaria, our strongest enemy. Cleanliness is the most important factor, though staying clean will be hard as water is rationed. You sounded so hopeful in your letter of January 12, and surely I am grounding all your hopes. It's no use for me to try to make you feel better. It doesn't pay in this case. I don't like it any more than you do. This is something that has been postponed up until now.

_____ so this is something worth sweating and waiting for.[*]

You have more nerve than I to try to skate backwards. I understand how you started out the new year with a bang. Fortunately, your head was not hard enough to crack the ice (no hard feelings).

I think perhaps you will like these two Hawaiian pieces: "Akoka Falls" #1642-A and "For You a Lei" #533-B. Will you try and get the records to add to the collection?

As always,
Herb

Herb heeded the army's warning about avoiding disease and rightly so. In both world wars, disease caused the most casualties, when counting those incapacitated for any reason regardless of the length of incapacitation. The tropical areas where Herb and his buddies were headed crawled with harmful microorganisms. Even

---

[*]The blank space in the preceding letter represents one of many censor's cuts, which ribboned Herb's letters starting in early 1944.

though the soldiers got inoculated, the damp climate fostered disease, making decent rations and clean water imperative.

Along with jungle rot, malaria and dengue fever plagued soldiers in the war. Contracted from the bite of a female anopheles mosquito, malaria recurs several times even years after initial infection and can kill. More often, though, it causes a prolonged high fever, the shakes, and spells of feeling extremely cold or intensely hot. During the war, soldiers in malarial areas had an infection rate of 85 to 95 percent. Military doctors treated malaria mainly with Atabrine, though it was only partly effective and turned the skin yellowish. Severe cases had to be evacuated from combat. Dengue fever, on the other hand, was rarely fatal and did not recur. Also born by mosquitoes, dengue caused a debilitating fever and throbbing pain.

February 1, 1944

Dearest Ann,

Received your letter dated January 5. The cold I have is one of the worst I've ever had, but it is breaking up at last. I feel pretty well. There have been so many men with colds recently that one would have to have superior health not to have gotten one.

You will probably get one more letter from me while I'm still at A.P.O. 953 [Hawaii] as I am leaving in a few days. So, the next four months are going to be a great change for me. I'll be washing in a steel helmet, sleeping in a foxhole, and enduring other hardships too numerous to mention. I hope you won't worry. There is a good possibility that I can come home to rest after a few months. I will probably see the rest of the South Seas before the war is over and have a lot to write about. The trip will make time go faster for me but will be the opposite for you.

I have plenty of work to do before blackout, so I better stop this letter for tonight.

> Your loving husband,
> Herb

In the Marshall Islands campaign, the Seventh Air Force got a nickname: "Hale's Handful" after its commander, Gen. Hale. The force, along with naval aircraft, had blasted those islands for 70 days before invasion day. From January 29 until the invasion three days later, they hammered Kwajalein, Wotje, and Maloelap from dawn until dusk, dropping 3.5 million pounds of bombs. The bombing destroyed or damaged every above-ground fortification on Kwajalein but left many machine-gun positions untouched, and the enemy stayed put in well-hidden foxholes.

The Battle of Kwajalein—the first assault on what Japan regarded as its soil—raged for four days, from January 31 to February 3, 1944. On invasion day, heavy bombers from Herb's command furnished part of the ground support for assault troops, scorching the northwestern part of Kwajalein. Though Japanese defenders mounted stiff resistance there, they were outnumbered and underprepared. Invasion forces landing in the southern part of the atoll faced rifle, machine gun, and mortar fire but secured the area in a week. One step forward in the drive to Japan, the battle gave the United States a significant victory.

> February 3, 1944

Dearest Ann,

There is no mistake concerning the allotment: $80 is correct. I made a mistake; if this isn't enough, I can make out another allotment for $90.

If you are trying to save, it's okay, but please, don't go without anything. I shall try to send you more money in the next few months, for _____ is not much in need.

A friend of mine is coming there for a furlough, and I want

you to introduce him to Ginny. He is from Virginia, has never been to Pennsylvania, and is a total stranger to Norristown. He plans to stay there for about a week and would like to meet and date Virginia. He is a grand fellow, clean cut, doesn't drink except on special occasions as I do. He's 22 years of age, tall, dark, easy to look at. I'm sending you a picture to give to Virginia when you tell her. This will help you recognize him when you meet him at the station. I've shown him pictures of you, and he thinks he will recognize you. He is a corporal wearing an emblem on the left shoulder sleeve with a figure seven going through the center of a star signifying the 7th Air Force. You can't miss it as no one else will be wearing this.

He will appreciate anything you can do to start a friendship between him and Virginia. I hope Virginia doesn't mind and understands. He is not a fresh type of a guy—more of a reserved and quiet type. He will probably be lonely and need a friend. He is not engaged to any girl because he has not met the right one. He is contemplating going home after staying in Norristown for a week. He is getting a 30-day furlough after leaving San Francisco, thus getting more leave than I had. I hope you can make his stay worthwhile. When he contacts you on his arrival in Philadelphia, if possible and time permits, take Ginny with you to the station to meet him. If he doesn't contact you, forget about the whole deal. I'm hoping Virginia doesn't think badly of me by introducing her to Cpl. Bob Roane.

Your loving husband,
Herb

The insignia of the Seventh Air Force.

CHAPTER 6
ISLAND HOPPING

Just one damned island after another!
—Seventh AAF air and ground crews

On a warm morning on Ella Island, Tarawa Atoll, Herb took his mess kit from his barracks bag and went to chow. He waited in a long line for hot cakes, canned fruit, and watery coffee. A bomber roared overhead, off to strike some spot in the Marshalls. After chow, he and his tent mates tidied their six-man pyramidal tent. Some men straightened the lauhala mats on which they slept; others smoothed the sand. Wire spools left by the Japanese made wash stands for shaving. The holes cut in the spools held the men's helmets so the water didn't slosh out.

The sun rose higher, heating the camp like a blast furnace. At noon, Herb and his buddies ate corny willy (canned corn beef) and canned wieners and had a cool drink. They traded rumors about the Marshall Islands campaign. Their workday done at 4 p.m., they shed their shoes and clothes and jumped in the ocean to wash away their sweat. Dusk most nights found the men settling in to watch a movie, as more bombers zoomed off.

The tiny island flattened daily life. Unlike Hawaii, Ella Island had no Honolulu. Here, at the forward echelon of the VII Bomber Command, monotony ruled. The orderly room was a tent, the PX, nonexistent. A steady diet of C rations—precooked, ready-to-eat canned meals—sustained Herb and his colleagues. They arrived on Ella Island on February 11, 1944, to maintain signal communications for the command jointly with the navy and marines as flies and mosquitoes buzzed around them.

Sarcasm and gallows humor helped them cope with the

boredom. They dubbed their tents, foxholes, or offices Flabby Arms, Duffy's Tavern, Passion Pit, Hose Company No. 1, Bugbox, Hell's Hip Pocket, Wahine Haven, and the like. Other such names poked fun at themselves: Idiot's Delight, Moron's Mansion, and So What? It's Home. Still other names alluded to the stresses of combat: Sleepless Hollow, Neurosis Towers, Hallucination House, and Chamber of Horrors.

Herb's squadron moved around like a "circus troupe," he wrote, which helped to pass the time. But the constant moving made saving Ann's letters almost impossible, so few survived from Herb's island-hopping stint.

February 12, 1944

Dearest Ann,

I arrived yesterday safely and partly soundly, surprised to find these islands larger than expected. Although you can throw a stone from one side to the other, this island is much longer than it is wide. Everything I mentioned about the living conditions is true. I have been sweating like a horse since I arrived. Everything is damp and soggy, and it will take time to get acclimatized. Nothing is more uncomfortable than putting on damp clothes, like the ones I'm wearing now. Everyone tells me sooner or later I will get dengue fever.

The scenery is beautiful; the palm and coconut trees are much more plentiful than at A.P.O. #953. And you really can't forget that you are on an island.

The natives speak little English but seem friendly. Some of them wear nothing but cloth around their waists, giving the GI wolves something to howl about. They are brown skinned but not as dark as Negroes. Before we got here, they were under Japanese rule and forced to do heavy and tiring work. They hate the Japanese but seem to like Americans. We treat them much better and they get more to eat than before.

Please don't worry when you don't hear from me because, under the circumstances where everything is uncertain

200

and disorganized, it almost is impossible to write.

The mosquitoes are unbearable. Right now, it's hard to write as they are biting my hands and face. I assure you I am safe and all right. I will have some worthwhile experiences here, but tonight I can't go on. I am exhausted and will feel better after a good night's sleep, if possible.

Your loving husband,
Herb

By this time, Herb's command began bombing targets farther west to set up future amphibious assaults. Raids of the Caroline Islands and enemy-held positions in the Marshalls would preoccupy the command in the coming months.

On February 14, Liberators from the command flew their first bombing raids over Ponape, 385 miles east of Truk Atoll, the largest of the Carolines and Japan's main base for all South Central Pacific operations. Truk lay 1,085 miles from the command's forward echelon. After 11 days of blasting, Ponape lost its importance to Japan.

February 24, 1944

Dearest Ann,

It has been hard for me to start a letter. In the last four weeks, my schedule has completely changed. Several times we had to get up in the middle of the night, which isn't pleasant when you are half asleep and trying to fight off mosquitoes that you can't see biting you. The next morning everyone feels groggy as if they could sleep for ages.

One day last week, I hunted for some shells on the beach for a necklace for you. Other fellows have made necklaces, and after I get the knack of twisting the wire, I'll make you one.

We are paying Great Britain the grand sum of $50,000 a day for the use of these islands. When you think of the American soldiers and marines killed here, they sure aren't worth that much. In addition, for every coconut tree that is cut down, the United States pays $2.50 to the British government. I can see why as the coconuts are one of the few sources of food for the natives. Beyond this, the island is of no earthly good to us and never will be.

We are encouraged to catch the rain water that falls from the tent into a bucket or whatever we have. This is the only water we have for washing ourselves and doing laundry.

The ocean is dangerous for swimming because of sharks, electric eels, and all sorts of sea vermin. The day I swam, I came in contact with an electric eel. I tried to kill it, but the darn thing was too fast and slippery for me. The strong undertow has also pulled a few people out.

One night last week, while I was lying in my cot, the natives in the nearby village started some kind of pow-wow ceremony, pounding on drums and howling at the top of their voices. It sounded weird, and, after listening to this, especially while trying to sleep, it started to get on my nerves.

I'm reading *So Little Time* in my time off. So far, it's great. I get a thrill reading in bed at night with a flashlight, but it's not good for the eyes.

I received your letters dated January 31 and February 1 and 2. Down here a letter means much more to me, and whatever that scent is, it sure does get me. Please don't worry, and remember, I'll always love you.

Have you met Bob Roane yet?

Your husband,
Herb

Vol. 1. No. 11   FEBRUARY 15, 1944,   Price 15c

Cover of *Brief Magazine* from February 15, 1944,
showing a soldier bathing from his helmet on the
Gilbert Islands.

In March, the military decided to invade the Mariana
Islands. Bombing raids by the Seventh and the Thirteenth Air
Forces to Truk Atoll began in earnest that month.

At 6 p.m. on March 28, Herb's squadron boarded a landing
ship transport (LST) bound for the Marshall Islands. Traveling at
about 12 knots or about 13 miles per hour, the LST wallowed from
side to side rather than plow through the water like a regular ship.
Bunks were stacked three atop each other but many men slept on
deck at night to escape the sweltering heat and the smell of vomit
below. They spent seven days on the ship before disembarking at
the forward echelon in the Marshalls. When the doors of the LST
opened and the ramp lowered, the surf soaked their shins and feet
as they held their rifles overhead, wading ashore.

The islands needed a massive amount of cleaning up, with

few staff to do it. Piles of dirt and debris covered the foxholes in the street leading to the camp of Herb's squadron. After finishing their regular work, soldiers cleaned up and policed the area. They filled in the old foxholes and dug new ones between the tents and moved the theater area, creating a suitable street.

The squadron operated its own water distillery and generators for electrical power, both cobbled together by a sergeant and a corporal because no engineers were on site. These contraptions offered a supply of water and electrical power for lighting buildings, operating teletype machines, telephone switchboards, and photographic lab equipment. The men installed a volleyball net for recreation; the space couldn't accommodate other sports.

By early April, U.S. forces had captured about 90 percent of the Japanese positions in the Marshalls and dominated the 330,000 square miles of sea in that area. Bombing of sites in the Marshalls and Carolines would nonetheless go on until the war's end.

Somewhere in the Marshall Islands
April 12, 1944

Dearest Ann,

When you get this letter, notice the change in rank and address. I have requested this as I have given up trying to bear it. I will be happier this way and think it is best for me. With no cooperation from the officers, there was no use in going crazy trying. I hope this isn't hard for you to understand and think perhaps you will. This has happened before and is not out of the ordinary. The bonds will continue and the allotment will decrease to 50 dollars a month. Believe me, Ann, it was not my fault.

Before leaving the Gilbert Islands, I received a lot of letters from you all at once dated February 14 to 29. A lot has happened since, but I can't mention anything about it.

This place is a little better than the Gilbert Islands; it's not as damp and a little cooler but very dusty. Conditions for lungs are poor, and, under these circumstances, it's about all I can bear.

Hope you are happier than I. Remember, whatever happens, I love you. It's hard to write letters in this frame of mind.

Thanks for the Easter cards. The pictures of you and Marge are good.

I don't get much time anymore to write long letters but will write another short one soon.

Your loving husband,
Herb

Herb most likely lost his staff sergeant stripes by choosing a demotion over performing a certain duty that he couldn't stomach. In general, a soldier was demoted as a result of a punishment administered by his commander on the basis of the authorities allowed him under the Articles of War, that is, his inherent power to discipline his troops. In most cases such a demotion occurred when a soldier refused an order or the responsibilities required of his rank or when he talked back to a superior. Today, such a case requires a hearing, generating a record, but not then.

—★—

The most crucial source of information for my father's military career, his Official Military Personnel File, burned in a fire on July 12, 1973, along with those of most U.S. World War II veterans. The file would surely have had more information about his demotion.*

To ensure that I got all of the information on my father's service that I could, in 2013, I hired a researcher specializing in securing veterans' files. After a few weeks of digging, he informed me that the Veterans Administration (VA) had a file on my father

---

*The National Personnel Records Center in St. Louis, Missouri, keeps such files.

and, to get it, I'd have to file a Freedom of Information Act request with the VA. I filed the request and waited 13 months for the file. When it came, it had nothing about my father's time in the AAF—only copies of his enlistment and discharge papers and some medical and other benefit records.

The VA file did, however, dispel the notion that my father had post-traumatic stress disorder (PTSD), which might explain his rages. Mother said he had nightmares for several months after his discharge from the AAF. I knew of one man whose father's PTSD from the war had damaged him so that he beat his wife and children, making family life unbearable. But my father's VA file had no record of treatment for "psychoneurosis," the term used for post-traumatic stress, or anything related to mental health.

—★—

Somewhere in the Marshall Islands
April 21 (I think)

Dearest Ann,

Because my last letter was so short, I'll try again. I received three letters dated March 1 to 5. I'm expecting some mail today.

I never knew you were interested in Red Cross work. Maybe you're becoming too conscientious as if you're not doing much for the war effort. I hope not, but if you like Red Cross work, you may as well do it.

We have been eating Spam, Spam, and more Spam. I'm sick of it and never want to see or taste it when I get home. If you want to keep on my good side, please use Spam sparingly in our meals. I didn't mind it so in Hawaii. I could go to Honolulu and buy something good to eat once in a while but you cannot buy anything like that here. The soldiers waste more Spam than they consume. I can't see why they keep feeding it to us because no one eats it.

I probably won't be at one permanent station from now on. It is going to be hard for me to write steadily to you. We have been on the move constantly since we left Hawaii. There is so much work to be done when we make our camp, which is pretty nice. Then comes another move and we again start the process of packing, crating, loading, and so on—in other words, one hell of a mess.

April 22

I held this letter up purposely, thinking I may have more to write because I received three of your letters dated March 7 to 12. Some mail, like the last few letters from you, comes by boat from the Gilbert Islands and some, by plane. I'm expecting more to come by boat until you use my present A.P.O. I am in the combat area, where there is plenty of disorder.

Why don't you write to Bob Roane, asking him why he didn't show up? I'm sure he fully intended to come there and meet Ginny. I don't have time to write him but if Ginny wrote to him, he would reply.

I know it's hard for you not hearing from me. But I'm doing the best I can under the circumstances. You don't have to write as often. I know how it is. I guess the only solution for me is to take notes from time to time and then write a letter when I can.

Although the Marshalls were Japanese mandated islands, we can't afford to let up. The Japs had strong fortifications, having controlled these islands since 1918.

The weather you have been writing about sounds invigorating. It has been about four years since I have seen or felt snow. I'd be tempted to scrape some up in my hands and rub it on my face if I were home. By this time you should be enjoying the beauty of the coming spring, the season when a young man's fancy turns to love. Beware of the 4-Fs—I'm not really worried about this.

I suppose you are wondering how I'm making out. I do expect to be a private in the future. I hope you won't think me unfair to you. What has happened is worse than you can realize; however, I'm still holding on.

I love you always,
Herb

Three days before Herb wrote the preceding letter, heavy bombers from his command, venturing even farther west, flew 2,900 miles round trip from Kwajalein to Saipan in the Mariana Islands, escorting navy photo planes. They dropped 100-pound bombs on Saipan; one B-24 crashed in the ocean but the crew was rescued.

Pushing toward Tokyo, bombers from Herb's command and navy Liberators raided Guam, the largest and southernmost island in the Marianas on April 25. In the first strike on Guam from land bases, U.S. airmen dropped bombs and viewed enemy installations and planes. Not one U.S. plane was intercepted.

Wednesday, 8 p.m.
April 26, 1944

Dearest,

Your letter from the new location has arrived. What a relief to know you are safe. I felt you were too ill to write and was very concerned.

I wrote your Mother telling her about your new location. She suspected you had moved to the Marshalls. She is worried about your safety, though, since the news broadcasts say fighting is still going on there. If you can ease her mind in any way, she'd feel a lot better.

I don't know what to say about the change in rank. You ask me to understand but I don't. The news did disappoint me. I can't exactly explain what I mean, and I hope you appreciate what I'm trying to tell you. I was proud of your rank because it was visible proof, some evidence, that I'm right about you—that you are intelligent, capable, and conscientious. On the other hand, I cannot rightfully judge because I know little of Army regimentation, discipline, methods, rules, and regulations and nothing of the particular circumstances in your case. Do what you think is right and make the best of it, and it's all right with me.

I'll love you always, Herb.

Your devoted and
loving, Ann

In the last days of April, the Seventh continued to raid Truk, points in the Marshalls, Wake Island, and Ponape—then the most bombed spot in the Carolines. By May 1, squadrons of the Seventh Air Force had established bases from which to conduct the next phase of its operations—the seizure and occupation of the Mariana Islands, 1,500 miles from Tokyo. The occupation would then enable more bases from which to bomb Japan, secure control of sea communications through the Central Pacific, and isolate and neutralize the central Carolines. Truk remained the main target of Herb's command from May to July 1944, though it kept other islands under observation.

Someplace in the Marshall Islands
May 3, 1944

Dear Ann,

Bob R. has arrived here where I am, and he seems happy since his furlough. He was disappointed about not meeting Ginny. While in Philadelphia, he telephoned the orchard as you instructed and no one answered. Being a stranger there, he slept in the station all night. The next morning he took the train home to Virginia. Surely if he had phoned the orchard the next morning or sent a telegram everything could have worked out. I had the directions written down for him—a 6-year-old could have followed them. He wants to come home with me after the war and meet her then (provided Ginny is willing). By this time, you should have received a letter from him to give her. I hope you won't mind.

I have completed your necklace of shells from the Gilbert

Islands. I've been looking for a small box in which to send it to you. I'm sending along two bracelets to match the necklace. You will have to take the necklace and bracelets to a jeweler to have him attach a fastener. If I get enough shells from this place, I will make you another one. The one I made prior is more or less amateurish. Perhaps you are wondering how I find time to make necklaces but not write letters. . . .

I received four letters from you all at once dated March 6 to 20 and April 25, and I meant to answer them the next day, but the Army had other plans for me.

It's going to be a long time before I can enjoy life as one should. There is no other person with whom I'd rather be alone than you. When this is all over, we are going to find a remote place where I can rest completely and try and forget these four awful years. It would be wonderful to forget horrible memories and remember only happy ones.

It's not advisable to send anything as I said before. We are not in a permanent place and won't be from now on. Who knows? We may be on the road to Tokyo.

I hope your visualizations of the circumstances "down under" are realistic, but perhaps you are apt to be a little off. I don't mean to criticize you. I merely don't want you to overrate them. Although there are many things I would like to have, most of us get along on bare necessities, such as our steel helmet for washing, one blanket for sleeping upon, soap and towel, razor, toothbrush, mess kit, and rifle. Do we care? You bet your life we do. But once in a while we can drive down to the Stork Club for a good dinner and afterwards take in a stage show. But this gets boring. Then we go to some other place and have cocktails. This also gets tiresome; one meets so many beautiful girls.

May 5, 1944

There is little I can write about. My resignation has been submitted; I'm waiting to hear how I made out. It seems to be taking a long time. The executive officer called me into his office, asking me if I wanted to go to another section. He thinks it may go easier for me. I wish I could agree. I can't see how. I need more than a change of section. A change of environment would be more like it.

I'm growing accustomed to the dirt here and don't seem to mind it as when we first landed. It seems more natural to be dirty than clean anyway. We can go native to a certain limit. Short pants are permissible as this place has fewer mosquitoes than the Gilberts and such pants are almost a necessity. They are much more comfortable than long pants, so many of us wear them.

You are correct that we are a day behind your time, and speaking of time, no one pays attention to it. In fact, none of us has the correct hour. It's so unimportant.

If and when I get back to Hawaii, I have a good chance for another furlough. The War Department passed a law that men who have been overseas for two years or more be granted a 30-day furlough.

I have not been working as hard as before. I have decided to take it easy for a while. I don't like to think of the consequences. But I want to write more letters to you, and the only way to do this is to stay away from work. I haven't written to anyone except you and Mother for six months. I guess some people think I'm lost or killed in combat.

Speaking of which, I got a letter returned today that I sent Johnny Quillman before he died. I wish he would have received it as I only wrote him once since in the Army. I'm glad you met his wife, Kathy, and I sure sympathize with her. Johnny was a good friend of mine. It's hard to believe he's gone. All the wrong people are getting killed.

Thanks for writing as often as you do, dear. I feel guilty for not keeping up with you. Another guy here wants to correspond with one of your girlfriends. His name is P.F.C. Edward Hart, age 24, height 5 feet, 11 inches—same address as mine. I told him I didn't know many of your girlfriends and would ask you if Virginia would care to write. Bob R. doesn't know about this. Even if he did, it wouldn't make much difference.

I love you so much,
Herb

Although Herb termed his loss of rank a "resignation," only officers could resign—not enlisted men. This supports the idea that he chose a lower rank rather than perform a certain duty that he did not want to.

In May, bombers from Herb's command continued to target mainly Truk. The bombers flew night missions until mid-June. By then, the airmen noticed fewer interceptors and searchlights and less antiaircraft fire: the bombings were taking a toll on the enemy, they believed.

Also in May, army and navy heavy bombers, flying more than 2,000 miles round trip, raided Guam. U.S. planes downed, destroyed, or damaged almost half of the enemy's 25 interceptors that met them. All U.S. planes returned safely.

Somewhere in the Marshall Islands
May 14, 1944

Dearest Ann,

All the mail that I expected has arrived. I received four letters from you dated March 31 to April 9 and two from Mother.

You are correct about where I am. Why did I have to be sent to places no one ever heard of before the war? I would rather be in Europe than on a speck in the Pacific Ocean.

The other day one of the fellows caught an octopus, weighing about 60 pounds, its eight long tentacles squirming all over the place—one of the largest I've ever seen. The ones in captivity couldn't compare with it. It must have been hungry because they never come near the shore to shallow water. I like adventure, but swimming next to an octopus is uncomfortable, and this one could have waged a good fight.

I like your new stationery. But the stationery means less to me than what you write and after that, it's the perfume that haunts me as if you are near. In fact, I sleep with the ones that smell of perfume until the smell goes away. You'll never know how nice it is to experience this amongst the worse things in life.

We have constructed an outdoor theatre, quite a ritzy place, seating approximately 100 people. I mustn't overlook the best feature of the theatre, that is, all seats are reserved and can be carried with you at show time and parked any place in the sand. We get all the latest shows, such as *The Smart Girls Grow Up*, with Deanna Durbin. I remember seeing this at least 10 years ago, and if you ask me, it took a long time for them to grow up. These movies do help a lot, and we look forward to them. I read in *Time Magazine* that up-to-date shows are scheduled to be sent over for us and should be here in the near future. I asked the Special Service clerk about this, and he said that a few shows such as *Let's Face It*, with Bob Hope and Betty Hutton, and *A Thousand Cheers*, have come in. Have you seen any of these?

> Missing you so much,
> Herb

> Somewhere in the
> Marshall Islands
> May 17, 1944

Dearest Ann,

This evening I am a little stiff from digging foxholes. My hands are blistered so please ignore the penmanship. When you're not used to such work, it sure stiffens your shoulders in a short time. I will sleep better than usual tonight. The last few nights I have been restless, waking up and having a hard time getting back to sleep. I hate this as I get to thinking and wondering what you are doing. The sunset this evening was beautiful, with the most vibrant colors I've ever seen.

Mother wrote and told me you went to church with her on Easter. She thought that was sweet of you.

It's cool this evening after a very hot day. It feels like a spring night back home. I like the evenings here much better than the days because of the coolness and because the darkness of night hides the surroundings.

Our movie tonight was *This Was Paris*, starring Ann Dvorak and Ben Lynn. It was a stinko but better than nothing. It's much more pleasant to look at Ann Dvorak than a bunch of G.I. faces. I haven't seen a white woman in six months. On this island, there are no women at all, not even Army nurses.

All the natives live on another island, having been sent there after the bombardment. Many natives were killed when this fell under our control. This is bad but can't be helped in an invasion. The natives were left helpless against any shelling and shooting we had to do. The Japanese were busy protecting themselves and had no time for saving natives.

Well, Ann, Dear, this will have to do until I think of something else. I'm still unhappy and disgusted. The only thing that can cure this is to get out of the Army. . . .

Loving you dearly,
Herb

BY MARK HELLINGER

THE MARSHALLS MAY 22 (DELAYED)

I PACKED THIS MORNING. TIME NOW TO SHOVE TO OTHER FIELDS, BUT I'M
SORRY TO BE LEAVING. THAT IS STRANGE, BECAUSE OF ALL THE PLACES IN
THE WORLD, THIS IS PROBABLY THE SPOT TO WHICH YOU'D BE MOST HAPPY
TO WAVE GOODBYE. IT'S CRUELLY HOT AND THERE ISN'T A BLADE OF GRASS
THE FOOD HAS A CHRONIC SAMENESS, THE ACCOMMODATIONS ARE PURELY
PRIMITIVE AND YOUR FRIENDS FLY OFF INTO DEATH. YES, I'M SURE YOU
WOULD NOT CARE MUCH ABOUT IT. YET THERE ARE THINGS I AM TO MISS.
MY COT FOR EXAMPLE. IT'S JUST AN ORDINARY ARMY COT, WITH NO
MATTRESS. WHEN I MOVED IT AROUND IN THE MIDDLE OF THE NIGHT, TRYING
TO FIND A DRY SPOT IN THE TENT, IT COMPLAINED SQUEAKILY. WHEN I
PUT A CLEAN SHEET ON IT SOME TEN DAYS AGO, IT DIDN'T LOOK NATURAL
AT ALL.
BUT THE ALL IMPORTANT THING IS THAT I WAS ABLE TO SLEEP ON THAT COT,
MAYBE BECAUSE IT SAGGED A BIT IN THE MIDDLE--DOGGONE IT, SO DO I.
I'M GOING TO MISS THE BREAKFASTS. YOU WERE PRESENT AT 7:30 OR YOU
DIDN'T EAT. THE MENU BARELY CHANGED--HOT CAKES, WHITE BREAD, THAT
INFERNAL PARAFINED BUTTER THAT STICKS TO YOUR MOUTH AND PLENTY OF
COFFEE. ON ONE MEMORABLE MORNING EVERYONE GOT A FRESH EGG, A FRESH
EGG, MIND YOU, NOT A POWDERED EGG BUT A GENUINE FRESH EGG, TENDERLY
FRIED SO THERE WAS EVEN A BIT OF YOKE TO BE SOPPED UP WITH YOUR BREAD.
AH, MY FRIENDS, WHAT A MORNING THAT WAS. I'M GOING TO MISS THE WONDER-
FUL GUYS WHO FLY THOSE GIANT LIBERATORS FOR THE 7TH BOMBER COMMAND. I
GUESS I'LL MISS THEM MOST OF ALL BECAUSE I HAVEN'T KNOWN MEN LIKE THEM
BEFORE. JUST SO LONG AS OUR NATION PRODUCES BOYS LIKE THESE, OUR
COUNTRY WILL MOVE ONWARD. WELL, SO IT GOES--AND NOW I MUST GO TOO.

Herb included this piece by journalist Mark Hellinger in the preceding letter.
Hellinger worked as a war correspondent, writing human interest stories
about the troops, after repeated rejections for active service because of a
congenital heart condition.

Somewhere in the Marshall Islands
May 30, 1944

Dearest Ann,

I received two of your letters dated March 26 and 30, really late getting here. By the look of the envelopes, they went around the world three times; they have so many different addresses on them. Three more are recent, dated April 13, 16, and 18, and after I read them again, I may have something to write about.

In one of your letters you sound troubled, Ann. I assure you, if I had the time and place to write more often, I would not give up the privilege. This is not like Hawaii, where I had plenty of time. I am not sick as you thought, and if anything serious happened, the War Department would let you know before I could. Please don't worry.

It sounds as if your friend who works at the bank is writing to someone in Hawaii because of all the pleasant things he is doing. This locale has only our open-air cinema. Last night we saw *Rationing*, starring Wallace Beery and Marjorie Maine. I didn't enjoy it because it dealt too much with the Army for my taste. In fact, I left the show and went to bed. I don't see anything funny in the problems of war. Maybe I was in a bad mood last night. The show before that was *Doctor Broadway*. I can't remember who starred in it because it was a Class CCC, though it was much better than *Rationing*, even if it was about five years old. At least it stayed away from the war.

I would have been mad, more so than I am now if I read the article in *Life Magazine* on the Gilberts. I wish I knew where the hell the writer was—probably not even there. There should be a law against articles that consist of lies. Why didn't he mention that we caught the rain water from our tents in order to wash? And why not mention we washed from our steel helmets? The things he mentioned are exaggerated. For example, a portable drinking fountain is only a blister bag filled by hand with fresh water and hung on a tree so it's easier to get the water. It's made from canvas and lined with rubber to

216

prevent breakage, thus giving the water a delicious rubbery taste. I could go on criticizing the article, but what's the use? He probably got a kick out of the sort of life there. He lied when he wrote about tennis courts and few mosquitoes. Why did we get dengue fever? True, we had and still have a telephone system, but it's not what most people think. It is a field phone that you have to crank to get your party. About the cool breezes—why do we wear shorts? The only thing in the article I agree with concerns the beaches, which are beautiful but dangerous. As far as the fishing is concerned, the only ones who fished were the natives—for food. I don't know what the fish tastes like as I don't care to eat fish raw. Enough on this subject—I'm pretty angry about it.

Bob Roane is no longer here but has gone back to A.P.O. #953 to attend radio and gunnery school. I don't think he is going to write to Virginia. We had an argument, putting our friendship on thin ice. I told him he better change if he's going to correspond with Virginia, and he said he didn't care about writing. I guess I'm to blame for that. I hope Virginia doesn't mind, and if he does write to her, tell her to be casual with him. He's not a good man.

The islands that you mentioned in one of your letters are where I was—three of them. I hope this passes the censor. I don't see why it shouldn't. . . .

Your lonely husband,
Herb

—★—

The envelope for the preceding letter contained a snippet of paper, which read, "I am on Kwajalein." The censors had again failed to stifle Herb.

Battle-wrecked, Kwajalein during the war was no Eden. Choking dust, stirred up by vehicles on the roads, filled the air, smelling like cinders from gunpowder. Difficult to wash away with scarce water, it coated soldiers' skin. Shredded trees, rubble from concrete buildings, dud ammunition, shrapnel-riddled tanks amid blighted taro patches, remnants of a railroad line, and piles of war debris covered the atoll. Everything metal had started to rust. In the dugouts, soldiers found tin boxes with portraits of the enemy's loved ones and their souvenirs to send home, toothbrushes, breath freshener, slippers, and socks.

In June, the soldiers in Herb's squadron improved their camp. They gathered rocks and scrap wood and hauled them away. They filled in craters in the ground with sand and gravel to prevent water from the constant rains from pooling. They built a covered framework to house the blister bags for showering and dug sewage pits beneath the bags, which proved inadequate for drainage. So the soldiers dug new sumps and filled them partly with rocks, leaving about 3 feet to the ground surface, covered with a thin layer of dirt and topped with sheet metal.

Flies vied with soldiers for their meals. The mess hall had baited fly traps, and soldiers sprayed the area around and under the mess daily with a solution of creosote, kerosene, and diesel oil. They also fly-proofed the latrines and sprayed them daily with the same solution.

Headless bodies of the Japanese killed by aerial and naval bombardment on the Marshall Islands in February 1944. (Photo courtesy of the U.S. Air Force)

At the nightly movies, an officer reported the latest news of the war, and a private reviewed sports news to those gathered. Every night more and more soldiers showed up for the movie, making seats scarce. They replaced the old seats with steel ones, former frameworks for the bomb fins obtained from the bomb dump. The squadron opened a day room for enlisted men, with a radio, record player, current newspapers, magazines, pocket-sized books, and athletic equipment supplied by Special Services.

Constant shipments of fresh fruit and vegetables from the rear echelon supplemented the rations, which were fair. Each section could mix up and serve ice cream on special occasions, but the lack of freezers prevented everyone from having it at once. The PX supplied the most prized privilege of all: a daily bottle of beer per man.

Somewhere in the Marshall Islands
June 6, 1944

Dearest Ann,

I received your letters dated April 23, 21, and May 1st. Having read your letter concerning my being reduced to a private, I know you don't understand (and see why you don't). I am sorry you don't and wish you could. In fact, your letter on this subject made me angry. It's silly for me to feel this way. Many other people feel the way you do. I just wish you knew the truth. I shall not write any more on this subject. But please don't think highly of someone because they achieved a certain rank in the Army.

We have just heard by radio the news of the invasions in Europe. Things are going to happen fast from now on, and the war may be over sooner than predicted. I would like to know how Japan could last if we sent 2,000 planes over there, as we did in Germany. I'm sure they could not stand it as long as the Germans. Now that we're getting more control in Europe, we will start to gain control here. The soldiers over there will have a tough time of it for a while.

The boys in Europe are better off than those stationed on these atolls in the Pacific. They have more interesting things to see and places to go to than we have. When you see one atoll in the Pacific, you have seen them all. The only difference is the shape of the atoll. And the boys in Europe have had more furloughs than we have.

I hope someday we can have a house like this one in the picture you sent me. The bungalow is just right. It felt good while home just to be inside a private home once more. However, I did feel cramped even when sitting alone. I suppose it's perfectly natural to feel that way after spending time in the open air. It's going to be hard to adapt to civilized surroundings and wearing civilian clothes. When I get to wear such clothes again, they will be for comfort only; the looser and baggier they are, the better.

We saw *Riding High* last night. Even though it was more recent and in Technicolor, I did not like it. The acting was poor as well as most of the scenes and music. Dot Lamour and Dick Powell co-starred—never did like either of them. . . .

Your loving husband,
Herb

Somewhere in the Marshall Islands
June 12, 1944

Dearest Ann,

Mail came in on June 4, and I received four letters from you dated May 3, 5, 7, and 8; two from Mother; and one from a friend. I am on duty with a few moments to spare now and then to answer them.

I gave the letter for Bob Roane to a guy who is returning to Hawaii, asking him to give it to him. I don't think Bob will correspond with Virginia. He is writing to several girls, one of whom is married. He met her on the train while heading home. Perhaps if you mention this to Virginia, she would appreciate it.

The rationing of some meats sounds good. I wish they would send some down here. We do have roast beef once a week and other days, hot dogs and delicious Spam. It's amazing how some of us stay alive.

I have heard discouraging news about the furloughs that we are supposed to get after completing three years. The A.A.F. is furloughing 22 men per month. This is not good when there are thousands of boys here who, like me, have three and more years.

If you want some of the Hawaiian dishes at Wanamaker's, don't hesitate, Ann. I think I know what you have in mind about the modern dishes made from the Hawaiian monkey pod trees. I like them a lot. . . .

Your loving husband,
Herb

After almost two weeks of night raids, on June 13, Liberators from Herb's command based in the Marshalls flew their first daylight mission over Truk, accompanied by three navy photo planes. The Liberators encountered about 15 enemy fighters, destroying and damaging more than half of them. Japan's fighter strength at Truk was less than presumed, the air crews concluded.

Army and marine forces invaded Saipan on June 15. Despite flies, mosquitoes, searing heat, and choking dust, U.S. troops gave the Japanese no rest during a prolonged 25-day battle. They captured or exploded vast stores of ammunition and supplies intended for bases throughout the Pacific. The Japanese fought almost to the last man. During the invasion, the navy fought the Battle of the Philippine Sea, destroying several hundred Japanese fighter planes. The continuous piercing of the Carolines by Herb's command had rendered unnecessary a slow and costly series of invasions of those islands.

More deadly than Tarawa, the Battle of Saipan cost the Americans 3,426 lives, with 12,000 men wounded and missing. Among the approximately 24,000 Japanese dead from the fighting was Vice Admiral Chuichi Nagumo, who led the attack on Pearl Harbor. He'd shot himself in the head.

To the astonishment of U.S. troops, 5,000 Japanese committed suicide as a result of the battle. When captured, Japanese civilians and soldiers often asked, "Why don't you kill me here?" Occasionally, they died unnecessarily as when six Japanese soldiers in a mountainside cave used hand grenades to blow themselves up after hearing a U.S. officer call for his flame throwers. Japanese propaganda about the brutality of the Americans as well as the Japanese culture explained the suicides. Other Japanese civilians committed suicide on the rocky northernmost tip of Saipan, dying as "shields for the emperor." Some used grenades furnished by their own soldiers. Others joined hands, waded into the ocean, and drowned.

Saipan was to Japan what Pearl Harbor was to the United

States except that the island lies 1,000 miles closer to Japan's coast than Pearl Harbor does to the U.S. coast. Once Saipan fell, large B-29 Super-Fortresses could reach Japan easily from nearby bases.

Engineers of the Seventh Air Force landed with the first support troops on Saipan and began lengthening and filling in the shell holes in Aslito Airfield at the southern end of the island, working under shell and sniper fire. The Americans renamed the airstrip Isley Field after navy Commander Robert H. Isley, killed while strafing the base. It soon hosted the Seventh Fighter Command's planes for use as sweeps against other islands in the Marianas.

This sign at Isley Field shows the sign for the VII Bomber Command on the bottom left. (Photo courtesy of the U.S. Air Force)

Marshall Islands
June 16, 1944

Dearest Ann,

Since receiving your letter (this morning at 8) telling me about your throat operation, I have been impatient and anxious and thought about you constantly. By this time, you are in the hospital or recuperating. I hope you don't have any pain. Removing a thyroid is serious, but, if as you say, it's getting larger, the operation seems necessary.

I don't want to discourage you, but any chances for a furlough look gloomy.

I can't name the general whom I am going to write about, but he is mentioned in the clipping you sent me. He is unpopular amongst the men here and in Hawaii. Not long ago, he toured one of the military camps in Hawaii. The men threw shoes and other objects at him when he was about to make a speech at one camp. In addition, he isn't at all popular amongst the civilians in Hawaii. To keep a man down here when he is so disliked is more than I can understand.

I easily understand the bitterness some boys feel toward military life. But some civilians, especially women, find this attitude entirely incomprehensible. Some of them take it as a joke and laugh it off. Others think it is a good thing for one to experience the military.

I hope it won't be long before this whole mess is over. The news of the last few weeks has been encouraging. The latest bombing of Japan by the new B-29 AAF bombers staged in China has definitely helped to weaken Japan. It won't be long now.

Your husband,
Herb

Marshall Islands
June 20, 1944

Dearest Ann,

Your letters indicate your operation was on May 21. I have received two letters from you dated May 19 and 21. I

224

hope you are not suffering.

I'm glad you have played tennis. When I get home, you will probably defeat me. I haven't played tennis for 6 months and don't believe I will be able to play again soon. I miss playing a lot.

[Half of the page cut by censor.]

. . . about the showers that have been constructed. The shower room and building are okay. Someone discovered water 8 to 10 feet down; this gave us the idea for the showers. The water is of a brackish solution, half salt water and God knows what else. The odor of the water is sickening, and no matter what fragrance of soap one uses it is impossible to kill that smell. It takes a half a bar of soap to whip up a lather. The color of the lather is grayish, making it seem as if you didn't bathe in a while. Everyone is forbidden to brush their teeth with this water as it is poison to take internally. A few men did not know this and have taken sick, becoming thin and weak.

Some say the odor of the water is from the bodies of Japs who are buried here. In many places on this island, sections of land have been fenced off and marked with signs saying, "E.D.," [Enemy Dead] followed by the number of dead. These look more like public dumps than burial grounds.

I hope you haven't forgotten the picture you promised me. I'm sorry I can't send you any snaps of me. We are not permitted to have a camera here. Some boys have one, though, and once in a while you see someone taking a picture on the sly side. If they got caught, they would lose the camera and get a lot of punishment besides.

P.F.C. Hart has left here, so his writing to Mary is out. I don't like playing cupid for these guys and mean to stop. I'm sorry Virginia wrote to Bob R. and hope nothing comes of it. If so, I will feel sorry for Virginia and that I am to blame. Well, Ann, give all my regards. I love you and will write soon again.

Your loving husband,
Herb

Somewhere in the Marshall Islands
June 24, 1944

Dearest Ann,

It is 11 o'clock—one more hour to go before a good night's sleep. I'm wondering how you are, thinking of you constantly.

I received three letters yesterday dated May 23, 28, and 31. This is fairly good time, and some mail is coming in tomorrow.

I am glad you like the necklace, although it looks amateurish. The other one I sent you is better than the small one. Mary and your Mother should have received their necklaces by this time.

Thanks for taking care of my friend, Andy Beyer. I haven't written to him for a long time. I did receive his wedding invitation. But the A.A.F. had other plans for me. They seem to have it pretty good in Texas. I wonder if he and his wife realize how fortunate they are that they have been together so long.

From what I hear from my brother, he is unhappy and has requested to go overseas. I wish he wouldn't be such a sucker.

A couple of days later—

It got too late for me to finish this the other night, and I was falling asleep while writing. I have a few minutes before the movie starts, so I'll finish up.

Today, I cleaned some sea shells to make a necklace for my sister and will make you another from a different color and rarer type of shell than the others. I buried them in the ground for 10 days so no one else could get them. The odor is not pleasant, almost strong enough for a gas mask. . . .

Your loving husband,
Herb

Two days before Herb wrote the preceding letter, 22 fighter planes of the Seventh Air Force took off from an aircraft carrier and landed on Saipan. Along with other aircraft, they began a series of bombing, strafing, and rocket-firing missions on enemy positions on the island, under sniper fire. Ground crews and airmen on Saipan endured long nights of rifle fire and shell bursts. Four days later, 300 enemy soldiers and some saboteurs broke through infantry lines and reached Isley Field. Fighter crews fought like infantrymen to hold their own. By dawn, the enemy had left, having destroyed only one U.S. plane. The bombing and strafing of Saipan continued until Allied forces secured it on July 9, as well as missions to Tinian, only 3 miles across the water from Saipan.

Somewhere in the Marshall Islands
July 10, 1944

Dear Ann,

At last, I have relief about your operation. I am glad the whole thing is over. Mother wrote that you look well and had a comfortable room and that your voice was husky. I am glad you liked your nurse and that she took good care of you. I would not worry about the incision scar as it will heal and in a few months be unnoticeable.

Today I sent you a grass skirt that I bought in Tarawa—also a rug made by the natives, which I traded for two cartons of cigarettes. I wanted to send it before I left Tarawa but didn't have time.

My watch is also in the box in case you may overlook it. I think the mainspring is broken, and it was beginning to rust so it's best to send it back. This is no place for a wrist watch.

I received an apologetic letter from Bob R. in Hawaii. He said he was sorry that he lost his temper and that he was too hot headed. He left a box of socks here and wanted me to send them to him. This may be a made-up excuse as no one remembers seeing any socks that he left. Both of us were hot headed when we argued. I should write him and tell him I am not mad, but I don't have time. This affair with the married

227

woman may be nothing, but I don't think it is wise of him to write to her and Virginia.

I spoke out of turn when I told him not to write to Virginia, saying I'd tell her he was writing to a married woman. This really made him mad, but it was not what we argued about. Your letter, in fact, helped Bob. You are his Dear Miss Dix.

The shows have been coming along exceptionally well. I've seen *Jane Eyre*, *Girl Crazy*, *No Time for Love*, *Up in Arms*, and *His Butler Sister*. I liked them all but *Jane Eyre*, the best. Because most of the shows have been musicals, I enjoyed seeing something serious for a change. *So's Your Uncle* is another show I saw, but it was poor.

I suppose you have read the news that Saipan belongs to the United States. Remember this place. I can't say too much as the censor will cut it out. At last, we are sending some bombers to Japan, and it won't be long before the end.

The problem with our shower is mostly solved. We dug a well from which we get water about 50 feet from our "private bath house." The water is brackish and full of bacteria, but it's nice to know we are not washing in water with people's waste in it.

The clipping that I am sending you is a good description of this island [Johnston Island]. Many personnel are sent there for punishment. Most of the sailors sent there stay for a year and six months. We stopped there overnight on my way to Tarawa, but after being here, Johnston Island seems good. While there, I did see the two cups with lipstick that the article mentions.

Give my regards to all.

Your loving husband,
Herb

Cherchez la Femme: In the Pacific It's a Feast or a Famine

Two NEWSWEEK *war correspondents in the Pacific recently visited two bases that the war has left behind. William Hipple stopped by an almost unknown island in the Central Pacific. Robert Shaplen returned to one of the most famous bases in the Southwest Pacific. Here is what they found:*

Johnston Island . . .

This is a pile of sand and coral in the middle of the Pacific Ocean—717 miles southwest of Honolulu—where transport planes en route to or from Tarawa, Kwajalein, or Guadalcanal stop over to fuel their engines and feed their passengers.

The stiff-legged passengers crawl out, take one look, and invariably exclaim: "What a place! Boy, would I hate to get stuck here!"

Other spots have made claims, but J. I. would certainly survive in the finals of any contest to pick the smallest, loneliest, and most desolate outpost where Americans are serving in this war.

The foliage here is scattered patches of bunch grass, dry and brown. The sailors and marines have to hang up pictures of forests just to keep in mind what trees look like. California redwoods are as popular this season as Betty Grable.

Barracks, mess halls, and offices—Quonset huts or wooden buildings—stand on the small knoll which runs down the center of the island, nowhere more than 15 feet above sea level. There once was a rise called "Summit Peak" near the eastern end, but it has been shaved down. It towered 44 feet.

All the buildings are a dirty Confederate gray, mostly from the coral dust, which whirls and penetrates everywhere. The airfield runs down one side and a taxi-way and plane-dispersal area down the other. That's your island.

Until the conquest of the Marshalls and Gilberts, Johnston was rarely visited by more than one plane a week and one ship a month. Now it has become important in the air route for Naval Air Transport Service (NATS) and Army Transport Command (ATC) planes and as a stopover for combat bombers heading to or from the fighting zones.

So civilization's problems have come to Johnston, including the female problem. On the rare occasions when nurses stop here, a special warning system goes into action. A modern Paul Revere mounted on a jeep sweeps down the beaches shouting: "Women are coming! Women are coming! Take cover!" Nude bathers clothe themselves speedily or take shelter immediately in the nearest building.

Women are regarded with awe. Many of the men haven't talked to one for more than a year. This statement includes native women, because there have never been any natives on Johnston.

One mess hall has a proud trophy—two cups with lipstick lip prints on the rims. They were made by Army evacuation nurses Alice Kirsis of Arlington, Mass., and Elsie Nolan of Middletown, Mo., first women ever to set foot on this island.

In the Quonset officers' club a sign says: "On March 1, 1944, the first lady to enter this club was Second Lt. Jewell R. Ellis, U. S. Army evacuation nurse. She stood on this spot."

"This spot" has been memorialized by two small footprints presumably made by Miss Ellis—in the Grauman's Chinese theater manner—on a floor plaque.

Enlisted Navy men now stay on Johnston nine months, officers a year. They have movies nightly, a salt-water swimming pool as well as beaches, fishing, reefing parties, volleyball, softball, boxing, table tennis, a library, a soda fountain, rations of beer, good chow, and regular airmail delivery.

But what a place! Boy, would I hate to get stuck here! *William Hipple*

Somewhere in the Marshall Islands
14 July 1944

Dearest Ann,

Your letter of June 18 came today. I hope you are enjoying your rest at home. I wish I were there with you. The days that you didn't write makes it seem like years since I have heard from you.

When I mail the necklace I shall put in a few loose shells as you suggest. A jeweler could make earrings and also keep the wire on the first necklace from rusting by putting a chemical solution on it. It makes the wire appear gold and should prevent it from turning your neck green.

Go ahead and get the maternity insurance. It's a good idea providing it doesn't make you short of cash. I want you to have the best when it comes to anything such as this. Would you want to make use of it that soon after the war? This seems sort of soon, but, of course, this is up to you. I shall talk to the censor to see if I may send you a copy of a lecture on sex given by a professor at Columbia University. It has an excellent view of sex relations between man and wife, though it's a little raw in parts and states the facts. I hope you won't think it embarrassing, but you are intelligent enough to understand it all.

Had you noticed any change in me while I was home? The time was short so it might be hard for you to comment; if that's the case, never mind. I feel changed and it is an uncomfortable feeling, which I hope time will cure.

It must be pretty bad for people when things occur such as that described in the enclosed clipping. This is only one of many cases that happen daily. A soldier here committed suicide the other night by shooting himself in the brain. Easy way out, isn't it? I'm sure the poor guy had a good reason.

U. S. Soldier Is Shot for Murder

LONDON, May 31 (AP)—U. S. Army headquarters announced today that Private Alex S. Miranda of 1821 West Eighth street, Santa Ana, Calif., was shot to death "by musketry" yesterday for murdering First Sergeant Thomas Evison of Port Norris, N. J. A court-martial convicted Miranda of shooting Evison through the head with a carbine.

Colmeyer, who sleeps in the same tent as me and four others, wakes us up at night with his nightmares. Last night, one of the fellows entered the tent at 12 after work. He used a flashlight and made as little noise as possible. Nonetheless, Colmeyer was aroused and must have been dreaming that he was a captive of the Japs. Raising himself up in bed, he yelled, "What's this? Jesus spare me!" waking us all up with his outburst. But this case is just a mild one. This morning we mentioned it to him, and he didn't remember anything about it. He has us all wondering. It's amazing what sort of people you meet in the Army. There's never a dull moment—even in your sleep.

Well, Ann Dear, I guess this is it for now.

Your loving husband,
Herb

Of all of the American casualties in World War II, 20 percent had post-traumatic stress, though the term was not used, and other battle-induced mental problems. By 1944, the military evacuated from the Pacific theater an average of 22 soldiers a day suffering from severe psychosis.

Let There Be Light, a documentary film directed by John Huston and commissioned by the army in 1946 referred to such soldiers as "casualties of the spirit . . . forced beyond the limit of human endurance." Symptoms of those diagnosed as neuropsychiatric ranged from trembling, insomnia, amnesia,

231

depression, unceasing fear and apprehension, hopelessness, stuttering, battle fatigue, isolation, impending doom, and nightmares. A fear of death was common. Some soldiers had conversion hysteria—an inability to walk or move in some way with no physical reason why. Hospitalized soldiers typically stayed in a psychiatric ward for 8 to 10 weeks. Their psychotherapy included hypnosis, the use of sodium amatol, Rorschach tests, and electroencephalograms. In addition to individual psychotherapy, soldiers attended group and occupational therapy, where they made crafts or painted and drew pictures, worked in a wood or machine shop, and played sports.

Through the summer and fall of 1944, Herb's command continued raiding Truk, Nauru, and Ponape. And the Seventh's fighter planes on Saipan hit Tinian, Pagan, and Rota in the Marianas. By July 17, the Seventh's fighters in this area had flown more than 2,500 sorties—without seeing one enemy plane.

U.S. marine and army troops landed on Guam on July 21. Heavy fighting as well as round-the-clock air strikes conquered the enemy on August 10, with 1,400 U.S. soldiers dead or missing. While the battle raged on Guam, more ground forces prepared to land 121 miles south on Tinian. Preinvasion air strikes of Tinian reached a peak on July 23 as the Seventh's fighters, for the first time in the Pacific, dropped napalm on Japanese caves and pillboxes, firebombing to bits what had been impregnable positions.*

Somewhere in the Marshall Islands
22 July 1944

Dearest Ann,
    I hope by this time your friend Sara has heard better news about her friend, Charlie Giambrone. Mistakes can happen. The Army generally waits six months until it

---

* Pillboxes were small, low shelters from which soldiers could fire weapons.

announces someone killed. During that time, it lists him as missing in action (six months to hope for the best).

I am glad your throat is returning to normal. Do you answer the telephone now? People may think you are the famous Lamont Cranston (The Shadow). Business may pick up.

Mother wrote that you look fine and that the scar is hardly visible and in time would be unnoticeable.

The great battle of Saipan is over. This is the nearest island to Japan—the most important base for us to operate from. Many Japanese have been killed and some captured. One Japanese soldier found hiding in a cave ran to one of our officers, begging not to be killed. The officer, not having great love for Japs, hesitated and spared his life, thinking he could be used to gain military information.

For the number of Japs on Saipan, a small percentage has been taken prisoner. Garapan, the capital, seems completely destroyed from pictures I've seen. Snipers gave soldiers the most opposition. Some snipers tied themselves to trees; others hid in caves. A soldier is a perfect target for snipers, and his chances are only 50 to 1 of surviving. Many snipers were found on top of palm trees, dead, tied to the tree—more or less a human sacrifice.

You seem to mention the word furlough in every letter. I wish I could tell you that I'm coming home, which I want more than you. No one is leaving this place; everyone seems to be getting further from rather than closer to a furlough and, as we near Japan, the chance for furloughs is going to lessen.

No one has received any mail for six days; the last letter I got from you on July 16 is dated June 25—better time than before but fewer letters. I don't know which is better. You at least get my letters within 10 days. I'm beginning to think I am fortunate just to receive your letters. I think they are holding the mail up until after a certain incident.

Remember, I love you very much and miss you more
than you'll ever know. Give my regards to all.

                                        Your loving husband,
                                        Herb

During July, Herb's squadron prepared to move to Saipan,
and most of the squadron left on July 28 aboard the USS
Livingston. Key men kept their departments operating back in the
Marshalls. One of the cargo planes headed to Saipan crashed into
a lagoon after takeoff, killing nine men.

                          Somewhere in the Marshall Islands
                                        30 July 1944
Dearest Ann,
    I'm glad to hear you are getting back into the swing of
things (tennis, that is). When I start again I shall have to take it
easy and work up to the point where I don't feel tired from
playing. You will take it easy on me, won't you? What make of
racket are you using? I played with a Shessinger (Australian
make) in Hawaii but had to leave it when I came here.
    We know where we're going and are anxious to get there.
It is much bigger than this atoll we're on now. It is an island,
not an atoll, so it has better facilities, providing the structures
have not been destroyed.
    Our greatest problem is still water for washing. The
pump we have been using is broken. The 2,000-gallon tank that
was holding the water is on a platform 12 feet high. We don't
intend to form a bucket brigade to fill it. We've got enough
work to do. We now draw water by dipping a bucket into the
well and then washing from the bucket.
    The heat seems to be getting worse. Everyone sweats a
lot. If not, something is wrong with him. Lying in the tent at 6
o'clock in the morning with the sun just rising, you can feel the
heat gradually penetrating the canvas until it gets so hot you
cannot stay there for long. Yesterday, one fellow who was
standing around talking to someone at about 2 o'clock blacked

234

out from a sun stroke, his first, and it scared him. He had no covering on his head. I understand why he fainted. The heat at noon is terrific.

A pig left here by the Japs has been walking around the island just like a dog would. He is a friendly pig and likes to be petted. All the men feed him, and he eats anything you give him. He is black with white spots and about 15 inches high. One of these days, I won't be surprised if the cooks have killed him to eat as we never get pork, and this pig is getting to be the right size. I guess he and the handful of natives were the only beings left here after the battle.

Walter K., I presume, is still at A.P.O. #953 and Wagner also. I never heard anything definite. Sgt. Hibbard's brother [Gerald] was one of the fortunate ones to go back to the states. While he was there, he married his sweetheart, and, when he returned, told me what a good time he had.

I dream and think of you constantly. If you only knew, you would think me crazy. I love you very much and miss you terribly.

Your loving husband,
Herb

Although most of Herb's squadron sailed to Saipan, Herb flew in 26 days after its capture, arriving on August 4, at yet another camp rife with rain, mud, flies, mosquitoes, and confusion. Vehicles furrowed the water-soaked cane field, and the men had nothing to use to fill in the ruts. Despite soaking rain and the lack of tools and materials, the men set up pyramidal tents sufficient to house everyone soon after arriving. The flight surgeon declared the field kitchen unsatisfactory, so the soldiers ate C and K rations. When the mess was declared useable, the men had some meals of B rations—canned, packaged, or preserved food normally prepared in field kitchens without refrigeration—but mostly C rations.

The battle had ravaged Saipan's sugar cane fields,

refineries, and flame trees; tore coconut palms; and flattened its flimsy towns. Plenty of work remained for the troops on Saipan in the weeks after the battle, including using flame throwers, shovels, and dynamite to rid the caves of remaining Japanese fighters.

The men built roads of coral and erected tents for the offices with wooden frames and screening during their first week there. By the end of the month, the enlisted men's and officers' showers had been built. The men also had a day room that housed not only Special Services but also the mailroom and the squadron barber. The chaplain got a chapel put up. The men had no laundry facilities, but the mail service and movies rated well. For recreation, the soldiers played horseshoes.

Herb and some buddies went to the prisoner internment camp, Camp Susupe, on August 12. The camp held 18,000 people, mostly Japanese, along with Koreans, Mongols, and Filipinos. The civilian internees lived in a camp separate from the Japanese soldiers. Herb wrote, "I could not help noticing the inferiority . . . of these people, who are living like animals—men, women, and children alike," with 20 to 50 people in one shelter. "I feel sorry for the innocent children." Between 10 and 15 babies were born every day in the camp. Built from materials salvaged from the ruins, the shelters consisted of tents or ramshackle huts. "The women and girls stay at the camp and help to keep it clean. At least, they are supposed to . . . but it looks like a pig pen," wrote Herb. The internees wore whatever clothing was available, including Japanese uniforms.

The internees ran the camp themselves and provided some of their food by fishing and farming, though most of it came from stores the Japanese military had hidden in caves. "None of the internees speaks English—most speak Japanese—but they have no trouble saying 'food' and 'cigarettes.'" wrote Herb. "They like the army's good rations in cans and cigarettes. They all look sickly, thin, undernourished, and filthy. . . . The male internees are jailed in a labor battalion and sent out under guard to clean up the island; they earn 40 cents a day. None of them overworks. They just mope along as if they were sick."

Japanese civilians on Saipan suffered from 14 years of occupation by the Japanese military, which confiscated all the island's milk and fresh vegetables, leaving the civilians only rice and dried fish to eat. Almost all had gum disease, according to Wendell Rookstood, a dentist with the Seventh Air Force who surveyed the internees. Japanese and American doctors treated 1,200 patients a day, most for malnutrition.

Organized enemy resistance ended early in that same month on Guam and Tinian. Airfields to accommodate giant B-29s for the final assault on Japan were built or improved on Saipan, Guam, and Tinian as soon as the fighting died down. Herb's command moved its heavy bombers from Kwajalein to the Marianas as the airfields went into operation. Less than a week after Herb arrived there, B-24s from his command flew their first mission from Saipan, blasting Iwo Jima in the Volcano Islands to begin its neutralization. Two days later, the bombers hit sites on the Bonin Islands and Northern Marianas, taking the fight onward toward Tokyo.

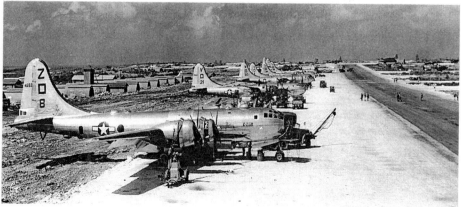

B-29s lined up on Saipan (c. 1944).

Saipan

13 August '44

Dearest Ann,

Your letters dated July 5, 9, and 12 have been forwarded to me here. I have been here 10 days. Flying from A.P.O. #241 [Marshall Islands] made the trip shorter than going by L.S.T., which would have taken days. L.S.T. stands for Landing Ship Transport, and these are used for just that. They are ships with a flat bottom that go right up to the shore line. You probably have seen pictures of them in *Life Magazine*.

I arrived in Saipan 26 days after its capture, but fighting goes on at the other end of the island, and many snipers live in caves up in the hills. This is the nearest I have been to actual war and I don't feel comfortably safe.

It has rained constantly since I have been here as it is the rainy season until October. The whole place is one hell of a mess. We are sleeping in tents where the mud is thick and deep, coming up to the rims of our high shoes. This is the worst place I have ever been, and it won't get any better. Mosquitoes and rats are the worst pests again, with more here than at Tarawa, which I thought was the hell hole of the world.

Not a building remains untouched in Garapan, the big city here. We didn't mean to destroy it so much as we could have made good use of it. The Japanese civilians had plenty of time to evacuate the city and the lucky ones did. Since the Japanese army would not leave, it took the consequences, after forcing half the civilians to stay for use as human targets and killing those who refused. Toward the end of their defeat at Garapan, the Japanese, seeing no escape, forced men and women to stand in front of them for protection from our guns, thinking the Marines and infantry would not shoot them. As a result, many women were killed. The marines say they will never forget during the final push at night the anguished cries of women and children whom they killed or the Japanese were torturing.

We are a few miles from Garapan in a district consisting of, from the looks of the poorly constructed buildings, farmers'

238

and sugar workers' dwellings. The building we work in used to be a hospital (a poorly built one), and all around is evidence of this. Men in other organizations who arrived before us are fortunate to have buildings for their living quarters and mess halls a lot sturdier than ours that protect them better from the rain and mud.

I visited a demolished Shinto Buddhist temple, which must have been in a beautiful place. The Japanese used this as a military stronghold. Many buildings, such as a sugar mill and others with nonmilitary uses, were turned into ammunition storage areas. Snipers in caves in the hills are believed to have some ammunition and have considerably injured our personnel and damaged planes. The snipers are dangerous, and I am a perfect target for one while working at night. We capture 40 to 50 snipers a day. Some are giving themselves up and others remain in the caves to be burnt alive by torch throwers or hand grenades.

The island is scenic, with green trees, grass, and mountains, a pretty sight after being on Kwajalein and not seeing such scenery for a while. In fact, if Saipan were larger, it would be another Hawaii. The climate is about the same, except it's a few degrees hotter and damper with many more rats and mosquitoes.

Our first year of marriage, ha! It seems a joke. Neither of us was around to make it bad anyway. It was pretty hard for me, and I hope I never see another one like it.

I am looking forward to fulfilling all the plans we are making. The day cannot come soon enough for me. I love you very much and miss you. Give my regards to your parents.

Your loving husband,
Herb

Saipan
20 August 1944

Dearest Ann,

The censorship regulations have been eased. You probably noticed from my last letter. I guess they think the Japanese know where we are now, as if they never did. We can say much more about this place and our experiences here than at A.P.O. 953.

We had an air raid last night at midnight, a ghastly hour to get up, especially when it's raining. It's hard to say which was worse, the mosquitoes or the bombs. A.P.O. #240 [Gilbert Islands] and Saipan have much in common, namely, plenty of malaria and dengue. Many are afflicted with both and are being sent to Guadalcanal.

We have worked all day on our tent, trying to make it livable and homey. It's no use; there's too much mud. We built floors to put our bunks on, which is better than having them sink into the mud when we get in them. The Marines, however, have slept in pup tents on the damp ground since the invasion, so what we have isn't too bad. The sleeping arrangements for the Marines and many other such situations that are not publicly known are hard to swallow. You said it's just as well these issues are not known, but I disagree. There are some good people left in this world who could do something about these conditions if they knew about them.

Having a baby is up to you, with a little help from me. Twenty-three does seem to be a good age to have a baby. I do think, though, that we should get settled awhile after I come home and maybe take a trip. I do not want to wait too long to get a job. After that, I may be able to rest and then think about a baby.

Hoping this letter finds you well and happy.

Loving you truly,
Herb

Saipan
26 August '44

Dear Ann,

The mail is somewhat delayed. I received two letters dated July 23 and 27 on August 22 and one more today dated July 30. I guess you are wondering why I've waited almost a week to answer. I didn't exactly wait. I hardly had time with so much work to do. I'm writing this one at work now. Things have quieted down to half-normal conditions for a few hours.

Dengue is common here, and I'm fortunate not to have gotten it, but it is not contagious. One can only get it from a mosquito infected with it. More than 60 percent of the men have had it twice and spent seven ungodly days in bed each time. Something about my constitution has prevented my getting it. I was told that people with type B blood are not susceptible to it. My blood type is B+. Sometimes I feel I am getting sick, but it doesn't worry me because it is natural not to feel healthy here.

It now rains off and on, not constantly as before. There is still plenty of mud, and after the rainy season, there will be lots of dust. I prefer the mud. Tonight there is a beautiful moon, and it's much too beautiful to be in this hell hole of the Marianas.

My sense of humor, which you referred to, comes and goes. I have grown more serious in the last four years, only a natural adaptation after seeing and experiencing all this. You will notice a great change in me when you're with me for a while. My strongest characteristic is being too temperamental, and it's not to my advantage. I hope you can overlook this and understand when we start living together. Outside of this, I'm easy to get along with.

Let me quote a few lines from an article I read. I wish I could send the whole thing, but it's not mine, so here it is:

241

My idea of living in the country has not changed. If I have to live in a city, I'd prefer one like New York or Philadelphia and not like Norristown. I would want someplace where we can build an outside grill so we can have some charcoal-grilled steaks and barbeque occasionally.

The Roane and Detwiler affair is beyond me. I hope Virginia knows what she is doing. I don't plan to write to Bob. I am not sore or anything. But Virginia is one of many girls receiving his love letters. Any guy who asks a girl whether she loves him only on the basis of letter writing, in my estimation, doesn't show much sense. Wise up, Virginia. I hope everything will turn out okay. Bob seems to be a natural Romeo. He has good morals and seems to be honest. But this mania that he's gotten into with writing to different girls is beyond me.

Sorry to hear that Sara has received no word concerning [Charlie] Giambrone. The fact that he was reported missing on invasion day in Europe does not sound good.

Loving you as ever. I must go to work and bring this letter to an end.

Your loving husband,
Herb

242

The U.S. government waited a year before declaring anyone missing officially dead in the war. So for months, people held out hope for survivors of the Normandy invasion of June 6, 1944.

On that day, the churches in Norristown scheduled services at noon for people to come to pray for our troops. Sara asked Ann to meet her and attend a service with her to pray for her beloved Charlie Giambrone. Ann wrote, "Of course, we found out later, our prayers were too late—European time being ahead of ours." Charlie had already died. The landing craft bearing him and others of the army's 29th Field Artillery Battalion, 4th Infantry Division, hit a mine and exploded off of Utah Beach. He was one of 4,413 Allied servicemen killed that day and was buried in the Normandy American Cemetery in Colleville-sur-Mer, France. About Sara, Ann wrote, "His death had a profound effect on her. She was never again the lighthearted, fun-loving girl she had been before Charlie's death."

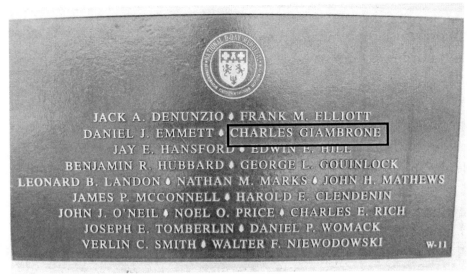

A plaque at the National D-Day Memorial Foundation bears the name of the boyfriend of Ann's friend, Sara Garges (the outline was added by the author). (Photo courtesy of James Morrison)

In late summer and the fall of 1944, Saipan-based Liberators from Herb's command continued bombing targets in the Carolines and Northern Marianas and hammered sites in the Bonin Islands. The Seventh's fighters bombed and strafed and fired rockets on the Northern Marianas.

Saipan
4 September '44

Dearest Ann,

Thanks for the birthday card. I received it today with two letters dated August 2 and 5. Have you been receiving my letters from here in less time than from the other address? I have been writing fairly regularly since I've been here.

The news of the events in Europe has been so good; it's like reading a fairy tale. It won't be long now.

I never went to the Fiji Islands so I could not get a fan like the one you mentioned in your letter. After seeing most of the islands in the Pacific, I have less desire to see those islands. If things go right, this may be the last island I will ever see.

The Lieutenant that I work with has the same birthday as you. He asked me to send you his congratulations. He seems like a good person and hasn't any great love for the Army.

The other day, he took us up to the mountains. We saw many interesting things, but we all felt uncomfortable. The roads are narrow and mysterious, a perfect place for a sniper. Although we were armed, the snipers have all the advantage. Many of the caves have not been cleared out and contain plenty of dead Japs in them. You can find lots of souvenirs if you feel like venturing into one to these ghastly caves. I would rather not. One never knows what may be inside. Lots of guys go in them and find souvenirs on the bodies of dead Japs. It's an unhealthy ordeal. The stench from the caves when you stand outside them is terrific. The only way to go in would be to wear a gas mask.

I was looking at the pictures of you today, the one where you are standing by the bridge in a white sweater and a plaid skirt. My favorite one, though, is the one with your hair the way I like it. I'm not even going to mention the one in the bathing suit. But what's the use of telling you which pictures I like? It would be all of them. I remain

Your loving husband,
Herb

Give all my regards, and, oh yes, I almost forgot, if this will make you feel better, they made me a corporal.

Saipan
7 September 1944

Dearest Ann,

Happy Birthday, Dear. This is the best I can do. I sent you a necklace but don't suppose it will get to you in time for the event. Your mail has been coming through faster than usual. Two of your letters dated August 7 and August 11 got here yesterday. And you would be wise to use 6-cent stamps, not 3-cent-ers.

This damn place is the dampest place I will ever live in. There's nothing like it. Getting acclimatized back in the states

245

is the least of my worries. Of course, coming home in the heart of winter, one would have to be cautious to dress for the cold. When they start sending us home, we will probably have to spend time in Hawaii and go through California. This way, we would get acclimatized gradually. I would like to gain more weight. I have lost 8 pounds since I have been here from perspiration and the food, which is putrid.

Don't worry about the Christmas package. It is not wise to send anything here. Hawaii was different; it wasn't as far. I want a package more than anything and appreciate your concern.

This isn't much of a letter because I have no time for more. I took this time to let you know I am thinking of you on your birthday as always. I'll write soon again.

Your loving husband,
Herb

The food Herb and his buddies ate on Saipan was as bad as the conditions, with C rations prevailing. But tasty baked goods compensated for that, along with a trickle of fresh apples, pears, and oranges arriving from Hawaii.

At times, the men ate only K rations: nonperishable, high-calorie, ready-to-eat meals that fit in a soldier's pocket. Intended for short-term use, they consisted of hard biscuits, hard candy, dry sausages, and chocolate bars and had about as much nutrition as a fast-food lunch. Despite this, use of K rations remained common in the war, especially for soldiers fighting in extreme conditions.

Saipan
9 September '44

Dearest Ann,

Just a few lines in remembrance of our anniversary: Wishing I could be home on this day more than any other. No one in the world could have been happier on that day than I. I wish I could give you something, but I cannot, much to my sorrow.

The news about Marge and Merrill Gander divorcing surprised me. It's really too bad. They impressed me as being happily married. I knew Marge worried a lot when Merrill went on trips for months at a time; she's a nervous person who could not stand much. Marge was lonelier than people thought. I know how Marge feels because I've been lonely, too. I am sure the divorce will be easier on Merrill than her. Give her my regards and wish her the best of luck. The divorce should not change our friendship. This is when she needs a friend. What kind of work is she doing in the laundry?

I am getting another damn tropical cold. My nose has been dripping all day and is sore from my rubbing it. I'm surprised I didn't get one sooner after all the rain here. I hope it doesn't spread to my chest—then I will complain. I feel miserable and have to work until midnight, which doesn't help.

I told you to send nothing but I have changed my mind. If it would be possible for you to disguise it, I would like to have a quart of rum or Scotch whiskey. I can't think of anything that would taste better. Something like this would help the morale of a few of us.

Loving you truly,
Herb

Saipan
15 September '44

Dear Ann,

I got two of your letters from Cape May. I hope you had a good time and made the best of it. Accommodations at such places are not good during these times. You really can't expect them to be, with all the shortages.

The current rumor involves a new station at Hawaii. So far, nothing official has been said, but it seems believable. I have not thought much about this, but I have an excellent chance for sergeant and won't hesitate to request it, if the rumor proves true. I won't get optimistic and hope you won't.

The "medicine" that I asked you to send me seems like a

247

bad idea unless you can disguise it thoroughly. One way that has been effective is to put it inside of a tall candy cane with pieces of candy on the outside of the bottle. If you don't think you can do this, forget about it.

I read *Christmas Holiday* and enjoyed it. Maugham is one of my favorite writers. *Time Magazine* did not give the picture a good write-up. Have you seen the miniature magazines printed for overseas shipment? I enjoy getting them even though they are a little late.

Speaking of pictures, I haven't seen *Going My Way* and don't think I will get the chance. It was playing at Kwajalein the day after I left. The shows we've had are fair. We saw *Show Business*, *Flesh and Fantasy*, and *Four Jills and a Jeep* (terrible). For the last few nights, the power has been weak. Last night, *Harvest Moon* was playing but we could not hear it well. I was pretty sore because Ann Sheridan is one of my favorites.

Writing on the beach is not the easiest way to write a letter but one of the nicest. I've done it many times and seem to think better.

The rains have not stopped. Everything is still muddy. The narrow roads are slippery and some cars have chains on their tires to stay on the road. We often see a truck or Jeep stuck in the mud up to the rims.

I have been a doctor and nursemaid for the last two days. One of the boys in the tent has dengue fever, and the rest of us take turns bringing him meals and drinking water and the like. It is nice to take turns as no one knows when he is going to get it again, and we would want the same service. Thank God it only lasts for seven days, and at the end you think all the blood has left you. . . .

Your loving husband,
Herb

Saipan
22 September '44

Dearest Ann,

I received three letters from you at one time, dated August 18 and 22 and September 4. If you wrote any letters between August 22 and September 4, I have not received them yet.

It is impossible to rid this place of mosquitoes. A couple of miles from here is a stagnant pool, a perfect breeding place for them. Oil has been put in the pond with no results. Disinfecting not only the ponds here but also rain barrels and tin cans full of water is hard. Plus, all the rain adds to the problem.

Yes, I am still working in an office doing communications work and the message center.

An air raid chased us from our beds a few nights ago and into foxholes and bomb shelters. Fortunately, it wasn't raining at the time. The Japs like to come over when the moon is commencing to be full, so as long as the moon is full, we will be susceptible.

Did I tell you I planted tomato plants? They are 3-1/2 inches high—and sure look good. Some of the boys brought seeds from Hawaii and gave me some. It's hard to say whether I will eat them if we move before they ripen. I won't plant anymore because I don't think I will be here long enough.

I saw a sight yesterday that I never saw before and will probably never see again. A tame, black, homeless chicken has been hanging around our tent area, maybe because this was his home before the war. The boys have named him "Tojo."* After much fussing and scampering around, Tojo caught a mouse. While the mouse screeched, very much alive, Tojo swallowed it. I would not have believed this if I hadn't seen it.

I hope you have fully recovered from your vacation, Labor Day, and gay weekends and will spend your next

*The chicken was named after Hideki Tojo, Prime Minister of Japan during the attack on Pearl Harbor.

249

vacation with me.

Your loving husband,
Herb

Two days after Herb wrote the preceding letter, a friendly patrol fired on four soldiers in his squadron, shooting three of them. The soldier who escaped injury, Pfc. Pamerto Ancheta, and an officer who happened on the scene got one of the injured men to the hospital. Then Ancheta ran to the camp to get help, thinking they'd been struck by the enemy. The surgeon and squadron's commander accompanied Ancheta back to the scene. They found one soldier dead and another shot in four places but still alive. Unfortunately, friendly fire incidents were common in the war.

Herb, thinking that snipers had hit the soldiers, wrote, "Three boys were fired upon a few days ago while venturing into the sniper vicinity looking for war souvenirs. One was killed, the other two, seriously injured. One of the injured has had two blood transfusions. We were warned not to hunt for souvenirs because of the possibility of getting shot, not only by snipers, but also by marines on patrol in the area, who don't take chances with anyone. Quite a few accidents and deaths have occurred when a marine has heard something stirring in the brush and fired at one of our own men."

Saipan
1 October '44

Dearest Ann,
You will have to excuse me for not writing for a while; I've not been in a happy frame of mind. I've let five of your letters accumulate. I hope this isn't too hard for you to understand.

The pictures you sent are good. You look well and healthy but as if you're gaining some weight—what about this? Do you know how I feel about fat people? My opinion is not flattering.

Bob R. is here and came to see me the other day. Our misunderstanding seems to be resolved. He is a gunner in a B-24, a tough position, but he seems to like it. He showed me a picture of Virginia. It wasn't a good picture of her, but he likes it.

The pictures in *Life Magazine* of the Japanese family on the rocks getting ready to drown themselves are sad. Can you imagine how they must have felt and the memories the children are going to grow up with? This is one of many cases here in which civilians believed what the Japs told them about our intentions to torture them.

Monday, October 2, '44

The anniversary letter came today. It was sweet of you to remember. The reason you're my wife is simple: You're attractive, with pretty hair, a nice figure, good spirit, and you can cook (I hope). But, I really don't know much about you, and you know little about me. Some people say I am hard to understand. I hope you won't think so. I'm sure of one thing. I love you and the day we will be together cannot come too soon.

A hurricane has been reported coming in our direction. We are getting the start of it now, and if the wind gets much stronger, I am afraid we are going to lose our tent. The last news we heard, the wind was blowing 65 miles per hour 10 miles off the island south of us. I feel like taking a walk and feeling the rain and wind against my face. I would if I were someplace besides Saipan.

I have just read *The Robe*, by L.C. Douglas. Have you read it? He is a fine author, and I enjoyed reading it. It deals with different Bible stories along with a love story.

The mud and rain are blowing strongly, and I'm having a hard time keeping the paper I'm writing on from blowing around so I must end this letter. We shall have to better secure our tent. . . . The rain came.

Your loving husband,
Herb

251

Somewhere in the Marianas
7 October 1944

Dearest Ann,

I don't have anything important to write but having received three letters from you dated September 11, 17, and 20, you might like to know they made it in exceptionally good time.

They have started to give us vitamins with all meals, which is a good thing because we don't get nutrients from the food here. Some of the boys say if it wasn't for bread and peanut butter, which we have at every meal, along with the other food, they would starve. One of them exists solely on this, and I can't blame him. I have had to be satisfied with bread, peanut butter, and water.

Concerning the rumor about the rotation policy—if not this time, the next time we move, it will not be to another island. No one has gone home yet everyone expects to. Many boys are going to be disappointed.

The house that you wrote about sounds perfect. By all means, if they want to sell, we want to be the first in line. How about finding out more details? Moving into an old farmhouse and fixing it up can be fun. I think we better stay on the friendly side of Mr. and Mrs. Post. Where is this house? I'm interested.

I wrote Mother and told her to send a fruitcake and a few cans of nuts. If you could bake another fruitcake like you did last year, I would be grateful for it. If it is too late to send it, don't feel bad about it. If you put it in a good strong box, it would reach here okay.

Bob R. must be a busy guy. I expected him to visit a couple of times. As far as I know, he is still here and probably flying over different targets. You really have to take your hat off to him.

My cold is better and I feel good again. Mentally, well, this remains to be seen.

The shows we have seen are *Sweet and Low-Down* (poor), with Benny Goodman and Linda Darnell, and *The Man from Down Under*, with Charles Laughton, which wasn't bad. We have also seen *The Heavenly Body*, starring Hedy Lamarr and William Powell. It was light and silly but better than sitting in the tent. *In Society* is scheduled for tomorrow night, but I shall take your advice and not see it. I never did like Abbot and Costello, anyway.

Well, Ann, I am tired and am going to bed and dream of you.

Your loving husband,
Herb

Somewhere in the Marianas
13 October 1944

Dearest Ann,

I'm glad to know you are feeling okay and your throat is returning to normal. We had a little time off today, and we played volleyball. I feel more relaxed than usual.

To be with you on those autumn days would be a gift from out of this world. Time seems to be going by so fast, and all seems wasted.

Nothing new has developed about the rotation. A few marines are leaving soon, but they are under a different category that only pertains to marines and navy personnel. This is one advantage the navy has over the army. They give the men a break before it's too late.

The office that I am working in has gotten a shortwave radio set, and we have been picking up signals from many different places, including Australia, Japan, the Philippines, and San Francisco. Right now, I'm listening to a Vienna waltz coming from Australia, and it sounds very nice. If only I could be anyplace but here. [Several sentences cut by censor.]

Work has been rather slow the last couple of weeks. We are getting ready to move to a new camp site, which means plenty of work in the next few days. They say it isn't as hot or muddy and has fewer mosquitoes. This could be true because it is on a mountainside.

About 2 miles from our new area is a restricted area,

which you can enter on your own. This area has many caves in which snipers are still hiding. The latest reports say we are capturing as many as 100 to 150 [cut by censor] daily. You probably have noticed we are not permitted to use the name of the island anymore. We do not know why.

I'm making you another necklace from a different type of shell. Hoping there is a letter on its way. I remain

Your loving husband,
Herb

Somewhere in the Marianas
17 October 1944

Darling,

That I keep receiving your mail in such good time means that conditions in general are getting better. Your letter of September 29 came on October 15. I have been busy answering the last few letters.

We are preparing for the move to the new area, or I would have answered sooner. I am glad you like the snapshot. I was fortunate to get a picture taken. Film is impossible to get here. The guy who took the photo used his last roll, which he brought from Hawaii. Pictures are allowed to be taken providing there is no military information shown.

The rotation plan is taking effect. Some boys who had five years in Hawaii have left there. At least someone is going home. I hope my time won't be too long and am willing to wait if I'm sure to go. It would be grand if I could make it by Christmas.

I am sending you some copies of the 7th Army Air Force Magazine, called *Brief*. Some issues have good information in them. After you read them, do with them whatever you want.

Please save the two sketches in ink that I sent. They are typical tropical scenes. Someday, we can frame and hang them in our house. I could have done better if I'd had the proper supplies to work with.

The censor cut up the letter you got before this one in a couple of places. He called me in and told me I must bear in

254

mind the morale of the civilians back home and not say anything that may lower it. I really don't think it would have affected civilian morale. . . .

Your loving husband,
Herb

Somewhere in the Marianas
20 October 1944

Dearest Ann,

I got your letter of October 1 yesterday. I have just finished eating chow (God knows what it was—some kind of salmon cakes, which were almost impossible to cut with your knife, let alone chew). After one taste of these and a swallow of something that they call coffee, I was ready to leave. I ate a piece of bread with jam and once in a while sipped the so-called coffee.

Will you please send me some olives, sweet pickles, a jar of cheese, and crackers—or anything that you think may be a delicacy? If they tell you at the post office it's too late for Christmas, tell them it's a necessity. All kidding aside, I would appreciate it if you send me those things.

I went to see Betty Hutton and her troupe of entertainers last night, and she really put on a good show. A juggler and guitar and accordion players and an attractive girl acrobatic dancer came along. She sang songs that no one else could have sung any better than she. She acts just as crazy in person as in the movies. She is a cute (chic) girl, and I give her a lot of credit for coming here and performing four times a day for five days. Last night was her last performance, and toward the end of the act, her voice was beginning to get hoarse and the strain starting to show.

I'm glad you got yourself a new suit and look forward to seeing you in it one of these days. . . .

Loving your always,
Herb

Two days after Herb wrote the preceding letter, three men from his squadron sweated in the steamy air to clear unexploded enemy shells and booby traps from the area around the camp when they discovered a Japanese soldier. Shouting and gesturing, one of the men conveyed to him that he was captive. One soldier started to grab a canvas bag next to the captive, while another aimed a pistol at him. When the Japanese soldier removed a bayonet from his belt, the third soldier wrested it from him and threw him to the ground. They struggled until the other two joined in to secure the prisoner. They took him to the orderly room, while other soldiers looked on, muttering amid the commotion. A soldier who spoke some Japanese questioned the captive, but he refused to answer any questions and was sent to Army Garrison Forces for interrogation by that headquarters' intelligence officers.

Somewhere in the Marianas
23 October 1944

Dear Ann,

I received your letters dated October 6 and 20. I'd better answer these before any others come. I hope the package you sent me gets through all right. I have learned that there is a fine of $100 for sending such things in the mail. If I'd known this, I would not have asked for it. I appreciate your efforts and know you probably had a hard time getting it.

Bob R. was here to see me yesterday. He asked me a lot of questions, such as if he should start getting more personal with Virginia, telling her he loves her. He doesn't show much sense. He told me that he was in the hospital having a kidney stone removed, which he got from drinking the water here. He mentioned that he wrote Virginia telling her that you would probably see me in about two or three weeks. This peeved me and I told him he should not have said anything like that. He knows less about reassignments than I. Some guys are getting ready to be reassigned and waiting for their orders. I hope all this optimism is not in vain.

They made me a sergeant. They don't know what they are doing.

The movie last night was *Stand by for Action*, with Robert Taylor and Charles Laughton. It was an odd picture with too much bull____ and glory. . . .

Your loving husband,
Herb

Somewhere in the Marianas
28 October 1944

Dearest Ann,

Your letters dated October 8, 9, and 10 came yesterday. I am glad you have the time to write me, but if it means neglecting your work, you don't have to.

I don't know if Bob will stay here; so far, his stay looks as permanent as mine. The last time he came to see me, I gave him a few shells for making Virginia another necklace. He plans to send it as a Christmas gift.

Don't feel sad about anyone here. Just feel fortunate it isn't you. Telling you what we have to bear is an escape. And I want to end the notion that we are having a picnic. If I had to live these four years of my life over, I would rather die, and I believe this sincerely.

The movie last night was *Government Girl* with Olivia DeHaviland. Tonight's is *Suspicious*, starring Joan Fontaine and Cary Grant. *Government Girl* was too patriotic and flag waving for my taste. It is time for me to leave to get a seat so I can see the show well. I shall continue after the show.

After the show: First, I was misinformed. It wasn't *Suspicious* but *Above Suspicion*, with Joan Crawford and Fred MacMurry. Once in a while these shows about Nazis and the Gestapo are all right. This was better than the rest of them, maybe because the actors were better than the usual ones who play in these movies.

I think the rainy season is about over. It hasn't rained for five days, and everything is getting dirty and dusty. We are working by a road used constantly by trucks, tanks, tractors, and jeeps. Our tents are on the other side of the same road, so there is no escape. At least the mud from the rain was more welcome than the dust.

I did some wash today, which has been accumulating in the tent for about a week. It made me sort of tired so until the next letter, sweetheart, I love you.

Your loving husband,
Herb

Less than a week after Herb wrote the preceding letter, the air raid alarm sounded, rousing him and his buddies from bed at 1 a.m. Under a full moon, they scurried for their clothes and headed for their foxholes, cursing. Planes roared overhead and ack-ack lit up the sky. "Boom!" cracked the air not far from them, loud and clear, an enemy plane being shot down. The next morning, the soldiers learned that the enemy, dubbed "Bed check Charlie," had dropped no bombs, apparently confused and under fire from our antiaircraft. Two additional enemy planes had been downed. "Our old camp area," wrote Herb, "was strafed—it's right next to the airfield, the perfect target for the Japs. Luckily, we moved out when we did or we would have some casualties today. It was the longest and most exciting raid I ever went through."

Somewhere in the Marianas
3 November 1944

Dear Ann,

This is the first chance I've had to write a letter after moving into the new area.

It has been hard moving all of our squadron's equipment, but everyone seems satisfied with this new camp site. It is a lot cooler, the mosquitoes are fewer, and there is less dust than in our last camp. Our tents are brand new and have wooden floors built a foot from the ground, and, last but not least, screening on all sides of the tent. It's going to be a nice place to live compared with our old area. It may just be the best area on the

258

island.

I received the first Christmas package today from Mother containing a can of tuna, jar of marshmallows, fruit cocktail, and the like. Only one thing went wrong. The box also had a bottle of citronella that leaked onto the crackers. Since I wouldn't like the mixture of crackers, tuna, and citronella, I threw the crackers away. I already enjoyed the tuna. And as for the citronella, I have no use for it as we have plenty. Of course, Mother, not knowing this, meant well. . . .

> Your loving husband,
> Herb

One week after the bomb attack, the air raid siren blared at 1 a.m. Herb and his buddies threw their clothes on, grabbed their helmets, and headed for their foxholes. Japanese planes zoomed above, and ack-ack rattled their ears. Once the all-clear sounded, the soldiers climbed out of their foxholes and headed back to their tents, crawling under mosquito netting, fearing the enemy would return. They placed their shoes, helmets, and clothing nearby where they could get them quickly. Again the air raid siren sounded, at about 4:30 a.m., and the soldiers jumped up and scrambled for shelter. "I hope I never see another night like last night," Herb wrote. "I've had a headache all day thanks to the damn Japs. But we expect them again tonight, so I want to get to bed early. . . . When they come over just enough to cause an alarm, making us get out of bed—this really makes a fellow sore. But we have learned it is safer to get out of bed on such occasions."

13 November 1944

Dearest Ann,

As you mentioned, the landing of allied troops on the Philippines is good news for you people to read and talk about. For us and others in the war, we see the war less clearly, talk of it less often, and think of it far less. We are living war, so why talk about it?

A few of the boys have received packages, and I am expecting mine almost any day. I hope you made the fruitcake you sent and that it is as good as the last one.

Russ Stinson, who is in the same tent as I, received a package from his girlfriend consisting of tuna and a jar of peanut butter. We managed to chisel some K ration crackers from the mess hall, which taste like dog biscuits and are just as hard. But with tuna and peanut butter, they may not taste so bad. We plan to have a snack after I finish this letter.

We have read about this point system that the newspaper publicized. So far, it's gone no further than the newspaper. No one believes in the deal. Please don't believe all you hear and read in the newspaper. If you remember, all this happened just before the election. Another thing—the War Department ordered sending men home who have been overseas a certain length of time. Rarely, we do hear of a guy with seven or eight years over here at last getting to go home, after he blows his top.

I have claimed a discontinuance to cancel the allotment you are getting. As soon as they fill the thing out, I shall go in and sign it. I will have to pay back the extra money that you have been getting. It's best to deal with this because, sooner or later, they will see their mistake.

Bob R. came to see me yesterday. He had a hard time finding this area. He sounded disappointed by Ginny's letters. I gather they were not mushy enough. I asked him what he expects from her. I believe he thinks she should tell him how much she loves him. I told him this is silly.

Give my regards to the family and loving you always. I remain,

Your loving husband,
Herb

The point system Herb so disparaged, known as the Adjusted Service Rating, sorted servicemen according to their length of time in uniform or overseas. Men received points according to the number of months in service since September 16, 1940, and whether they had a Purple Heart, decoration, or children under 18.

A soldier needed 85 points for a discharge. After those who had at least 85 points were discharged, the army slowly lowered the total number of points needed for discharge. This resulted in men who had served overseas being discharged first, those who had seen combat receiving priority.

In November and December 1944, Saipan- and Guam-based Liberators from Herb's command continued striking targets in the Bonin, Caroline, and Volcano Islands. They also hit Iwo Jima almost daily from December 1 until its invasion on February 16, 1945.

By November, rainy seasons, bombing raids, and disgusting food began to fade in significance for Herb like yesterday's mail call. The raid that gave him such a headache was his last. In mid-November 1944, after nine months on combat duty, Herb said sayonara to Saipan and left for home on furlough—in time for Christmas. Courtesy of the AAF, however, Herb still had one more beach in his future.

CHAPTER 7
COMING HOME

And the end of all our exploring
Will be to arrive where we started
And know the place for the first time.
—T.S.Eliot

After spending Christmas and two weeks at home, Herb looked forward to even more rest: a 30-day R&R. He and Ann entrained in Philadelphia on a Sunday afternoon in January 1945, arriving on Tuesday for R&R at the Patrician Hotel in Miami Beach. They were under "orders" to have fun: lounging on the beach, shopping, deep sea fishing and going to dog and horse races at Hialeah Park. Sopping up sun, sand, and neon-lit streetscapes soothed the soul, the AAF figured.

After his R&R, Herb reported for work at the Pancoast Hotel, while Ann returned to Pennsylvania. Herb's new unit, the one from which he mustered out, was HQ 1075 Base Unit P, Section A. He worked at the AAF Redistribution Center #2, which spanned Collins Avenue from 24th to 42nd Streets. At the center, the AAF calculated the pay of returning combat veterans, processed their records, and discharged or reassigned them.

"The best hotel room is none too good for the American soldier," announced Secretary of War Robert P. Patterson in 1942. From then until 1945, nearly 500,000 servicemen, including movie star Clark Gable, descended on Miami Beach, leasing 300 hotels and other buildings for housing and training headquarters under the AAF Technical Training Command. By the time the war ended, one-fourth of all AAF officers and one-fifth of the Air Corps' enlisted men had been trained in "the most beautiful boot camp in America"—Miami Beach.

January 29, 1945

Dearest Ann,

    After leaving you, I got back in time to have some breakfast at the mess hall consisting of two soft boiled eggs, some toast, and milk. After that, I returned to our hotel (good old Patrician) and made your bed. While we were at the station, someone stuck a note under the door, telling me to report to the C.O. [commanding officer] at once in the Coral Reef to sign the alert notice.*

    I am writing this letter in the writing room in the Coral Reef. Do you remember it? After signing the alert notice, I went back and brought my bags down to the lobby, turned in the key at the desk, and after an officer inspected the room, I got my quarter refunded. He told me to wait in the Coral Reef lobby for a truck that would pick me up at about 9 o'clock. At 9:30, a truck came and took me and some others to the brown building next to the Pancoast Hotel. Do you remember that building? After once again being interviewed and classified, I was assigned to the personnel section of the unit I am now in. I spent the morning answering questions to determine what I can and cannot do. I am supposed to report to work tomorrow morning at 8 o'clock and work until 5. I can't yet tell you anything definite about my likes and dislikes of this new setup.

    My sleeping quarters are at the used-to-be Roberts Beach Hotel.§ It is directly across the street from the Versailles. The Cornell Hotel is on the other end of the same block, and the Indian Creek Apartment House is directly across on the other corner.

    I spent this afternoon unpacking my barracks bag and getting everything ready, such as getting a sheet from the supply sergeant and one blanket and a pillow case. I finished at about 3:30 and had some time on my hands, so I went up to the P.X. to buy another towel and a wash cloth, but they did not

---

*Signing an alert notice signified that you knew not to go anywhere that you could not be reached.
§The Roberts Beach Hotel was renamed the Atlantic Beach Hotel in 1944.

have either, so I still don't have an extra towel, which I will have to buy sooner or later.

I ate dinner [a noon meal] at the Pancoast Hotel, which is where we are supposed to eat. I wasn't hungry, and the place seemed strange to me, although the food was excellent and better than at our mess hall. I can't seem to stay away from the Patrician and the Coral Reef. It brings back memories of our being there together. I ate my supper at the mess we used to eat at, and think I will continue to eat there until someone tells me I am not supposed to.

I miss you, Ann, very, very much, even more than I did last time when I went back from furlough. Probably this is because I spent more time with you this time, and I think you are going to find the same thing. I wish you hadn't cried this morning. I wouldn't have felt so bad when I left you. I have to admit I am already lonely but hope to snap out of it in the near future. When I used the elevator, the girl asked me where you were, and it made me feel bad to tell her, but I didn't show my feelings.

After eating, I came back to the Coral Reef and sat on the porch. I have not met any of the three other fellows who are sleeping in the same room as me. We are sleeping in double bunks, one on top of the other. I am on the top but would rather be on the bottom. The room is larger than ours at the Patrician, and it is on the first floor in the back where you can't see anything. The bathroom is the same size as ours was, and the living quarters are okay.

I am writing this after coming home from the show at the 41st Street Theater.[*] I saw that professor who spells words backwards. Buddie Walker was the M.C. as well as your friend, the heavy-set one, remember? They also had Willie Howard, Hilde Simmons, who is the queen of boogie-woogie (your favorite type), Sara Basquett, a dancer, Lynn Pareé, and singer Nee Wang.

---

[*]The 41st Street Theater was owned by Lou Walters, father of future TV news star, Barbara Walters.

Ann, it is 11:15, and I am tired, so I'll close now, missing you too much. I shall write tomorrow night. I stopped in at the drug store and bought you the pen you wanted. They are sending it to you.

> Your loving husband,
> Herb

All of the hotels noted by Herb in the preceding letter sat on a narrow isthmus of land between the Atlantic Ocean and Indian Creek, from 23rd to 44th Streets in Miami Beach. The AAF had taken over nearly all of the hotels in this area.*

Pancoast Hotel, Miami Beach, Florida   70

A post card of the Pancoast from Herb's collection. It was one of many hotels in Miami Beach taken over by the AAF during the war.

30 January 1945

Dearest Ann,
Today was my longest day since I've been here. I just

---

* The entire area is now part of the Collins Waterfront Historic District of Miami Beach.

finished showering and had a cup of coffee in the P.X. I worked till 8 o'clock and it is 9 o'clock now. The work I am doing may become interesting when I'm familiar with it. Today, I was working on the Form # 20's, the long yellow card that you were looking at. The fellows I work with seem okay; three of them have been overseas, and the other three may be sent over sooner or later.

I guess I have what you call writer's cramp. My fingers feel that way anyhow. I did about 400 Form 20's, making an entry on every one, so you can imagine the cramping. I shall put off until tomorrow night writing a letter to my folks.

I walked to the drug store after my shower this evening to see if the pictures were ready. They will be ready tomorrow night. I found a compact that you wanted in one of the stores in that district. It cost $2—a little more expensive there. I bought it, anyway, because I don't know when I will get into Miami.

I hope you got home okay and enjoyed the ride. Did you have to change trains? How is your tan holding out? Today was warmer than yesterday, and I was wishing as I worked that I could be on the beach at the Patrician playing volleyball or throwing the medicine ball to you know who. Will you keep the promise you made about losing those five pounds?

I ate breakfast at our mess hall where we used to eat. I ate dinner and supper at the Pancoast, where I am supposed to eat. I think the food is better there, but I do miss the ice cream and cake at the old place. While eating dinner, I noticed a few prisoners of war doing K.P. in the kitchen. I asked someone if they were German prisoners, and he told me they have a few here. They are wearing a gray work uniform with "PW" on the back of them, meaning prisoner of war. They look young and a little stubborn and bull headed. I guess this is my imagination.

I stopped at the tennis courts during my noon hour; they are right across the street from where I work. No one was playing or around to get any information from about playing. I would rather play here than where we played as it is closer to where I live.

Well, Ann, I hope it won't be too long before I can see

267

you again. I feel a little better today, but I think it was wise and the best thing for you to return home.

Remember me to your folks, and I love you.

Your loving husband,
Herb

Florida held 10,000 of the 378,000 prisoners of war (POWs) who fought for Hitler and ended up in almost every state. Most POWs were ethnically German, but many came from such countries as Austria, Czechoslovakia, Yugoslavia, and Poland. The POWs, such as those Herb saw, worked in Miami Beach hotels and in timbering and agriculture and on military bases. On the military bases, POWs gardened and painted and did mechanical, electrical, and hospital work and KP. Though Florida had 27 POW camps, the prisoners Herb saw were most likely from Kendall, which housed 264 POWs on the outskirts of Miami.

1 February '45

Dearest Ann,

I presume you have fully recuperated from your time here. It's amazing how much fun you can have here. But it's not all fun after you return to the Army routine. So far, it isn't half bad. Our working hours are long, but after we get caught up with work, we won't have to work at night.

If you want me to send my letters to you by Air Mail, I will, but am sending this one with 3 cents because of the pictures, which I think came out well. Notice how your tan shows up. It really looks good, and I wish you could be here in the flesh instead of a picture. I guess these pictures will bring back memories for you as they have for me. The light I saw in Room 600 this evening made me a little lonely. I find myself looking up to the window unconsciously, then wishing I were on my way up.

It is so chilly here tonight, I have my sweat shirt on underneath my shirt and am still a little cold. How do you stand the cold weather up there?

Bob Hope performed at the Air Field here. I have not had a chance to see him. If he comes out to this district, I may go. Edward G. Robinson is his guest.

Some of the soldiers are running around here at nights. By that, I mean going out and having a wild time. It's not a good idea to make a habit of this. Some of them have been deprived of this sort of life for so long, they are taking advantage of it. They have all the opportunities they are seeking, but they will be losers and sorry later. Just having a nice place to sleep and plenty of good food is all I care about, plus being in the states.

Writing letters to you again makes me wonder how long it will be until I see you. We are spending more of our time writing letters when we should be together. I hate this more than anyone, but believe me, Ann, I have been honest and loyal to you since we have been married and shall continue to be. I hope you have no worries of this sort and believe me when I write this. You may start to think about this after being here and seeing the opportunities a soldier has, but remember, I'm no ordinary soldier. Some think it natural to run around, but I disagree if you are married. I love you and I guess I always will. I hope you feel as I do. I'm just waiting for the day when we have our own place in the country. The little time that we had together makes me certain of this and of my love for you.

It's almost 11 o'clock, Ann, and I am tired. I shall write again on Saturday. . . .

Your loving husband,
Herb

February 2, 1945

My dearest Herb,

I got home and I'm back at work, right in the old routine. The train trip wasn't bad and would have almost been as tiresome as the trip down except that the girl sharing the seat with me turned out to be a good companion. Her name is Olive White from Akron, Ohio. Her husband is an aerial photographer and was overseas only six months. He's stationed at Boca Grande, and they have a 2-year-old girl. She liked to talk as much as I do, so we enjoyed each other's company. The train was due in Philadelphia at 8:30 Tuesday morning, and we didn't get there until 4:15 that afternoon—eight hours late. The "Champion" didn't have a diesel engine and went only 30 miles per hour. It took 37 hours to come back and I think it took 38 to go down—not much difference. I finally got home at 7 o'clock.

I spent Wednesday at home resting, and yesterday, I went to work. Of course, Mother and Dad were tickled to see me again. Everybody at the bank seemed glad to see me. But almost all of them and especially the ones who had visited Florida, said, "What did you come home for? When are you going back? Why did you leave?" . . . . and a lot of, "We didn't expect to see you back here" or "We didn't think you'd be back so soon."

I've gotten nothing but compliments on my tan. I've been touched by everyone's kindness to me and by their candid welcome. It's good to be back even though I'd give a lot to be there in that wonderful sunshine with you. Even though I'm here in body, my heart is there.

You say it would have been better if I had not cried when I left. It would not have been so hard on you. You know, I didn't feel so good myself. You'll never know how I hated to get on that train or how I hated to leave you. It would have taken only the least bit of coaxing to get me to step right off before it pulled out. I didn't want to cry; I fought not to, but I couldn't help myself. I'm here at home with those who love me, but don't think I'm not lonely—I am lonely. I'll always be lonely when I'm not with you.

I phoned your mother when I got back and told her you were staying there. She wasn't too surprised. She asked me, too, why I didn't stay.

You must have just about spent that $20 on the pen and compact. They haven't gotten here yet, but I expect they'll come next week. I haven't found the pen I lost so I do need a fountain pen. I'll be happy with the one you're sending and the compact, also.

Well, I think I've written enough for one night. I miss you, Herb, terribly, and just wish I were there with you as you say—throwing the medicine ball (I even miss that thing) and playing volleyball. Until the next time, all my love.

Your loving wife,
Ann

The Coral Reef Hotel, Miami Beach, in the 1940s. The Patrician is next door, on the left.

Saturday night
3 February 1945

Dearest Ann,

Tomorrow I have off, and you can guess where I shall spend the day, either playing tennis if I find a partner or going to the beach at the Patrician.

Miami is having what they call a brownout, which means the street and hotel lights are extinguished at night, and it's not lovely the way it used to be. The streets appear gloomy, and the last few nights I had to wear my O.D.s [olive drabs] because it was cold. We are probably getting some of that cold weather

271

from the North. Damn Yankees, why don't y'all keep that cool weather up there?

I am glad to have tomorrow off as I have been working long hours. The time seems to drag since you left, but not half as much as when I was overseas. I will be willing to stand much more crap since I am in the states, and from what I have seen so far, there is going to be plenty.

I think I know now the function of the organization I am assigned to. The first couple of days were a whirlwind and I didn't know what people were trying to do. It is this: Assigning returning convalescents to organizations in the states. I am working in classifications, where we keep records of officers and enlisted men assigned to the command that I am in. There is probably more to it than I have mentioned, but this is all I have learned so far. I know that fellows stationed in the states the whole time don't like returnees working here and knowing more than they do about such work.

It's wonderful to write freely, knowing that nothing will be cut out of your letters and saying the things you want to.

My eyes have been burning a lot, and I have decided to go see about this on Monday morning. Maybe the next time you see me, I, too, will be wearing glasses. My eyes have been redder than usual today. I look as if I was out on an all-night drunk last night.

Your loving husband,
Herb

February 3, 1945

My dearest Herb,

So we're back to writing letters again. At least when we were together, I had no letters to write. But since we can't be together, letters are all we have.

Ever since I've reached home, so much has been going on that I haven't really had time to feel lonely, but as things are quieting down and the newness of being home wears off, I can see I'm going to miss you terribly.

Virginia stopped by after work on Wednesday and stayed

for the evening. She let me read the last letter she'd gotten from Bob, and things seem to be going along for them. Bob writes a good letter. He does include some affection, but now that they've been writing for this length of time and seem mutually interested, it does not seem improper or bold that he should write affectionately to her. He doesn't overdo it as he did at first—just a phrase here and there throughout the letter. He said to tell you they have moved to a new site and it's much nicer than the previous one. He's close to a beach—a much nicer one than Waikiki—and can take a dip before breakfast and lunch. He has about 22 more missions to fly.

Thursday evening, one of the girls from my department at the bank got married. I read their names in the marriage licenses listed in Tuesday's paper when I got home, and I was floored. She wasn't even engaged to the guy and she married him just like that. The wedding was nice, but of course, didn't compare with ours. They left the next day for Tampa, Florida, where he's stationed. She's gotten a three-month leave of absence. I think he's scheduled to go overseas after that.

That package that arrived here while we were at the Patrician is the briefcase containing your artwork. I opened it and looked through it. It looked good and it must be according to the favorable grades marked on it by the instructor. Is there any chance you could finish the course now after so much time has elapsed since you've worked on it? You seemed to do well with it.

I see I can't write all I had intended so I'll continue in the next letter. . . .

> Your loving wife,
> Ann

> February 4, 1945

Dearest Herb,

I found out that Bea got married while I was in Florida. Sara and Ginny told me about it and said I didn't miss too much. She was married in a street-length dress, had only one attendant and no vocalist, and it wasn't a showy affair. They went to New York on a honeymoon. They got back Friday and tomorrow leave for Maine, where he's stationed. We girls went over this afternoon to see their gifts and say goodbye. They got a lot of lovely gifts. She seems so much in love and he seems to care for her, too, but there's something about him that makes me wonder if it will work out. I surely hope it does because she's a sweet, good-hearted, and good-natured person who deserves the best.

Gee whiz, it's started snowing again—I think it's another blizzard. Oh, well, that means a day or two at home. I sure wish I was down there with you—nice and warm—instead of here.

I started, or rather, tried to start *Storm to the South*, the other book [your sister] Dorothy lent us, but I couldn't seem to get interested. One of the girls at the bank told me she had *Forever Amber*, the new talked-about novel, and I immediately asked for it. I started it yesterday and so far (page 135—of 972) it's good.

I stopped at your mother's yesterday and left the jug of honey (a bit of it seeped out in my suitcase on the way home) and the shell for [your brother] Bud. They both seemed pleased—your mother liked the pig a lot. The dates for your father had come that morning, but he hadn't been home yet to see and taste them. The candy reached the bank on Saturday morning also.

Well, that's really bringing you up to date and seems to be a good signing-off place. . . .

Your loving wife,
Ann

4 February 1945

Dearest Ann,

At last a letter from you—it came this morning. I stopped in to see if I had one on the way to the hospital to see about my eyes. I will not have to wear glasses, but I contracted a fungus in my eyes when overseas, and the Doc has given me some drops to put in them four times a day. They feel fine now, and some of the redness has faded. They should be cured within a week.

I went down to the G.I. main house tonight and saw *Music for Millions*, with Margaret O'Brien, June Allyson, and Marsha Hunt. I am sure you would enjoy this picture. José Iturbi was in it, and the music was the best thing about it.

You probably wonder what I did yesterday when I was off work. I got up at 9 o'clock. I went down to the tennis courts, thinking I'd play some tennis. No one was around, except for one guy who told me that I would not be allowed to play until 10 o'clock. I felt pretty bad about this, but I didn't want to sit around until that time, and there was no one to play with. So I went up to the beach and played shuffleboard with myself and knocked myself out, so to speak. Only one couple was on the beach then, and they asked me to take a picture of them, so I did. At 11:15, I went back to my room, took a shower, and went to chow. They had turkey—the same thing every Sunday. I was hungry since I did not eat breakfast. By the way, how are you making out on that eating business?

After chow, I took *The Valley of Decision* and a beach chair and got myself comfortable. Do you remember the couple who were, as you said, good dancers—that last night at the dance? They were on the beach yesterday, and she asked me where you were and when you left. I found out they are from Pittsburgh, and he has been in the hospital at the Pancoast doctoring for malaria. She received a notice to leave by tomorrow and seemed sad about it.

Ann, please stop misinterpreting what I say. First, I did not say, "I do not want you to live where I am stationed." I want to live with you more than anyone in the world. Please believe this. This is not my idea of living, and I thought I made myself clear on this. I'm sure you would get tired of living in one room with a bed and a chair for five or six months, sitting around, eating your meals at a corner drug store, or maybe working in some strange place. Our time together here was more or less a vacation, all play, which could not last forever. If I were a M/Sgt. or a Lieutenant, we could afford to pay $60

275

or $75 a week for an apartment, but you are married to a mere Sgt. Are you sorry?

This is a lonely place without a wife or friend. When I see people walking around, it makes me feel sad. It's hard going into a new organization to work, not knowing anyone. After being overseas with the same guys for so long, it's hard to forget them. The friendships really stick with you. I think I should be alone for a while, anyway. I can judge better and find out more about what's going on here.

This will be too heavy to send by Air Mail, thus the 3-cent stamp. . . .

Your loving husband,
Herb

February 6, 1945

My dearest,

I sure was glad to see your letter of February 1 on the table when I got home today. I felt awfully low yesterday when I came home looking for that familiar envelope and not finding one. It seems I'm lonely without you all the time except when I see a letter from you waiting for me and the few hours after reading it until I go to bed. And then I'm lonely again. So while I'm writing this, I don't feel quite as alone as I did all day. I thought when I got back to work and began to work hard, I would lose myself in it and wouldn't have time to think and would recover from missing you. But, no luck. I go about my work mechanically, giving it the least attention necessary to get it done. Constantly my thoughts return to Florida and you. The only cure for my loneliness is to have you home, for keeps.

Half the people I bump into only encourage my longing. It seems everyone's been to Florida at one time or another, and they're willing to sit right down and tell you all about it. Today, D. Rae Boyd (the undertaker here in Norristown), whom I know from the bank, came in to see my boss. D. Rae noticed my tan and asked where I had been. He promptly sat down and told me all the merits and wonders of Miami Beach. It seems he took ill several years ago and went there for his health. He stayed at the Ocean Grande and later bought a home there—a bungalow out at 95th Street, somewhere near the new golf course. Right away I asked if it was rented and was disappointed when he said, "Yes, it's rented." He says if he ever retires, he's going to live there. After hearing all that, intermittent daydreaming ruined the rest of this afternoon.

So I sure welcomed your letter when I got home. And the compact came today also, so the two of them together helped lift my deflated spirits.

You say you presumed I had fully recuperated from the life of leisure I led down there. No, I have to admit those six weeks I didn't work, and more so the three weeks in Miami Beach, just about ruined me as far as work is concerned. I see I take to that sort of life easily.

This seems like a good signing-off place. Most likely, you'll hear from me again the day after you receive this. Until then, good night, sweet dreams.

Yours,
Ann

February 7, 1945

Dearest Herb,

What do you think of the pen? It writes smoothly, and I've already written one letter tonight—to Sis—and no ink stains on my fingers yet. It's wonderful! And I still think it's extremely good looking. I'm so proud of it. It was sweet of you to get it for me. You do buy me the nicest things, darling. You're sweet and I love you dearly.

Before I forget again, I've been meaning to tell you this in every letter, but it slips my mind. No $80 check came for December. The $50 check for January (dated February 1) came on Friday, and I put it in the bank. I guess the $80 Class E allotment has been stopped. I also cashed the $80 check I brought home with me and have the money, thinking that there may have been a stop-payment issued for that check and the money may be requested returned directly through the bank. If this doesn't happen, in about a month, I'm going to bank the money. The present bank balance is $1,837, which is better than we had thought.

So you're having a little chilly weather! Listen to a weather-beaten Northerner for one moment. Yesterday and today when I left the house for work at 7:45, the thermometer shivered on the porch, registering a very cold 0°. The bank and the house at night are probably colder inside most of the time than the temperature in Miami Beach outside! So, please don't complain of chilly temperatures to us Yankees, especially don't attempt it with that *?!!XQD@X rebel accent. I was so tired of hearing it, and it is a relief to be back where I hear only "damn Yankee" talk.

The brownout seems to be universal—we have it even in Norristown.

I wondered whether you would be working with fellows who hadn't been overseas. I can see how friction might occur between you returnees and them. They're probably scared to death they'll be replaced by returnees and sent overseas,

Darling, it is a relief that your letters don't have to be censored any longer, and I don't have to ask questions in an around-the-bush fashion. Please feel free to say anything and everything you wish to me. It's a relief, too, to get your letters in four days, and I know it's a relief to you to get mine in only a few days instead of weeks. . . .

Your devoted wife,
Ann

7 February 1945

Dearest Ann,

Your letter dated February 3 came today—four days for Air Mail. I guess my letters would take just as long with 3-cent stamps as they would to send them free. I will send them Air Mail if you want.

A small handful, about 20, fellows from this station left today for overseas. I don't think they have sent any who have been here for six months yet. But I heard a rumor recently that they are going to start sending them. I think if the war in Europe ends soon, there will be some great changes made.

If my time comes, which I hope it never does, I am undecided about what to do. If I have to go over again, it will be hard to bear, but I will be willing provided everyone here gets a crack at it. And believe me, certain guys here are doing everything in their power to stay in the states. To be in the same class as some of these guys makes me feel ashamed. None of them is worth fighting for. It is hard to take seeing how some of these guys live and act when better men are dying and suffering for them. I talked to a sergeant stationed here for five months, and he told me he would be glad to go over again and that this bad element has been here ever since he has been back from Hawaii.

They have also begun to transfer men to the infantry from the Air Corps for overseas duty, so now anyone going overseas does so as an infantryman. This is bad and will not be for me, I hope. This is why my friend, [Andy] Gregos has been disqualified from overseas duty. If you have flat feet, the infantry is no place for you. As I said before, I think I have flat feet, which in my opinion is a poor excuse to be disqualified from going overseas.

They had a show at the Pancoast, *Laura*, with Gene Tierney. It was someplace to go to pass the time. I shall stop for now; I love you more than ever.

Your loving husband,
Herb

February 8, 1945

My darling,

Yesterday, I asked T, my boss, to figure out my income tax—he likes to do taxes and figuring of any kind—so I always ask him to do my return.*

Sometime—maybe on your lunch hour—will you go to wherever you collected your pay and try to find out your total

---

*The name of Ann's boss was Trevisa T. Wolfenden, but everyone called him "T."

279

pay from the Army for 1944? That is, your total pay before the allotment was taken out—your gross pay for the year. Also, sign the return that I enclosed at the bottom. If you can't find out what your gross income was from the Army office there, send the return back to me signed and I will fix it up here somehow. T says you should forget about filing a return for 1943, 1942, or 1941 since your pay for those years did not exceed the $1,500 exemption. Servicemen pay tax only on income in excess of $1,500.

We had an adventure yesterday. We heard there were two old bachelors who do caning and basketwork living in the woods somewhere. Our rockers need new seats, and people who do this sort of work are few and far between. So we started out in the direction of where we thought they might be, and after asking only once we located their humble abode and I do mean humble. It turned out to be a house that is standing up only by the grace of God. Half the windows are out and the porch is rotted away. The old men were away at some sale selling their lowly wares (baskets) so we didn't see them. But we talked to a neighbor and he told us they live there almost like hermits except for the trip to the sale once a week. They nearly never cook their food or wash themselves or their clothes. I don't even think they have any furniture or heat of any kind. I don't see how they eke out an existence but they do somehow. How strangely some people in this world live.

Well, I have no more news to write, so I'll sign off. Hope to see you soon.

All my love,
Ann

9 February '45

Dearest Ann,

Your Air Mail letter got here (yesterday) one day before the one I am answering now. I don't see any need for us to use Air Mail and think free letters are just as fast as those with 3-cent stamps, but you are not authorized this privilege, are you?

I just came from the mess hall, where hamburgers and

milk were being served. They serve this every night, and that's why all the people were there that night we walked by.

I am glad Bea has gotten married. She is the girl who works in the beauty parlor, isn't she? I hope you didn't mind missing her wedding too much.

Earlier this evening I went to the show and saw *Tomorrow, the World*, a propaganda picture, but it had fine acting. You know the story: an American family adopts a nephew from Germany who as a child had been taught Nazism.

I was on C.Q. [charge of quarters] at the hotel where I am sleeping and had to stay up all night and keep an eye on the door and check people in and out.* I had time to write Bob R. a letter. Also, I read some more of *The Valley of Decision*. By the way, Greer Garson is in the movie version of this book.

I was up mostly all last night answering the phone, putting the lights out, and giving out linen for six newcomers, who came in at the ungodly hour of 2:30. After this, someone was expecting a call from Texas, which came about 3 o'clock, and at 5 o'clock someone wanted to be awakened so he could get to work. So you see how little sleep I got and, having to work after all this, I am tuckered out.

It got pretty cold last night and I needed two army blankets and one cotton one to keep me warm. Today, old man Sun came out and warmed everything once again. How is the snow up there? I wish I could see it. . . .

> Your loving husband,
> Herb

> February 9, 1945

Dearest Herb,

I got your letter of Monday, February 5, today. I guess my letters have begun to arrive regularly by this time.

From the sound of your letter, your day off wasn't bad.

---

*To be on C.Q., or in charge of quarters, meant to be in charge of the organization's headquarters, generally at night or when everyone else was away training.

Yes, I remember the couple you spoke of. What do you find to do on a Sunday night? Tell me of the things you do and places you go. Since I know some of the places, I try to imagine you here or there each night. What about the fellows you bunk with? Are they okay or don't you bother with them? Are they returnees, also?

How am I making out on that eating business? Well, I weighed 137 when I got home, and I'm still hovering between 137-138 pounds. I'm confident I'll get down to 135, but it's going to take a little time. I honestly am trying to be careful of what and how much I eat. The only trouble is that I get practically no exercise here at home. I think all the exercise I got down there did more to bring my weight down than the amount of food I consumed. And I won't be getting any exercise here until at least April—the weather is too bad.

I can't believe it's Friday already—time passes so quickly sometimes it frightens me. Sometimes I get the strange sensation that the days are spinning past so swiftly I'll go into a trance and suddenly one day wake up and realize my whole life has completely passed and I am old—and I have missed it all because it passed by so swiftly. Isn't that strange! Maybe that is how it really is. Anyhow, that's one thing about that job of mine—as much as I tire of it—it also makes the days pass quickly. The only trouble is that the weekends, which I look for so anxiously, pass just as quickly as the week days.

I'll be signing off here. Until the next one, happy days, Darling, and sweet dreams and remember I'll be loving you always.

Your loving wife,
Ann

February 11, 1945

Dearest Herb,

It's warming up, here; it's been about 45° today. Sure hope this is here to stay. Last week was my first one driving again. For two days I had a constant prayer on my lips that we would reach Norristown safely and get back home alive. I'm

282

not kidding—the roads were so treacherous I wondered whether I would live to see the next day.

We went out looking for some ice skating this afternoon but all the ice has been ruined by the recent heavy snowstorm. So I guess I had all the skating I'll get for this winter the night we went to the park with Jeanne and Archie. We had lots of fun that night, didn't we?

I spent last night with Gisella. Her mother had the most wonderful tasting spaghetti waiting for our lunch yesterday. Gisella told me how to make it, so I'm going to try it myself. We went to a girlfriend's wedding early in the evening. One of the girls from the bank married her fiancé, a Marine, in a beautiful evening wedding. After that, we saw *Tall in the Saddle*—John Wayne and Ella Raines—cowboy stuff, but Gisella and I loved it. John Wayne is terrific for my money. It was the first time I had seen Ella Raines act, and I agree with you that she's a good actress. She played a cowgirl and suited the part perfectly.

I've wanted to reply to one of your letters in particular, but I've put it off until I could devote more time and space to it. I refer to the one where you told me some fellows are having a wild time in view of the many "opportunities" available in Miami Beach. Yes, I realized that when I had been there only a few days. I haven't been concerned about it for I felt no need to be. These kinds of opportunities are everywhere for those who are weak and seek them. But I know you are intelligent and, moreover, you are strong, both physically and mentally. You have a good mind; you say you know what you want and what is worth wanting. All this I am sure of. You say you are no ordinary soldier. This I believe and think, too, that you are unusual and extraordinary and the wild life so attractive to the fellows you speak of would appeal only to those who are common, ordinary, in fact, low.

You know, being lonely isn't new to me. For four years, all my girlfriends had all the dates they wanted—dancing dates, dinner dates, parties, and all sorts of entertainment. The fun I had was listening to them tell me about their dates,

283

dances, and parties. It still makes me sad to see other couples together (especially since I've been home), and yet I am always alone with my parents. But I didn't mind too much for I felt I would receive the best reward of all by waiting. And above all, besides having respect for you, I had respect for myself. Oh, it isn't easy—it's hard, but then you don't ever get anything really worthwhile unless you have worked hard for it and sacrificed a great deal. . . .

> Your loving wife,
> Ann

> 11 February '45

Dearest Ann,

I had a full day off on Sunday. I started out by sleeping till nine o'clock. I went to the beach at the Patrician, though it is beginning to wear off. One person can't have a good time.

I read a little of *The Valley of Decision* and left soon after I got there. It was about 10 o'clock when I left the beach and started to walk down to the tennis courts (Collins Avenue) to see if anyone wanted to play. Both courts were in use and no one was sitting around. I stayed there and watched the game until 11:30 and then went to the Pancoast to eat my dinner, which tasted good—fried chicken and the like. After this, I went to the courts again and had some luck—a hospital patient recuperating from malaria was sitting there and asked me if I wanted to hit a few. So we played till three o'clock and enjoyed every minute of it. After this, I went across the street to the beach and had a swim because I really was sweaty, and it sure did feel fine. I stayed there till about 4 o'clock and then went up to the quarters and took a shower.

This evening, I walked down to the Miami library, but it was closed because it was Sunday. So, I am writing this letter at the information center—the building where the GI Theatre is, but I am in the back of it. There is a small library here and it seems like a nice place.

The sunburn I got today feels fine and I am a little bit tired from the workout this afternoon, which I badly needed. I have gained two pounds and now weigh 140 with my clothes on and shoes off. How high do you make the scale go?

The guy here assigned to the same place at the same time as me is waiting for me to go to the mess hall with him and have a hamburger and some milk. He is the only guy I know here, and I guess he feels the same way I do. He is from Kansas and is about 35 years old, a nice sociable fellow but he doesn't play tennis and has some funny ideas. He talks intelligently and is an interesting conversationalist, which is something. He hates the Army as I do and is not too keen on being stationed here. His wife left the day after you did. She is a stenographer.

Boy, it seems so natural and easy for you to write, "I hope to see you soon." It just doesn't seem right. Give my regards to all. I love you.

> Your loving husband,
> Herb

Some of the logos from Herb's stationery.

Dearest Ann,

I received the box of candy today and the Valentine card. Thank you very much.

Now what is this something of importance that needs to be attended to? I have been thinking about it for three days, wondering what it could be.

Too bad the checks had to stop. The extra money came in handy. Hold on to the check in case you have to pay it back. This is a good example of the Army's efficiency, isn't it? I signed a discontinuance of that allotment sometime last year on Kwajalein, and they just now caught up with it. There are a lot of rude awakenings in the Army. I have noticed this much more since I've been back in the states. Winning the war as soon as possible is the least worry for people in the states, civilians or otherwise. When more soldiers come back from overseas, someone will start to notice and clean house, so to speak.

We had a physical fitness test today for qualifying for overseas duty. No one overworked himself to qualify. Can you blame them? Nothing will ever come from this test anyway. A few fellows seem conscientious about going over, and others are downright cowards. I have no time for such men and they know it. All they think about is what pictures are playing (free) and who is appearing in person so they can go see them. Some may be physically unfit for overseas duty, but they look healthy enough for everything else. Even if they could go to some noncombatant place like Hawaii, this would make a difference. But they would much rather dilly dally around in the states. I don't blame the guys because it is not their fault that they aren't overseas. It is the fault of some damn generals who are having too good a time themselves to bother sending replacements. So we will have to wait until more men come back to get the ball rolling.

It has been hot here today, and I hate to think how hot it's going to be when summer comes. I was sweating all day. Right now the sun has gone down and it is just right. I have lost my tan and will probably never have time for another one unless I go A.W.O.L.

I guess I will have to wait six months and possibly more for a furlough. If only this damn war would end, I'd be the happiest man in the world and happier to be out of the Army. I hope I never, ever, ever have to serve again. I would rather die, believe me. The whole thing is rotten all the way through. But this is democracy and democracy is great. Says who?

Did I mention that I went to see about my income tax return? I was told I have no worries and will not have to file one. Will you? I hope this letter finds you well and happy. . . .

Your loving husband,
Herb

February 15, 1945

Dearest Herb,

So you would like to see some of this snow here. Well, I, too, would like you to "enjoy" some of it. But it is no good for skiing, sledding, or ice skating—and in fact only makes the roads and pavements impossible for safe travel. This week the weather has been spring-like on Monday, snow and cold on Tuesday, cold on Wednesday, and spring-like again today. We only have a month or more of this to endure.

The bags have not come yet, and I shudder every time I think of all the things I'll lose if they don't come—six dresses, two pairs of shoes, the camera, slacks, three blouses, housecoat, and that photo album you made. Not to mention my good alligator bag, my new brown hat and gloves, and three bathing suits. I sure hope you can find out something about them and that the Express Company left some receipts at the Patrician when the bags were picked up. We should have made sure we had receipts for them. If all those clothes are lost, it will take me a year of working to make up for it. Did you notice the last time you were at the Patrician if the bags were still there? Maybe they are.

Have you gotten paid, Herb? May I ask how much you get paid each month? You got $51 while I was there. Is this your monthly pay, after the allotment, insurance premiums, and the like are deducted? I got my pay today $47.90—$50 less $2.10 in deductions. I don't think they're taking enough out for income tax, but I guess I'll let well enough alone.

I don't understand parts of your letter. Either I misinterpret them or don't understand what you are driving at. I think sometimes you don't say exactly what you mean. For instance, you wrote, "I went over to the beach at the Patrician. It is beginning to wear off. One person can't have a good time." What do you mean, "It is beginning to wear off, etc.?" Here's another example: "Boy, it seems so natural and easy for you to write 'I hope to see you soon! It just doesn't seem right.'" I don't understand that one at all. Just what "doesn't seem right"—that I wish to see you soon? Or what? Please explain these, if possible.

I'm glad you found a companion in the fellow from Kansas. What's his name? Was he overseas and where—in the Pacific or Europe? Does he bunk at the Pancoast also?

You gave me a good idea of how you spent Sunday, but what do you do on Saturday nights?

I'll sure be glad when this snow melts so that I can get out more often. The succession of pages in this letter got mixed up, but I guess you'll be able to figure it out. Hope so. Until we meet again, here's loving you, darling,

Your loving wife,
Ann

15 February 1945

Dearest Ann,

This evening I met up with a guy who was at Hickam Field with me on December 7—Joe Ferrick. He's from Pottsville, I think. I will check this when I see him.* His picture is amongst the ones you have. I think you asked me once while

---

*Herb's friend, Joseph M. Ferrick, of Shamokin, Pennsylvania, rose to the rank of Tech. Sergeant, in charge of repairing teletype machines. Joe and Herb served together in the 324th Signal Company, VII Bomber Command.

looking at a particular one who he was. He is doctoring for stomach ulcers that developed while overseas. He said he may try to get a Medical Discharge and has been in the hospital for four weeks. We chatted all evening and saw a G.I. stage show, which was poor, at the 41st Street Theatre.

Mother wrote that she received the basket we sent her and that she has already used it for shopping. She sounded pleased with it. By the way, how does your Mother like the little bowl?

I wish this discharging point system would start. They could be waiting for the war to end in Europe. I may have a good chance for a discharge when the point system starts. If things don't look any brighter by about May, how would you like to come down here? Or maybe if I get a furlough around then, I could come home and bring you back with me. We would have to use some of the money we have saved and you would have to find a job, which would not be hard. I want more than anything to have a home in an area like the one where we were that day together, but things now don't look good. I want to be with you so much.

As for the fellows I bunk with, I don't even know their names. They are not sociable and neither am I. I just say, "good morning." They are ward boys, assigned to the hospital wards doing general cleaning work, I presume. One of them is from Virginia and married with a 14-month-old girl whose pictures he has on the wall.

This last week, I have been feeling heavy. I have been eating too much and not exercising enough. I really do miss it. I hope you mean it regarding the poundage you said you were going to lose.

It is about 12:30, and I am sleepy. Joe and I talked so much this evening, it occupied most of my time. But I was determined to write you before going to bed, reminding you that I love you.

Your loving husband,
Herb

Friday, February 16, 1945

Dearest Herb,

Your letter of February 13 and the second Valentine came today—the one with the box of matches—very cute. I don't understand the sentiments on that one, especially what you wrote—"too expensive for a sergeant." Is this a hint that I'm extravagant?

I'm glad you finally wrote to Bob Roane. I phoned Virginia and she told me again to ask you to write him. The letter of Bob's that you sent me amused me. He sounds like he's got it bad. Already planning the wedding—fast worker, I'd say. Aren't you thrilled to think we'll be their best man and matron of honor? Another wedding! But I think he's ahead of himself for I don't think Virginia will marry anyone that fast. But she's anxious for him to get back to the states; so I guess we can expect anything.

Your having a physical fitness test for qualification for overseas duty scares me. I was afraid that being stationed in Miami Beach might result in your being shipped overseas again because that station is principally a redistribution post. I think you'd have had a better chance of staying in the states for the duration if you were stationed someplace that wasn't a redistribution station. But one takes what one gets and learns not to protest, I suppose. I hope the events of the war will change things so you can avoid going overseas. And I hope you can get a furlough sometime this summer when your six months expire.

Well, I'll be writing again Sunday. Until then, I'll be thinking of you and loving you.

Your devoted wife,
Ann

Dearest Ann,

Thanks a million for the apples. I received them today in good shape. I've eaten three since 5 o'clock and they tasted swell.

Tomorrow is Sunday and a day off for which I am thankful. I hope to play tennis and get some sunshine. It has been hot all week and the nights are starting to get longer and lighter. Maybe I'll play tennis after work at night. I'd like to buy myself a good tennis racket; maybe I will someday. The rented ones are not so good.

Joe Ferrick came up last night, and we went down to Flamingo Park to see the show. It was the first time I was in that district since you were here. We got there late and sat all the way in the back. The shows are tiresome after you see a few of them. They are all in the same style, and the performers crack the same jokes. Afterwards, we came back to the mess hall and had a hamburger and some milk.

I hope the weather has warmed up by now and driving to and from Norristown isn't too bad. Don't eat too much of that Italian spaghetti. You know it's fattening, or don't you care? I like it a lot providing it is made right.

I'm answering your letter of February 15, which I received on Thursday. Am I too unusual to understand? I know you don't understand me and, furthermore, I do not expect you to. But I love you and know you love me, so what's the difference? It would be easier for you to understand me if I told you a secret about me that would clear up all your misunderstanding. But I shall never tell you because if I did our life would not be so happy. Don't try to think of what it may be; someday I may tell you. For now, just forget about it.

They had some excitement yesterday at the Cadillac Hotel, where a G.I. truck hit an officer and killed him instantly. The driver was drunk and didn't stop when he hit the officer until someone chased him in another car. I didn't see the accident but heard that the officer was a returnee from Europe. They are holding the driver for manslaughter, and he will probably get 20 years of hard labor.

I have hardly anything worthwhile to write about except that I miss you very much and am always thinking of you. As ever,

Your loving husband,
Herb

—★—

Six decades after Herb wrote the preceding letter, in 2007, my research of his army service was underway. On a Friday afternoon in October of that year, I rolled my suitcase up to the door of my sister's home in Wilmington, Delaware. I hoped talking with April would help me interpret my father's letters. And I also wanted to spend time with her because she had been diagnosed with pancreatic cancer the month before.

When she came to the door, she looked like Daddy's mother, whom I'd known only as an old woman. April's 61-year-old face had a gray cast, looking drawn and longer than before. Her short blonde hair stuck out all over her head. Her petite frame appeared shrunken, and her painted toenails accentuated the bunions on her big toes. She moved her boney arms and everything else more slowly than usual. Though everyone said we looked alike, the differences in our looks seemed enhanced now: for the first time, I noticed the roundness of the nail beds on her tiny fingers; mine were less so. Compared with her flat back side, my round one looked even fuller.

April's appearance shocked me, though for her sake I kept a straight face. As a child, I'd watched her sit at the mirror and apply makeup to a face so beautiful you couldn't look away. Her twinkly green eyes would shine brightly from the mirror back at me, under a fringe of thick blonde bangs. She'd put on her lipstick and smack her plump lips together to even it out. Then, she'd crinkle her mouth into a smile as bright as the sunlamp clamped to the headboard of the bed.

"How do I look?" she'd ask as my heart melted. I adored her.

When I entered her living room, about 40 cards from well-wishers stood on a round table. Many had included money to help with April's medical bills. Although her home decorating smacked of genius, thick dust coated every tabletop and knickknack. Debris covered the rugs. The smeared windows clouded the sunny day outside. The kitchen floor sparkled, however, a new floor of light oak laminate, and the kitchen was freshly painted—pink, April's favorite color. Still optimistic about her prognosis, she'd improved the kitchen.

We settled in her bedroom, where she perched at the head of her unmade bed—which she called her "command post"—with her pillows propped up behind her. Her hoarding tendencies on full display, catalogs and scraps of paper with information that might someday come in handy covered her bed. Pill bottles sat atop her night stand. The ever-droning TV glowed from its hutch. Next to the bed, I sat in a boudoir chair that had belonged to Granny, clipboard in hand with pages of questions about Daddy for her.

April told me the story of her taking the hand of the black man at the parade when she was small. She also recalled going to the park and playing on the swings while my parents played tennis. In fourth grade, she sat for a portrait that daddy painted of her. "I had to sit still and not talk—that was hard," she said.

When I prodded her for more about Daddy, she spoke in a small, halting voice, barely above a whisper. She looked down into her lap. Her tone implied that she'd never told anyone this before: "Daddy wanted to keep me to himself. . . . He was obsessed with me. I think sometimes he wanted people who saw us together to think I was his girlfriend. . . . He used to take me to Korvette's to shop for clothes, picking out tasteful things but not the latest fashion. . . . They were more for a younger girl. He wanted to keep me a little girl. . . . I wonder if that's why I've had so many problems with men." As she spoke, a faint memory surfaced of our whole family revolving around April, her frailties, her asthma, and other illnesses. Excited, I felt the haze surrounding my family's dynamics beginning to fade. Was this the cause of my sister's drinking, which waylaid her once promising life?

April got out of bed and opened up her blanket chest. She reached in and pulled out a photo album. Returning to her bed, she paged through it until she found a photo taken at the New Jersey shore, where our family had spent summer days during our youth. Pointing to a photo and handing me the album, she said, "Look at this."

I took the album and saw a photo of 16-year-old April, already glamorous, sitting on a beach towel, smiling but looking distracted. Her knees bent and pointing to the sky, she cupped her left knee with her left hand; her right hand rested in the crook of her left arm, her right forearm across her chest. It seemed a defensive pose. To her left sat Daddy, beaming, a bit closer than appropriate. The photo proved her point. Struck dumb, I thought: if she knew the exact location of this proof of her pain, it couldn't have been far from her consciousness. Yet she'd never talked about it. Instead, she'd donned that 1,000-watt smile, honed her humor, and wisecracked her way through life.

Agape, I asked, "Did he molest you?"

"No . . . there was no inappropriate touching. . . . When I was a teenager, one night I went to a party in the Myers's basement rec room. I happened to look up at one point and see Daddy peering in the window."

"Did your eyes meet?" I asked her.

"Yeah, and he backed away from the window."

"Did you ever ask him about this afterwards . . . or did he bring it up?"

"No, I was too embarrassed and afraid to ask and he never brought it up. . . . I never thought he was much of a man after that.

. . . Looking back, I think Daddy was gay or bisexual. . . . He had that 'crazy' friend Jack Bolger . . . and, you know, birds of a feather. . . ." she said, her voice rising higher with each syllable. Jack Bolger had been a bachelor friend of Daddy's from his hometown. I vaguely remembered him and made a note to ask Mother about him.

April's remarks aroused me as if I'd fallen under the spell of infatuation. I'd felt this way before when I'd heard an idea the profoundness of which I felt deep in my bones: I was having an epiphany. I felt on the verge of discovering not only my father but also the cause of our whole family's dysfunction. Everything around me took on incredible clarity, as if I'd just put on eyeglasses for the first time.

April's sense of Daddy as gay was heartfelt, not vengeful, despite her difficulties with him. As a flight attendant, she'd had gay friends as had I. Intrigued by the implications of April's words, I scribbled down them down exactly, without reacting lest April would stop talking. I would process them later. Surely Daddy had caused April's problems with men—she'd had three failed marriages—but I didn't know how exactly. I intended to find out, though.

After I returned home from my weekend with April, I searched in Daddy's letters for clues about his sexuality and found that passage about "a secret" in his letter of February 17, 1945, which I had not read before:

> It would be easier for you to understand me if I told you a secret about me that would clear up all your misunderstanding. But I shall never tell you because if I did our life would not be so happy. Don't try to think of what it may be; someday I may tell you. For now, just forget about it.

It sounded to me as if Daddy wanted Mother to know

him deeply and that he felt her empathetic enough to handle his "secret." After all, why—on the basis of Mother's asking him only to clarify a few sentences in a letter—would he even mention his secret if he didn't want to share it with her? Maybe he'd only experimented with a gay lifestyle in the past, making him feel secure enough to discuss it sometime in the future. On the other hand, saying he'd never tell her indicated he knew the risk involved.

After deliberating on the "secret" and April's suspicion, I called Mother to see what she thought, not mentioning my chat with April. I read her the passage from Daddy's letter.

"Mom, what do you think Daddy meant when he wrote that?"

"Probably that he was gay," she said slowly. "You know, he had that friend, Jack Bolger, who lived with his mother."

"Is he dead?"

"Yes, he was a little older than your father. Herb and I understood that Jack was 'that way,' even though we never said it. The friendship faded as we started child rearing and they hadn't much in common anymore. . . . But I remember conversations between Herb and Jack about male friends of theirs who were couples. . . . Jack Bolger used to have parties at his home. I went to one with Herb after the war. All the men at the party were effeminate. Jack's mother and I were the only women there."

"Did you know any of the men, Mom?"

"No, they were Herb's friends from before he joined the army."

"Did you ever ask Daddy about the men at the party?"

"No, I never did." She sounded pained. "What was I going to do, Liz? I had a brand new baby. I never suspected this about your father until after I was married. I was naïve about such things."

Though Mother defended herself, she had nothing to defend that I could see. How could Mother, a sheltered country girl, know anything about gay life in 1943, when she married?

"You have nothing to feel bad about, Mother."

"Does all of this upset you, Liz?" Mother asked.

"No . . . I find it fascinating." After all, Daddy had been dead for 37 years.

"Then there was that party in Miami Beach that we went to on R&R. Again, most of the guests were effeminate men. Besides me, only one other woman was there. . . . It was so sweltering hot that she took off her blouse and sat there in her bra." Mother realized that the woman felt emboldened to do so because it wouldn't arouse the men there.

"But I really think Herb was faithful to me. . . . He never gave me a reason to distrust him or his word. I always knew where he was. There were never any suspicious phone calls or letters. . . . He'd take a small amount of spending money from his paycheck and give me the rest to pay the bills."

I wrote down everything Mother told me, thrilled that she was so honest.

"We had a good sex life," she continued. I hoped she wouldn't elaborate. "I really think he put that life behind him when he got married. . . . Your father did not drink, gamble, or chase women. He took care of the yard. He planted flowers and shrubs and painted the house." That was enough for her.

After the conversation with Mother, I searched for more clues about my father's sexuality in his letters. One sentence written on November 26, 1940, caught my eye: "As I have told you before, I have never felt this way about any other person." Person? Why didn't he say "woman?" In his letter of April 28, 1943, my father wrote about Andy Beyer, whom he called "Andrew": "He's a swell guy and one of my intimate friends." Intimate friends? Is this how guys referred to buddies in 1943? As it turned out, Andy

297

Beyer, a.k.a. Bumbo the Clown, also had an artistic nature. But most likely, he was just my father's friend; he and his wife had four sons.

This photo, taken before the war, shows Herb, standing, second from the left. His friend, Jack Bolger, is kneeling right in front of him. His other friend, Andy Beyer, is standing on the far right. The others are unidentified. (Family photo.)

The military used techniques to screen out homosexuals and banned them outright in 1943. Nonetheless, gay men entered the service in significant numbers. In the army, many worked as clerks, and one of my father's MOSs was Clerk Typist.

Several authors have documented Honolulu's gay life among GIs in World War II. In an interview with Allan Bérubé, who wrote *Coming Out Under Fire: The History of Gay Men and Women in World War II*, one veteran discussed GIs cruising for gay sex on blacked-out Waikiki Beach. Gay GIs also found discreet gay men in the cocktail lounges of swanky hotels, including the Royal

Hawaiian, Moana, and Alexander Young. According to Beth Bailey and David Farber, authors of *The First Strange Place: Race and Sex in World War II Hawaii*, GIs went to certain restaurants and bars to receive free drinks and dinner from local gay men, even to the point of having sex for money. James Jones, author of *From Here to Eternity*, detailed such events extensively in that book, noting one bar in particular, the Waikiki Tavern, as a hangout for "queers."* While in Honolulu, I spoke with DeSoto Brown, historian and curator of the Bishop Museum on Oahu, who said that another hangout for local gays during the war was the Wagon Wheel, a restaurant that my father frequented. Could my father have known that Honolulu had an active gay life when he enlisted?

Months after my trip to Honolulu, a librarian at the University of Hawaii emailed me about an article she'd found. In the article, "George the Queer Danced the Hula," scholar Carol A. Stabile wrote about her father's gay sex life in Honolulu during the war. Stabile drew from her father's diary, which described a gay subculture among men in the close quarters of an army barracks with little access to women. In addition to gay sex among soldiers, Stabile discussed their friendships and sexual relations with local gay men. Stabile gave enough clues in her article about one such man that DeSoto Brown identified him for me: Samuel Amalu, who entertained GIs at his home on Barber's Point. Stabile's father referred to Amalu as "George" and also used that name as a euphemism for gay men in wartime Honolulu. This brings me to another quote from my father, in a letter of December 20, 1942:

> Incidentally, George, a well educated Chinese I met here,
> has offered to send you some tea. I mentioned that I really
> liked this tea, so he was happy to help someone else
> appreciate it also.

299

Was my father's friend, "George," Samuel Amalu, who gained post-war fame as Hawaii's most notorious con man?* Amalu, though Hawaiian, not Chinese, was a skilled liar. One author wrote that after Amalu's wedding to a red-headed socialite, "he tossed $10 in dimes out of his hotel window, declaring, 'It's an old Chinese custom.'" He could have told my father that he was Chinese. (The same author wrote that, according to the bride, the marriage was never consummated.) Famous for impersonation, Amalu once captured the attention of the Japanese press while touring Tokyo in a flowing black cape, claiming to be a Hawaiian prince.

Before that—in 1943—Amalu was discharged from the army for alleged homosexuality. Could the "George" who sent Mother the type of tea my father enjoyed at a Chinese restaurant be Sammy Amalu? In his letter of May 25, 1943, my father refers to "our tennis friend, the one who sent you the tea. . . ." Amalu did play tennis, according to a former reporter for Honolulu's *Star-Bulletin*, Ted Kurrus, whom I contacted by email. Kurrus had interviewed and befriended Amalu, who died in 1986. A link between my father and Amalu sounds plausible. But I can neither confirm that Amalu was my father's friend "George" nor dismiss it. Or was the "George" Daddy referred to another gay man, whom he euphemistically called George?

Servicemen engaging in gay sex could be court-martialed for sodomy and risked physical harm and a dishonorable discharge, not to mention disgrace. According to Allan Bérubé, the military

*After the war, Amalu falsely represented himself and some friends as officials of a Swiss presidium to convince several Hawaii businessmen of their intention to buy five Waikiki hotels and some land for $50 million. The hoax ended after Amalu, who had no money, wrote two bad checks and landed in prison.

had "queer stockades" in the war, where "undesirables" were incarcerated. Had my father seen these stockades? Even if he hadn't, he could not have missed the military's anti-gay message. With his strict Methodist upbringing, he would not have wanted to risk a dishonorable discharge. According to Mother, "Your father would never have disgraced his parents that way." If he engaged in gay sex in the army, he was careful. And because he functioned sexually within marriage, my father, if anything, was technically bisexual, not gay.

Suppressing one's gayness or bisexuality and living a straight life seemed a necessary adaptation in the 1940s and 1950s. At the time, homosexuality offended most Americans' sense of decency and violated social norms. The Judeo-Christian tradition considered homosexuality a sin; the law, a crime; and the medical profession, a disease. Exposed gays faced punishment and ostracism. Between 1946 and 1967, hundreds of gays were arrested for offenses such as "cruising," propositioning an undercover policeman, wearing sex-inappropriate clothing, or socializing in a gay bar.

As a married man with children, who genuinely loved his wife, my father could not risk losing his job or going to jail; he had to support his wife and family. And after years of marriage, he most likely felt loyal to Mother and would not want to hurt her. Furthermore, he had no way of knowing whether he'd be happier without her. Living alone could be worse. As he got older, he probably felt he couldn't attract a man or that it was too late to start anew. Maybe he felt trapped, which brings me to his tantrums.

To find out how suppressing one's sexuality can affect a gay man, I corresponded on a blog site (Gay Life) with several gay men who either kept their sexuality secret or knew men who did. According to them, the constant guardedness required to hide your sexuality produces stress. You have to avoid anything that

301

could give you away. You become ever watchful and obsessive about everything you do. Even a joke you hear regarding sexuality can strike a devastating blow. If married, you lack a private space where you can let your guard down. Such effort requires immense energy and causes massive stress.

Did a vigilant suppression of his sexuality cause my father's irritability and anger? He may have felt hopeless when marriage didn't "fix" his sexuality as he thought it would, a common belief in decades past. One man whom I blogged with who posed as straight described himself as depressed and his life as "miserable." Another wrote me, "Your father may have been depressed, which made him angry instead of withdrawn."

Psychiatrist Gail Saltz, author of *The Anatomy of a Secret: The Psychology of Living a Lie*, wrote that for gay people who feel, "The need for secrecy . . . daily life on the inside feel[s] like a battlefield." She goes on to say that the psychological tension between "concealing and revealing" creates "an urgency akin to the physical need to urinate, defecate, or reach orgasm."

Did my father channel his sexual longing into art, an acceptable pastime? According to Saltz, Tchaikovsky, the gay Russian composer who ultimately committed suicide, did just that.* Such channeling is referred to as sublimation: "the diversion of the expression of an instinctual desire or impulse from its primitive form to one . . . considered socially acceptable" according to the dictionary.

I found no one to interview who'd known my father besides family members. The trail, by the time I researched this book, had gone as cold as a Pennsylvania winter.

Growing up, I knew my parents' marriage had problems. After Daddy got home from working the night shift at a printing

---

*A controversy surrounds the cause of Tchaikovsky's death: some believe he was poisoned.

company on most Friday nights, my parents argued. April had already left home to work as a flight attendant with Allegheny Airlines (the predecessor of U.S. Airways) in Pittsburgh. My two younger sisters slept in their room. A teen-ager, I was the only one who heard my parents quarrel. Neither Mother nor I could remember what they argued about, but we both thought Daddy was fishing for a fight, provoking Mother, and she was trying not to take the bait.

After interviewing April, I studied parental obsession with a "chosen child"—dubbed "spousification" and "emotional incest" by psychologists. Such focus by a father on a daughter so stimulates her that, when she grows up, no man can ever measure up.* When Daddy took April clothes shopping, she was serving as his real-life paper doll, fulfilling his need for creative expression to dress her in clothes of his taste—not hers. Worse, he sought her companionship over his wife's, driving Mother and April apart. One expert, Dr. Patricia Love, wrote in *The Emotional Incest Syndrome: What to Do When a Parent's Love Rules Your Life* that such a child is always estranged from the nonintrusive parent. Often, that parent resents the child getting all the attention of the doting parent.

"Oh, poor April," Mother remarked when I told her April's tale of Daddy's spying on her in our neighbor's rec room. "I'm sure that's true because we'd heard that the Myerses were serving beer to kids who went over there. Your father called them and told them not to give April any beer."

Poor April, indeed. While my parents argued, she paid the price. Who was meeting April's needs while my father used her to meet his need for companionship? Growing up, she had no emotional support: she had only me, a kid sister. When she tried

---

*Of course, a mother can also "spousify" a son, often the case when her husband is absent or distant. And a same-sex parent can spousify a son or daughter if that parent depends on the child for companionship.

303

to forge her independence as a teen, Daddy condemned and punished her, severing the relationship forever. Feeling unloved, lonely, and ashamed, she rebelled and started smoking and sneaking out at night. In 1967—three years before Daddy died—she left for flight attendant training. She flew for 40 years—and drank her way through her marriages and divorces.

Hurt that the two people I loved most, April and Mother, didn't get along, I'd always wondered why April was so hard on Mother. Now I knew why: Mother hadn't protected April from Daddy. April had to play the role Mother should have played— Daddy's companion.

When I told Mother about how Daddy had damaged April, she got it. But she denied any resentment of April or just couldn't remember that far back.

"I was just glad Herb took an interest in April when she was little," Mother said. She was too inexperienced a mother to know that Daddy's focus on April was unhealthy. By the time April started acting out as a teen, the damage was done.

I know my father loved Mother; she always felt he loved her. Idealized by their long correspondence, my parents' love had nonetheless ended up in the dead-letter office.

"Daddy berated Mother about her weight," April had told me.

"He did?" I'd asked, unaware of this.

"Oh, yeah, he used to tell her, 'You eat as much as a man. . . You think because you're tall, you can carry more weight, but you can't.'"

Mother was a fan of food, a gourmand; she'd even joked, "Food is the love of my life." Years of childbearing fattened her figure, and she never slimmed down. Could this have repulsed my father so much that he turned to April for companionship? Had he denied his sexual identity to spend life with a fat woman?

304

Her husband's remarks about her weight must have stung Mother. They surely didn't help her reduce and may have made her eat more to numb the hurt. I didn't want to remind Mother of such a painful time in her life, so I didn't ask her about this. My father's letters had been clear enough: he did not like fat people. The letters and April's words had sufficed for my purposes.

Did Mother eat to comfort herself because Daddy focused too much on April? Or did Daddy focus on April because Mother ate too much? Those questions I'd never answer.

And it didn't matter. Yes, my parents had damaged my beloved sister. But, like all parents, mine did the best they could with the knowledge and choices they had.

Tragically, April never knew who she really was. But what she had denied herself, she'd given me: She'd unlocked the mystery of our family's dysfunction, allowing me to make sense of Daddy's temper and aspects of my own life. As Daddy had leaned on April, Mother had leaned on me, her "veritable brick." I'd been set up, just as April had. Thanks to her, I grasped the consequences of being a veritable brick. My whole life, needy people had flocked to me like the homeless to a soup kitchen, sometimes landing me in dubious relationships. Now I had my antennae up to ward off people who would only drag me down. On the other hand, I also saw advantages to serving as Mother's pillar: I had developed steadfastness, resourcefulness, and independence.

By the time I'd figured out why April drank, which probably spurred her cancer, it was too late for her to heal. I awoke from a sound sleep after midnight on the last Wednesday in September 2008. I lay there fully alert, feeling disconcerted. In a few minutes, the phone rang, and I knew why before answering. April's daughter, Missy, was calling to say April would die soon, according to the hospice nurse. And so she did.

On a crisp, sunny October 2, my husband and I arrived at the funeral home in Wilmington before anyone else. I wore a navy linen suit with a trumpet skirt. My hair had thinned with the stress of April's illness and my eyelashes had fallen out completely. I placed a favorite photo of April on a table next to the urn. April's friends from high school and the airlines arrived, all ethnicities, gay and straight, packing the chapel. Wearing pink to honor her mother, Missy came with her father, April's second husband, and his wife. Mother, her 86-year-old heart shattered, and my two younger sisters arrived, one with her two children. I hoped that somehow April could see through her photo all the people who loved her and came to honor her. I eulogized April, choking back tears, but gaining composure as I went. I talked about playing hopscotch and with paper dolls in our childhood, her quick wit, her toughness in the face of cancer. Others spoke too. Her lifelong friend, Jeanne, described how the men at her wedding tripped over each other to dance with April, a bridesmaid, who took it all in stride. Afterwards, Missy's father said, "This was the nicest memorial service I've ever been to." It was the least I could do for my hero, my darling April, whom I miss every day.

—★—

Three months after Herb wrote of his secret, on May 8, 1945, the war in Europe ended; Herb was furloughed the next day. He came home to visit his folks and returned with Ann to Miami Beach. They moved to Apartment No. 7, a furnished apartment, in the Sea Bay Apartments at 6875 Byron Avenue. Ann went to work as the secretary to the director of one of the field offices of the Red Cross. She and Herb began their lives together as well as April's life: Ann got pregnant in that Miami Beach apartment.

Peace came to the world on V-J Day, August 15, 1945. Herb's army career ended on September 20, and he and Ann came home to Pennsylvania and began the family they had so wanted.

—★—

And so ended my journey to discover Daddy, with my feeling compassion and love for him. He was not the horrible man I'd thought. Although I hated what he'd done to April, I forgave him. Society had prevented him from being who he really was; he did his best under the circumstances. He worked hard all his life, supporting Mother, my sisters, and me. He faithfully visited his disabled and institutionalized brother. He gave me an appreciation of art, music, and literature and a love of nature, along with some of his looks. He gave me my work ethic: I also disdained doing work I didn't love. Now sorry that Daddy had died so young, I felt proud to be his daughter.

Whether we know it or not, we want those we love to fathom our depth. We yearn for them to know our hearts and love us anyway. That's why my parents wrote their letters and why April confided in me. And when we listen to them—or in my case probe them—we quell the yearning. They heal and we heal.

The letters—from places I'd never been and a time I never knew—had taken me home for the first time. They had led me to discover Daddy as well as myself. But how much lovelier life would be if I hadn't needed the letters at all—if my father had felt free to paint not only fruit and landscapes but also his life in his own palette.

I store my parents' letters and photos unfolded with their envelopes clipped to them in archival folders. They will go to a museum someday. But, for now, I keep them safe with me, where they were meant to be all along.

EPILOGUE

Back home after the service, Herb went to Berté Fashion Studio in Philadelphia and completed a course in commercial art. He worked as an illustrator and then a linotype operator. He had only 21 years of good health after the army. The symptoms of his leukemia began four years before he died, stealing his senses of smell and taste. He could no longer appreciate the delicious dinners Ann cooked for him and the rest of us. One Sunday, he threw down his fork and stomped away from the dinner table, criticizing her cooking, when, in fact, his illness had prevented his enjoyment of the meal. In June 1970, Ann and Herb went to Oahu for vacation and stayed at the Moana Hotel. Herb's poor health cut the trip short. Back at home, he had one blood transfusion after another until it no longer made sense to do so. He continued to work until a few months before he died on September 8, three days before his 52nd birthday. Fifteen months prior, Ann's father died; her mother died two months before Herb.

On Herb's furlough in May 1945, his army buddy, Bob Roane, visited him and met Ann's fiend, Ginny Detwiler.* They corresponded for a while, but Ginny was also writing to a navy man, Richard Baldwin, from Texas, whom she married on April 14, 1951. Ann was Ginny's maid of honor. April, who turned five that day, attended with her father. The Baldwins were married for 62 years until Dick died in 2014. To this day, Ginny has a necklace made of shells that Bob Roane made her in the service. Ann and Ginny remained friends until Ann passed away on March 20, 2016. In her desk, I found a "Dear Children" letter, 14 pages long, containing her life story. About Herb, she wrote:

---

*Ann and Herb lost touch with Bob Roane, but he did marry a girl from New York, Ann believed. I could not find any children he may have had.

Your father had many good qualities. He spent a lot of time with you children, amusing and entertaining you, especially summers. I'm sure a lot of the creative side of your personalities comes from your father. He was a lot less serious than I and he could be quite witty. I hope you will remember your father with gratefulness and empathy. He was a good man, his family always came first with him, and though he may have been misguided at times, as was I, he did his best. Those terrible Sunday dinners when he would rant and rave I'm sure had something to do with his own inner rage.

Ann, Bob Roane, and Ginny Detwiler (left photo) and Herb and Bob (right photo) at the tennis courts at Schwenksville High School. In the second photo, Herb is pointing to the tennis balls Bob has put inside his jacket for laughs. (Photos from Herb's collection)

Ann and April at Ginny and Dick Baldwin's
wedding, April 14, 1951. (Family photo)

Mother's friend and bridesmaid, Sara Garges, married a
man who worked for the U.S. State Department. They spent two
years stateside and then two years in Ethiopia for most of their
marriage. They had one son, who was born without an opening
for a mouth and had many surgeries to form a functional mouth.
Sara and her husband divorced when he retired. Sara drank in her
later years, according to Mother, and died in 1996.

Eighteen months after I got the letter from Andy Beyer's
wife, Margaret, the minister of the First United Methodist Church
in Orange, California, started the memorial service for Andy
Beyer with a classic knock-knock joke.

"Knock, knock," said the minister.

"Who's there?" the congregants responded.

"Orange."

"Orange who?"

"Orange you glad you knew Andy Beyer?"

Inside the church, the congregants smiled, laughed, and clapped. Among the mourners was Andy's wife, Margaret, with the couple's four sons and grandchildren. Andrew M. Beyer, Bumbo the Clown, died in December 2013.

In 1945, John F. Gilmore, Herb's brother, worked as an Army Cavalry military policeman at a test site for the Manhattan Project, code-named the Trinity site, at the Alamogordo Bombing and Gunnery Range in New Mexico (now part of White Sands Proving Ground). One of 250 people working at Trinity, he and his colleagues dug a trench near the test site and lay face down under blankets for the test, told that if they looked they would go blind. On July 16, 1945, he witnessed the first detonation of a nuclear weapon conducted by the army. It exploded with an energy equivalent to about 20 kilotons of TNT. Afterwards, John guarded the crater on horseback. He wore a white jumpsuit and a film badge, which he turned in after showering when his shift ended. As a military policeman, John guarded Enrico Fermi, Robert Oppenheimer, and other famous scientists with a Thompson submachine gun. John mustered out of the army in 1945 and joined the merchant marines. After that, he worked at a battery manufacturing business in Conshohocken, Pennsylvania. Sometimes he got days off because his "lead count" was too high. John and his wife, Edna, had three sons, all born with birth defects, which haunted their father until he died at age 72 in 1993.

John F. Gilmore as a cavalry MP in New Mexico, 1945.
(Photo courtesy of Dana A. Gilmore)

SOURCES

Allen, Gwenfred. *Hawaii's War Years, 1941-1945*. Honolulu: Hawaii UP, 1950.

Arakaki, Leatrice R., and John R. Kuborn. *7 December 1941, The Air Force Story*. Pacific Air Forces Office of History, Hickam Air Force Base. Hawaii: 1991.

Army Air Corps. *Hickam Bomber, 1942: A Pictorial Review of the Hickam Bomber Command*. Territory of Hawaii: Army Air Corps, 1942.

Bailey, Beth, and David Farber. *The First Strange Place: Race and Sex in World War II Hawaii*. New York: New York Free Press, 1992.

Bergerud, Eric M. *Touched With Fire: The Land War in the South Pacific*. New York: Penguin Books, 1996.

Bérubé, Allan. *Coming Out Under Fire: The History of Gay Men and Women in World War II*. New York: The Free Press, 1990.

Billinger, Robert D. Jr. *Hitler's Soldiers in the Sunshine State: German POWs in Florida*. Gainesville: Florida UP, 2000.

Brown, DeSoto. Email correspondence. 19 March 2014.

———. *Hawaii Goes to War: Life in Hawaii From Pearl Harbor to Peace*. Honolulu: Editions Limited, 1989.

———. Telephone interview. 4 April 2013.

Chamber of Commerce. *Old Home Week: Official Record of the One Hundred Twenty-Fifth Anniversary of the Borough of Norristown, PA*. Norristown, PA: Chamber of Commerce, 1937.

Chambers, John H. *Hawaii*. Northampton: Interlink Books, 2009.

Coffman, Edward M. *The Regulars: The American Army 1898-1941.* Cambridge: Belknap Press of Harvard UP, 2004.

Craven, Wesley Frank and James Lea Cate, ed. *The Army Air Forces in World War II, Volume IV, The Pacific: Guadalcanal to Saipan, August 1942 to July 1944* (Washington, D.C.: Office of Air Force History, 1983),http://www.afhso.af.mil/shared/media/document/AFD-101105-010.pdf/.

———. *The Army Air Forces in World War II: Volume VI, Men and Planes* (Chicago: University of Chicago Press, 1984), http://www.ibiblio.org/hyperwar/AAF/VI/.

D'Emilio, John. *Sexual Politics, Sexual Communities: The Making of a Homosexual Minority in the United States.* Chicago: University of Chicago Press, 1983.

Ellis, Peter S.H. "Hale's Handful . . . Up From the Ashes: The Forging of the Seventh Air Force From the Ashes of Pearl Harbor to the Triumph of V-J Day." Thesis, School of Advanced Airpower Studies, Air University, Maxwell Air Force Base, 2000.

Fox, Myron. "Censorship!" General Article. *PBS.org.* Public Broadcasting Service, American Experience, accessed 20 Aug. 2013.

Gawne, Jonathan. *Finding Your Father's War.* Drexel Hill: Casemate, 2006.

Gessler, Clifford. *Hawaii: Isles of Enchantment.* D. Appleton-Century Company: New York, 1942.

Hickam: The First Fifty Years. Captain Kevin K. Krejcarek, ed. Public Affairs Division, 15th Air Base Wing, Hickam Air Force Base. Hawaii: 1985.

Higa, Jessie. Personal interview. 28 March 2013.

Hillenbrand, Laura. *Unbroken: A World War II Story of Survival, Resilience, and Redemption.* New York: Random House, 2010.

Huston, John. *Let There Be Light. 59 min.* Long Island, New York,1946.

"Interview with Ernest Galeassi." College of Arts and Sciences, University of North Texas Oral History Collection Number 778. 16 September 1988.

"'Keep the Home Fires Burning:' Florida's World War II Experience." The Florida Handbook, 2001-2002. 28th ed. Ed. Allen Morris and Joan Perry Morris. Tallahassee: Peninsular Publishing, 1999.

Klepser, Carolyn. Correspondence. 10 October 2013.

Kurrus, Theodore. Email correspondence. 25 May 2014.

Lambert, John W. *The Pineapple Air Force: Pearl Harbor to Tokyo.* Atglen: Schiffer Publishing Ltd., 2006.

Lord, Walter. *Day of Infamy.* New York: Henry Holt & Co., 1957.

Love, Patricia and Jo Robinson. *The Emotional Incest Syndrome: What to Do When a Parent's Love Rules Your Life.* New York: Bantam Books, 1991.

"Odds & Ends." *Hickam Highlights,* 5 Sept. 1941, vol. V, no. IX.

Official History, 400th Signal Company, Aviation, Air Force Historical Research Agency, Maxwell Air Force Base, Alabama, Microfilm Reel # A0422.

Olson, James C. *The Operational History of the Seventh Air Force, 7 December 1941 to November 1943.* Army Air Forces Historical Office, Headquarters, Army Air Forces, 1945.

———. *The Operational History of the Seventh Air Force, 6 November 1943 to 31 July 1944,* Army Air Forces Historical Office, Headquarters, Army Air Forces, 1945.

Organizational History Headquarters & Headquarters Squadron, VII Bomber Command, Seventh Air Force, May 1931–March 1944. Air Force Historical Research Agency, Maxwell Air Force Base, Alabama, Microfilm Reel #A7608.

Perret, Geoffrey. *Winged Victory: The Army Air Forces in World War II*. New York: Random House, 1993.

Pillion, Thomas J. Eyewitness Account for *Day of Infamy*. 9 Jan. 1990.

Rust, Kenn C. *Seventh Air Force Story*. Temple City: Historical Aviation Album, 1979.

Saltz Gail, M.D. *Anatomy of a Secret Life: The Psychology of Living a Lie*. New York: Morgan Road Books, 2006.

Seventh Army Air Forces *Brief* Magazines, Air Force Historical Research Agency, Maxwell Air Force Base, Alabama, Microfilm Reel # 41299.

Sherrod, Robert. "Saipan: Eyewitness Tells of Island Fight," *Life Magazine* XLIV (28 Aug. 1944): 75.

———. "Japanese Civilians on Saipan," *Life Magazine* 17 (6 Nov. 1944): 45.

Shilts, Randy. *Conduct Unbecoming: Gays & Lesbians in the U.S. Military*. New York: Fawcett Columbine, 1994.

"Signal Chatter." *Hickam Highlights* V (26 Sept. 1941): XII.

Spence, Charles F. *Wings Field Autobiography: The First 75 Years of the People, the Events, the Businesses That Wings Field, Pennsylvania*. Philadelphia: Pavilion, 2005.

Spiller, Harry. *Pearl Harbor Survivors: An Oral History of 24 Servicemen*. Jefferson, North Carolina: McFarland & Company, Inc., 2002.

Stabile, Carol A. "George the Queer Danced the Hula." *Intimacy and Italian Migration: Gender and Domestic Lives in a Mobile World*. ed. Loretta Baldassar and Donna R. Gabaccia. New York: Fordham UP, 2011.

Terrett, Dulany. *The Signal Corps: The Emergency (To December 1941)*. United States Army in World War II, The Technical Services, Office of the Chief of Military History, Department of the Army, Washington, D.C., 1956.

The Official World War II Guide to the Army Air Forces: A Directory, Almanac and Chronicle of Achievement. New York: Bonanza Books, 1988.

"The Saga of Sammy Amalu." *Presstime in Paradise: The Life and Times of the Honolulu Advertiser 1856-1995.* Ed. George Chaplin. Honolulu: Hawaii UP, 1998.

Thompson, George Raynor, Dixie R. Harris, Pauline M. Oakes, and Dulany Terrett. *The Signal Corps: The Test (December 1941 to July 1943).* United States Army in World War II, The Technical Services, Office of the Chief of Military History, Department of the Army, Washington, D.C., 1957.

U.S. Department of the Interior, National Park Service, National Register of Historic Places Inventory—Nomination Form, Hickam Air Force Base, August 9, 1984.

Wels, Susan. *Pearl Harbor.* Tehabi Books: San Diego, 2001.

Williams, Howard D. *Army Air Forces Historical Study No. 49. Basic Military Training in the AAF 1939-1944,* 1946, https://archive.org/details/BasicMilitaryTrainingInTheAAF 1939-1944.

ABOUT THE AUTHOR

Liz Gilmore Williams earned an M.A. in American studies while working as a writer-editor for the federal government in Washington, D.C. She spent nine years researching and writing *No Ordinary Soldier: My Father's Two Wars*. A native of Pennsylvania, she lived in Mexico in 2010 before moving to South Carolina, where she spends her days interviewing and writing about people who had a front-row seat to history. Follow her on Twitter @WWIIletterlover or go to her web site, www.lizgilmorewilliams.com.

CPSIA information can be obtained
at www.ICGtesting.com
Printed in the USA
FFOW01n0915281116
29742FF